D0436993

THE PIONEERS OF FLIGHT

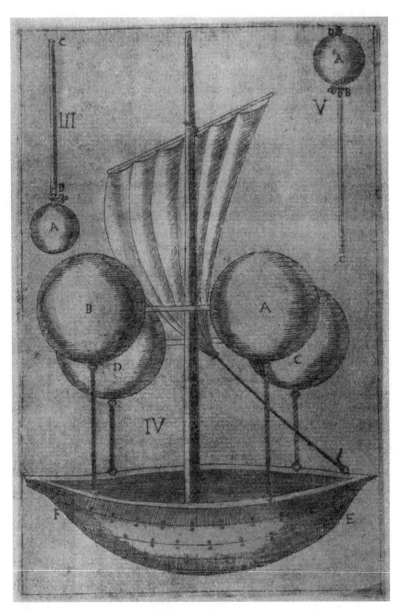

Father Francisco de Lana Terzi (1631–87) is recognized as the first to conceive of lighter-than-air flight. His Aerial Ship was supposed to rise into the heavens once the air was evacuated from its thin copper globes. From Prodromo, overo Saggio di alcune Inventioni Nuove. Brescia, 1670.

PHIL SCOTT

———⊷◈⊶———

The Pioneers of Flight

A Documentary History

———⊷◈⊶———

PRINCETON UNIVERSITY PRESS

Copyright © 1999 by Princeton University Press
Published by Princeton University Press, 41 William Street,
Princeton, New Jersey 08540
In the United Kingdom: Princeton University Press,
Chichester, West Sussex

All Rights Reserved

Library of Congress Cataloging-in-Publication Data
The pioneers of flight : a documentary
history / Phil Scott.
p.   cm.
A compilation of early aeronautical papers.
Includes bibliographical references and index.
ISBN 0-691-01117-6 (cloth : alk. paper)
1. Aeronautics—History—Sources.   2.
Aeronautics—History—Chronology.   I. Scott, Phil, 1961–
TL507 .C34 1999
629.13'09—dc21   98-38412

All photographs are courtesy of the National
Air and Space Museum, Smithsonian Institution,
unless otherwise noted.

This book has been composed in Adobe Caslon

The paper used in this publication meets the
minimum requirements of
ANSI/NISO Z39.48-1992 (R1997)
(*Permanence of Paper*)

http://pup.princeton.edu

Printed in the United States of America

1 3 5 7 9 10 8 6 4 2

*To Grandpa Scott, and to
Marcelle and
Christopher*

The only things that fly are birds and damn fools.
William Scott

CONTENTS

—————————

ACKNOWLEDGMENTS

To paraphrase somebody—I'm not sure whom—it takes a lot of books to make a book. More important, it takes a lot of people. First and foremost, there's Jack Repcheck, who conceived of this volume, and David Huang, who with Jack has labored to make it a reality. I also want to thank Tom Crouch and Robert Wohl of the National Air and Space Museum for their thoughtful critiques and additions to my initial proposal for this volume's contents, and especially Tony Bill, whose thorough expertise on the subject greatly assisted my final attempt to lock down the contents. John Rennie and Sarah Zimmerman kindly offered their criticism on the final manuscript. And, too, I profusely thank the staff of Princeton University Press, especially manuscript editor Bill Laznovsky and Senior Designer Jan Lilly.

Thanks, also, to Bill Garvey, Dick Collins, Jo Morris, Nancy Pallas, Winslow Browning, the effusive Beth Howard, Pat Luebke, Paul Barboza, Heather Dean, Terry Fagan, Peter Scallion, junior editor Perry Turner of *Escapade* magazine, Bill Wagstaff, and Robert Sadowski. And finally, thanks to Kitty, who complains a lot but somehow makes life more pleasant anyway.

THE PIONEERS OF FLIGHT

INTRODUCTION

―――→•←―――

The Origins of the Practical Airplane

―――→•←―――

The earliest airplanes weren't much. The one American history has agreed upon as the first arose from a few lengths of spruce and bent ash, a handful of screws and nails, some homemade steel fittings, lots of wire and spare bicycle parts (namely, wheel hubs and drive sprockets and a few feet of chain), a splash of aluminum paint, 127 yards of fine muslin, and a handmade engine of iron, aluminum, and copper that burned gasoline and cooled itself with water. By even the inventors' standards it barely flew: Just four flights of a total distance of less than a quarter mile across an especially sandy and desolate stretch of North Carolina beach before inadequate design, unskilled piloting, and an untimely gust of wind conspired to destroy it. The humblest bird, the meanest insect, could display infinitely more finesse.

Today near the same spot at Kitty Hawk, North Carolina, small four-seat airplanes continually circle from a nearby airfield, for a modest fee helping vacationers pay homage to the act that first occurred there. Right after Frequent Flyer Miles, nothing else so paints how commonplace the miracle of flight has become. But only a few who have skirted through the thin air in this machine made of plastic, metal, and man's cleverness have a bare concept of the complex forces and principles that sustain it. Even fewer are aware of the centuries-long struggle to understand and harness those principles. Our concerns are more basic and real. In the air we pray that mysterious laws keeping these craft aloft are somehow not repealed in our special instance. On the ground we justly lobby to remain out of the din of its lower paths, then rightfully grumble at the inconvenient distance to its infrastructure. Anchored in our present, we remain ignorant of its past.

It has changed our world in more ways than any invention before or since. It has reduced travel between continents from weeks to hours. In the bargain it has quickened our lives proportionately. Politically the airplane has shifted power away from massive armies and toward small but expensive air forces, and at the same time intensifying warfare to a hellishness brutal and unimaginable, even for humans. Too, it has spurred technology, leading the charge of devices with which we have stampeded through the twentieth century. To the airplane—and especially due to its usefulness in war—we owe ten thousand improvements to ten thousand devices. Without airplanes, we would have proceeded at a more leisurely pace with the development of radio (with which to communicate with airplanes); radar (with which to detect them), and so its bastard cousin television; and computers (with which to rapidly calculate the trajectories necessary to shoot them down). With the airplane we have gained sublime achievements in materials and design. Without the airplane there would have been no tail-fins on the '57 Chevy.

The airplane has become something that no one who helped bring it about could have possibly envisioned. Two years before their success one of its principal inventors, Wilbur Wright, a gentleman-inventor of quaint nineteenth-century conservative convictions, declared that it would be fifty years before men flew; the other principal, his brother Orville Wright, of similar convictions, lived long enough to see his frail and unique creation develop into the passenger jet, the rocket-powered aircraft capable of breaching the sound barrier, and the nuclear bomber that has helped human anxiety reach its distinctive twentieth-century frenzy. The Wright brothers, however, did not conjure their flying machine from the ether. So what were the steps by which human flight passed from myth to reality?

The process began centuries ago, evolutionary instead of revolutionary, largely because nothing quite like a successful airplane past or present can be found in nature. And yet it is obvious that the inspiration and the pattern came from birds. The ancients were careful birdwatchers, but the mechanisms keeping avians aloft defied observation through their simple appearance and complex reality. For just as the sun appeared to circle a stationary globe and some planets seemed to occasionally interrupt their orbit with retrograde motions, so too did birds seem to rely on their wings flapping down to hold the rest of their body up, while shifting their weight to steer and maintain balance. And so legends come down to us (namely, Ovid's Icarus and Daedalus) of ancient aviators who flew once they built themselves feather-covered wings for their arms. Though the point of Ovid's story was that man should avoid excess ("remember to fly midway"), the gullible flesh-and-blood Icarus would mistake a good story for truth and gather his feathers and his hubris and leap blindly from some height, usually with disastrous results. Even these reports contained a valuable lesson or two: That such "birdclothes" required a tail for stablity, that empirical experimentation was hazardous, or that the printed word is not necessarily a believable one.

Then, as now, there was a link between a nation's hegemony and its high level of activity in aeronautic experiment; a power achieves greatness and stability by, if not fostering experimentation and intellectual pursuit, then by not actively suppressing it either. (Or perhaps the reason is that history is written by the victors.) At any count, while the birds' secret remained undecipherable for the next few centuries, attempts to mimic their apparent actions continued. The Moor Armen Firman in ninth-century Cordoba and the monk Oliver of Malmesbury of the eleventh century, for example, both leapt with winged devices from tall towers. The Moor sustained bruising; the monk was crippled for life. Both suffered merciless skewering from their contemporaries.

The first extant sketches of a winged, heavier-than-air flying machine date from the fifteenth century, and emerged from the pen and the fertile mind of Leonardo da Vinci (1452–1519), the great genius of the Italian Renaissance. Though his design was subtle, his plans indicated little regard for economy of weight. Leonardo sought to mock with mechanics the flapping motion of birds that his normally keen eye discerned. What he didn't see was that, rather than flapping their wings simply up, then down and back, birds propel themselves forward with a twisting motion from their trailing edge feathers and control themselves also by flexing their wingtips. This motion, in fact, was only revealed late in the nineteenth century through stop-action photography, by which time the notion of the human-powered ornithopter had lost its hold on the minds of serious experimenters, having been scrutinized with reason. Mathematician Giovanni Alphonso Borelli (1608–79) of Messina compared the muscular strength of birds and man and found the latter sorely lacking in the pursuit of converting arms to wings. Humankind's strength, after all, emanates chiefly from the brain. And so it was that England's biggest, Isaac Newton (1642–1727), took the first step toward understanding how wings, unflapping and extended, move through the air and generate lift—one of the main secrets of flight—with his seminal exploration of how solid bodies react in fluids.

Newton, however, was not concerned with that particular aspect of fluid dynamics—lift—though a fellow Englishman named Sir George Cayley (1773–1857) was. The half-century that separated the pair saw the birth of one form of human flight, the lighter-than-air variety, thanks to the Montgolfier brothers of France. Ballooning was the catalyst for Cayley's interest in aeronautics, and he went on to become one of the deepest and most original practical thinkers in the field. It was he who first proposed the fixed wing—a vital, obvious, but apparently elusive conceptual leap—as well as the propeller; he devised a progenitor of the wind tunnel, and went on to fund the construction of the first glider. In 1853 his coachman became the first documented person to be lofted—albiet reluctantly—in such a contrivance. Cayley called it a "governable parachute" but that seemed more wishful thinking, since its control surfaces consisted solely of a cruciform tail to be operated tiller-fashion by the untrained, terrified coachman. For many years Sir George searched for a motor or some type of mechanism light enough to propel one of his governable parachutes, but he had the unfortunate luck to live in the dawn of the Age of Steam, a form of propulsion not given to a diminutive nature.

Cayley lived a long life; his later contemporaries included John String-fellow (1799–1883) and William Henson (1812–88), whose experimental vein ran toward relatively small models powered by cunningly engineered miniature steam engines. In the beginning they worked more or less together, then Stringfellow set out on his own and became the first to achieve powered—though uncontrolled—flight. In the larger scheme of things they achieved just enough to entice them to keep trying; but the bulk of science consists of small steps taken toward a larger destination. Only in rare instances does it attain giant leaps.

From England the progress in aeronautics shifted now toward the European continent. Most experimenters there at this time preferred to follow Cayley's lead by working on unpowered, manned gliding machines, often based on the planform of a species of bird that they had analyzed: There was Count Ferdinand Charles Honor, Phillipe d'Esterno, who designed, but never built, a birdlike ornithopter with wings that flapped, swiveled, and twisted to mimic the action of birds as did Leonardo's design; Louis-Pierre Mouillard (1834–97), who actually constructed a simple, straight wing that he slung over his shoulders and took into the air, albeit briefly; and Captain Jean-Marie Le Bris (d. 1872), who scaled an albatross up to more human dimensions, and who is believed to have made short hops in it on two separate occasions. The first and the third even had birdlike tail surfaces, but none of the aforementioned trio reached the degree of proficiency displayed later in the century by an engineer named Otto Lilienthal (1848–96) in the newly emerging nation of Germany.

Lilienthal gliders were disarmingly simple; his wings are notable in that they were not simply flat like most of his predecessors' but rather designed with a lift-enhancing curvature, or camber, derived from laboratory experimentation. He launched these lightweight machines from the Rhinower Hills outside of Berlin, and controlled them through shifting his weight. In a series of eighteen glider designs Lilienthal made an estimated 1,500 glides, the longest reaching 1,150 feet, and gained worldwide fame as "the flying man." But on an early August day in 1896, Lilienthal trotted off his hill as usual, pointing his glider's nose into the wind, when a gust lifted it straight up, and the little German struggled with all his might to shift the machine's nose down. His effort was in vain; the glider slid to the ground tailfirst, and Lilienthal's back was broken in the crash. He died the next day.

At the time of his death he held the endurance record—a few seconds—for unpowered flight. Of powered flight, only steam-driven models with a few seconds' endurance and with wings that spanned less than ten feet had flown, though for less than thirty feet, without control, and along a guide wire. The internal combustion engine was but two decades old. Propellers existed only as crude fans derived through empirical observation. No man had yet left the ground in true sustained, controlled flight. No one believed that humans were any closer to understanding the laws governing flight than they were a century before, or two thousand years prior, for that matter. Indeed, examiners at the U.S. Patent Office regularly applied the standard of "inoperable" to proposals for flying machines, the same standard assigned then and now to perpetual-motion machines, that holy grail of inventors the world over.

Such was the state of aeronautics when the Wright brothers entered the scene.

From their entrance they carried with them an understanding of the field and of its issues that all the others who had come before seemed to lack; too, they came with a surefooted confidence devoid of arrogance. Gifted inventors, but also methodical to the point of annoyance, the two introduced to the nascent art of aeronautics an approach that bordered on the scientific method: Regardless of their emotions they systematically recorded the results of an experiment; when the figures didn't mesh with what they had anticipated they sought an explanation before proceeding. None of their predecessors had been so orderly, so harmonious.

They began their foray into aeronautics by analyzing its goals and its shortcomings. Heavier-than-air flight was indeed possible, they said, though what was lacking was not a light but powerful engine. In fact, there were two things. The first was time and experience in the air; Lilienthal, they noted, had amassed but five hours' flying time after five years and more than 1,500 glides. The second, and most important, was complete control over the flying machine. The breakthrough for achieving the latter came early in their experimentation, before they even deigned to built a man-sized glider. Wilbur, observing the flight of buzzards, noticed that to right themselves in the air the birds twisted their wingtips in opposite directions—an observation that eluded even da Vinci. Without a doubt it was the most important of the Wrights' many vital contributions to the science. And too, it carried the Wright imprint, for no one in history would have thought to seek the solution to such a romantic notion as human flight from such an unsentimental, ungainly scavenger.

For gathering the necessary experience—time in the air through which to observe and understand how a flying machine flies—the brothers designed a small biplane glider that they hoped would be capable of hovering in the high winds above sandy Kitty Hawk, North Carolina. The glider's wingtips flexed in opposite directions through a cunning system of wires; the system would roll the glider level and even allow the pilot to turn it as they soon discovered. A moveable horizontal surface would allow the glider to climb and descend. It flew less well than expected, so the following year they came back with a bigger glider that performed much better, yet not as well as Lilienthal's tables of lift would lead them to expect. Though anyone else would have been satisfied with the second glider's performance, the gap between the tables and reality so troubled them that they nearly quit. That winter, however, they took the matter and tools in hand and built a simple wind tunnel. With it they performed a series of experiments intended to refine the aerodynamics of their gliders' basic planform. The result, their third glider, was the first air vehicle that relied more on experiment and experience rather than wishful thinking for its shape, size, and function. Along with the wingwarping feature and elevator of the previous two machines, this, the 1902 glider, also included a vertical rudder intended not, surprisingly, for turning, but rather to stabilize the glider in the air while the wingwarping feature did the balancing. From materials around virtually since the dawn of civilization, the brothers were able to fashion a fully controllable glider. So long had it taken for intelligence to catch up with imagination. Now it all seems as obvious as . . . as the Earth revolving around the sun.

By 1903 they felt they had refined their gliders and their flying skill enough that they finally thought themselves ready to attempt powered flight. That winter and spring they hashed out a theory of propellers and had their bicycle-shop mechanic hew and assemble a crude gasoline engine, which they mounted on a larger version of the glider of the year before. They made but four middling flights in the machine that December, but it proved that powered, controlled human flight was possible, and it gave them encouragement to continue.

The brothers spent the next two years perfecting their design and their understanding of how it flew, in a cow pasture outside their hometown of Dayton, Ohio (a small city that contributed a metropolis's share to the American consumer-industrial complex during that era, including the cash register and the automobile self-starter). It wasn't until 1908, after others had begun taking to the air—Glenn Curtiss in the United States and Alberto Santos-Dumont and Charles and Gabriel Voisin in France— that the Wright brothers finally demonstrated their machine before incredulous crowds of both nations. Though the others flew with less finesse than the brothers from Ohio, it showed that the airplane was an invention whose time had come. If the Wrights hadn't invented it when they did, it seems likely that someone would have come along and done so within a decade. After all, the Frenchmen flew what were essentially box kites (first designed by Australian Lawrence Hargrave in 1891) powered by indigenous marine engines of a much lighter weight than the ones that the Wrights had constructed from scratch. While their control systems lacked the sophistication of the Wrights', the others were much more willing to risk their necks in empiric experimentation. And so from that point forward the pages of aeronautical history are soaked with the blood of the fallen, who pushed their fragile machines beyond their unknown limits, who unwittingly violated some silent, involuable rule of physics and paid for it dearly. Even with Wright's cautious approach, it was with them that the first passenger died.

Despite the hazards, in 1911 *Scientific American* reported that "more than half a million men are now actively engaged in some industrial enterprise that has to do with navigation of the air." More than simply the realization of a dream, aviation had rapidly become an economic engine. Dangerous as it was, there would be no turning back.

. . .

While writing my recent book *The Shoulders of Giants,* a history of early aviation, my research was often aggravated by difficulties in locating copies of the early scientific texts and autobiographical materials. Even in the great libraries of New York City, subsequent history and advancements in aeronautics had relegated many works to obscure library storage spaces, where they languished for decades, laden with dust, forgotten.

Among aviation history aficionados, however, the titles of many of these same works are as familiar as household names—though entirely through reputation. Anyone who has read a biography of the Wrights, for instance, knows they were deeply influenced by such works as *Progress in Flying Machines* by Octave Chanute, or the shorter *L'Empire de l'air* by Pierre Mouillard, or *Der Vogelflug als Grundlage der Fliegekunst* by Otto Lilienthal. Yet in recent times few have personally gazed upon these ancient— often wildly inaccurate—texts, pamphlets, and articles. Instead, we rely upon the power of the historian to describe the works to us. Something invariably gets lost in the translation.

As I continually located my own copies of those early writings, I grew surprised and delighted by the depth and intelligence—or ignorance— displayed by the authors, and became charmed by their prose. Take, for example, this excerpt from the obscure Aeronautical and Miscellaneous Note-book of Sir George Cayley, the little-known English gentleman-farmer who discovered the principles of aeronautics through his acute observations of nature:

> I was much struck with the beautiful contrivance of the [seed] of the
> sycamore tree . . . so formed and balanced that it no sooner is blown from
> the tree than it instantly creates a rotative force preserving the seed for the

centre, and the centrifugal force of the wing keeps it nearly horizontal, meeting the air in a very small angle like the bird's wing. . . .

Thus, from a single seed sprang the airplane. Would today's scientist as personally and poetically describe orbital mechanics as it applies to the space shuttle? Cayleys' musing remings me of Henry David Thoreau's *The Dispersion of Seeds,* though Cayley does lack the great Transcendentalist's philosophical bent and his gentle insight into the nature of nature—but then the two have different purposes.

This isn't to say that everyone within these pages wrote with a silver quill. Henson's description of his Aerial Steam Carriage survives as a wordy, convoluted document, but his Proposal that follows offers the reader an exceptional view of the workings of his mind. Sometimes what a thing lacks in style it makes up for in charm. And when he and the others fumble we forgive them, for it is daunting work to set new ideas to words.

We have grown inured to the staccato techno-babble spouted from the modern aeronautical engineer and aviator, who often frankly deserve their popular reputations as icy, emotionless, quasi-articulate systems monitors. Our fliers and astronauts who now enter the public eye display a soulless facade borrowed from the pro athlete's post-game press conference, conditioned by the unblinking camera and coached by press agents to say exactly nothing. In contrast though, take this 1911 newspaper quote from Cal Rodgers, who more than a century after Cayley's observation made a beleaguered—but ultimately successful—eighty-four-day-long attempt to fly across the United States:

> Prize or no prize, that's where I am bound and if canvas, steel, and wire together with a little brawn, tendon, and brain stick with me, I mean to get there . . . I'm going to do this whether I get five thousand dollars or fifty cents or nothing. I am going to cross this continent simply to be the first to cross in an aeroplane.

These pioneers were visionaries, true; they also inhabited a world of letters instead of televised images and perhaps benefitted by having a somewhat greater ability to express themselves. Like celebrities of today, though, the early aviators—those who survived long enough—sought to capitalize on their fame and produced memoirs for public consumption. Our tastes have changed, and so there are no lurid tales of sexually abused childhoods and substance dependencies, but such omissions also tell a story: One of the sensibilities of a time past. Luckily, perhaps, we can still only speculate about the Wright brothers' sex lives. How refreshing.

This volume, *The Pioneers of Flight,* is filled with some of the most important written works in aviation's early history, the words of its earliest participants describing their observations and deeds. Beginning with the original account of Daedalus and Icarus from Ovid's *Metamorphosis*, through Cayley's writings, selected passages from the Wrights' voluminous correspondences, and those all-but-forgotten memoirs of the pioneer aviators, the volume traces the history and development of flight through the eyes and pens of its participants. The works that make up the bulk of this volume I chose primarily for the influence they and their authors had on the aeronautical history of the western world: those works that led to flight's successful achievement, and those who contributed to the airplane's successful spread from the U.S. to Europe. Sadly many items had to be omitted in a concession to space; my original wish list of papers, letters, and articles totaled nearly half a million words. And so in a bloodless triage I forced myself to sacrifice pieces by Samuel Langley on the successful unmanned flights of his steam-powered Aerodromes No. 5 and No. 6, a lengthy visit to Sir Hiram Maxim's home and a groundbound ride in his four-ton great kite by journalist H.J.W. Dam, and every drawing and word by Leonardo da Vinci on the subject. Someday soon they may be published again, their thoughts—and mistakes—preserved in bibliographic amber a little longer.

PART I

EARLY LEGENDS, ATTEMPTS,
AND CONCEPTS

1

Daedalus and Icarus

From *The Metamorphosis*, by Ovid, translated by Horace Gregory

Chinese legend has it that, as a boy, the Emperor Shun (2258–2208 B.C.) once escaped his father's enemies by stealing "the work clothes of a bird" and flying away. In the West, aeronautical legend begins with the tale of Daedalus and Icarus, laid down in Book VIII of *Metamorphosis*, by the Roman poet Ovid.

When Minos landed on the coast of Crete,
He bled a hundred bulls to mighty Jove,
And decked his palace with the spoils of war.
And yet strange gossip tainted all his honors;
Proof that his wife was mounted by a bull
Was clear enough to all who saw her son,
Half-beast, half-man, a sulky, heavy creature.
To hide this symbol of his wife's mismating
He planned to house the creature in a maze,
An arbor with blind walls beyond the palace;
He turned to Daedalus, an architect,
Who was well known for artful craft and wit,
To make a labyrinth that tricked the eye.
Quite as Meander flows through Phrygian pastures,
Twisting its streams to sea or fountainhead,
The dubious waters turning left or right,
So Daedalus designed his winding maze;
And as one entered it, only a wary mind
Could find an exit to the world again—
Such was the cleverness of that strange arbor.

. . . .

Weary of exile, hating Crete, his prison,
Old Daedalus grew homesick for his country
Far out of sight beyond his walls—the sea.
"Though Minos owns this island, rules the waves,

The skies are open: my direction's clear.
Though he commands all else on earth below
His tyranny does not control the air."
So Daedalus turned his mind to subtle craft,
An unknown art that seemed to outwit nature:
He placed a row of feathers in neat order,
Each longer than the one that came before it
Until the feathers traced an inclined plane
That cast a shadow like the ancient pipes
That shepherds played, each reed another step
Unequal to the next. With cord and wax
He fixed them smartly at one end and middle,
Then curved them till they looked like eagles' wings.
And as he worked, boy Icarus stood near him,
His brilliant face lit up by his father's skill.
He played at snatching feathers from the air
And sealing them with wax (nor did he know
How close to danger came his lightest touch);
And as the artist made his miracles
The artless boy was often in his way.
At last the wings were done and Daedalus
Slipped them across his shoulders for a test
And flapped them cautiously to keep his balance,
And for a moment glided into air.
He taught his son the trick and said, "Remember
To fly midway, for if you dip too low
The waves will weight your wings with thick saltwater,
And if you fly too high the flames of heaven
Will burn them from your sides. Then take your flight
Between the two. Your route is not towards Boötes
Nor Helice, nor where Orion swings
His naked sword. Steer where I lead the way."
With this he gave instructions how to fly
And made a pair of wings to fit the boy.
Though his swift fingers were as deft as ever,
The old man's face was wet with tears; he chattered
More fatherly advice on how to fly.
He kissed his son—and, as the future showed,
This was a last farewell—and then he took off.
And as a bird who drifts down from her nest
Instructs her young to follow her in flight,
So Daedalus flapped wings to guide his son.
Far off, below them, some stray fisherman,

Attention startled from his bending rod,
Or a bland shepherd resting on his crook,
Or a dazed farmer leaning on his plough,
Glanced up to see the pair float through the sky,
And, taking them for gods, stood still in wonder.
They flew past Juno's Samos on the left
And over Delos and the isle of Paros,
And on the right lay Lebinthus, Calymne,
A place made famous for its wealth in honey.
By this time Icarus began to feel the joy
Of beating wings in air and steered his course
Beyond his father's lead: all the wide sky
Was there to tempt him as he steered toward heaven.
Meanwhile the heat of sun struck at his back
And where his wings were joined, sweet-smelling fluid
Ran hot that once was wax. His naked arms
Whirled into wind; his lips, still calling out
His father's name, were gulfed in the dark sea.
And the unlucky man, no longer father,
Cried, "Icarus, where are you, Icarus,
Where are you hiding, Icarus, from me?"
Then as he called again, his eyes discovered
The boy's torn wings washed on the climbing waves.
He damned his art, his wretched cleverness,
Rescued the body and placed it in a tomb,
And where it lies the land's called Icarus.

2

The Short, Happy Flight of King Bladud

From *The History of the Kings of Britain*,
by Geoffrey of Monmouth, translated by Lewis Thorpe

In his history of the Kings of Britain written in 1136, Geoffrey tells of the pre-Saxon King Bladud, the ninth king of Britain (whose son's name Shakespeare spelled slightly differently in his famous tragedy), and his short aeronautical career in 863 B.C.

Hudibras's son Bladud finally succeeded him and ruled the kingdom for twenty years. It was he who built the town of Kaerbadum, which is now called Bath, and who constructed the hot baths there which are so suited to the needs of mortal men. He chose the goddess Minerva as the tutelary deity of the baths. In her temple he lit fires which never went out and which never fell away into ash, for the moment they began to die down they were turned into balls of stone.

At that time Elijah prayed that it should not rain upon the earth, so that for three years and six months no rain fell.

Bladud was a most ingenious man who encouraged necromancy* throughout the kingdom. He pressed on with his experiments and finally constructed a pair of wings for himself and tried to fly through the upper air. He came down on top of the Temple of Apollo in the town of Trinovantum† and was dashed into countless fragments.

After Bladud had met his fate in this way, his son Leir was raised to the kingship.

---

* Magic, alchemy.

† Trinovantum (New Troy), in Geoffrey's *History*, was settled by Trojans and later became London.

3

———⟩•⟨———

Oliver of Malmesbury, The Flying Monk

From *Histoire des Ballons* (1852), by Bescherelle,
translated by Octave Chanute

During the eleventh century a Benedictine monk tried a stunt similar to
Bladud's.

———⟩•⟨———

Having manufactured some wings, modeled after the description that
Ovid has given of those of Dedalus [*sic*], and having fastened them to his
hands, he sprang from the top of a tower against the wind. He succeeded
in sailing a distance of 125 paces; but either through the impetuosity of
whirling of the wind, or through nervousness resulting from his audacious
enterprise, he fell to the earth and broke his legs. Henceforth he dragged
a miserable, languishing existence, attributing his misfortune to his having failed to attach a tail to his feet.

4

The Saracen of Constantinople

From *Progress in Flying Machines,* by Octave Chanute (1894)

More lucky perhaps, was the Saracen of Constantinople, whose 1178 leap was recorded in his history of the city by Cousin.

He stood upright, clothed in a white robe, very long and very wide, whose folds, stiffened by willow wands, were to serve as sails to receive the wind. All the spectators kept their eyes intently fixed upon him, and many cried, "Fly, fly, O Saracen! Do not keep us so long in suspense while thou art weighing the wind!" . . .

The Emperor, who was present, then attempted to dissuade him from this vain and dangerous enterprise. The Sultan of Turkey in Asia, who was then on a visit to Constantinople, and who was also present at this experiment, halted between dread and hope, wishing on the one hand for the Saracen's success, and apprehending on the other that he should shamefully perish. The Saracen kept extending his arms to catch the wind. At last, when he deemed it favorable, he rose into the air like a bird; but his flight was as unfortunate as that of Icarus, for the weight of his body having more power to draw him downward than his artificial wings had to sustain him, he fell and broke his bones, and such was his misfortune that instead of sympathy there was only merriment over his misadventure.

5

The Aerial Ship

By Father Francisco de Lana Terzi, 1670

While progress in heavier-than-air flight remained as unproductive as ever, in 1671 an entirely new concept for human flight burst upon the scene. The idea came from Father Francisco de Lana Terzi (1630–87), an Italian Jesuit and distinguished scientist. After studying the recently invented barometer and his contemporaries' findings on atmospheric pressure and vacuum, de Lana wrote *The Aerial Ship*, the first serious description of lighter-than-air flight.

No one has . . . deemed it possible so to construct a vessel that it would travel on the air as if it were supported on water, insomuch that it has not been thought practicable to make a machine lighter than the air itself, which it is necessary first to do in order to accomplish the desired end.

Now I, who always had a bent for working out the most difficult inventions, after a long study over this, believe I have found the manner of making a machine lighter in itself than air, so that not only will it float on the air by its own lightness, but that it may also carry men and any other required weights; nor do I think it possible that I can be deceived, the whole thing being proven by tried experiment, while it can also be demonstrated as infallible from the 11th Book of Euclid, which is accepted by all mathematicians. I will therefore start by first making certain suppositions from which I will deduce the practical method of constructing the vessel, which if it does not deserve as did that one of Argus to be placed amongst the stars, yet will at least ascend upwards to them by its own efforts. I will, first of all, presuppose that air has weight owing to the vapours and halations which ascend from the earth and seas to a height of many miles and surround the whole of our terraqueous globe; and this fact will not be denied by philosophers, even by those who may have but a superficial knowledge, because it can be proven by exhausting, if not all, at any rate the greater part of the air contained in a glass vessel, which, if weighed before and after the air has been exhausted, will be found materially reduced in weight. Then I found out how much the air in itself weighed . . .

I assume that any large vessel can be entirely exhausted of all, or, at any rate, of nearly all, the air contained therein . . .

I suppose, with all the philosophers, that when a body is lighter or has less density, as they describe it, than another, the lighter one will ascend in the heavier one if the heavier is a liquid body. As is the case of a wooden sphere, which ascends to the surface of the water and floats there, because it is lighter in density than the water, so also will a glass vessel full of air float on the water, notwithstanding that glass in itself is heavier than water, but all the substance of the vessel—taking the glass and air together—is lighter than an equal volume of water, which fact is owing to its being, as a whole, lighter in density than water.

Presupposing all these things, it is certain that one can construct a vessel of glass or other material which could weigh less than the air contained therein; if, then, one exhausted all the air in the manner before described, this vessel would be lighter in density than the air itself, and, therefore . . . it would float on the air and ascend. . . .

Let us consider of what predetermined size it is possible to construct a vessel of copper beaten out thin, but not so thin as to be difficult to work, and let us suppose that the thinness of the copper be such that a sheet of the width and length of a foot weighs three ounces, which is not a difficult matter to do. Let us, therefore, with this copper drawn out to such a thinness, make a round vessel the size or diameter of which is 14 feet. I contend that this vessel will weight less than the air contained therein. If the latter be exhausted, the vessel, being lighter than its equivalent volume of air, will necessarily rise of itself and float in the air. . . .

It is thus manifest that the larger the ball or vessel is made, the thicker and more solid can the sheets of copper be made, because although the weight will increase, the capacity of the vessel will increase to a greater extent and with it the weight of the air therein, so that it will always be able to lift a heavier weight.

From this it can be easily seen how it is possible to construct a machine which, fashioned like unto a ship, will float on the air. Let us build four globes, each of which is capable of lifting two or three men as described above, and is exhausted of air . . . Then construct a wooden car fashioned like a boat, with its masts and sails and oars, and with four ropes of equal length; attach the four spheres after having exhausted the air therein, but keeping the vessel anchored to the earth so that it should not get away and fly off before the men have entered in the car; then release the cords gradually and all together, so that the ship may lift itself up with the car, carrying with it many men, more or less, according to the lifting power. The passengers may use the sails and oars to travel with great speed to any place at will, even over the highest mountains.

But whilst I write down these matters I smile unto myself, realising that seemingly it sounds like unto a fable no less strange or incredible than those made fantasies that issued from the fertile brain of Lucian.* Yet, on the other side, I clearly discern that I have not erred in any of my proofs, especially as I have conferred on these matters with many sage and well-instructed persons who have not been able to find any errors in my discourses, having only expressed a desire to have a visible proof by one of these spheres which would, of itself, ascend in the air. Which thing I would willingly have done before publishing these my inventions, had not my vows of poverty prevented my expending 100 ducats, which sum at least would be required to satisfy so laudable a curiosity. Therefore I pray those readers of my book who may be curious to try my experiments, to acquaint me if they succeed, or if any error committed in construction should prevent a successful issue, as no doubt I could show them how to correct any such errors. To encourage everyone to proceed on to the proof I will here smooth away some of the difficulties that may ordinarily present themselves in the practical working out of my invention. . . .

Difficulties may be experienced owing to the thinness of the vessel, because the great pressure of the outer air trying to force its way in to prevent there being a vacuum or, at any rate, an extreme rarefaction, would compress the vessel, and if not break it, at least flatten it.

To this, I reply, that it might so occur if the vessel were not round, but being spherical the outer air could only compress it equally on all sides, so that it would rather strengthen it than break it, which has been shown by experiments with glass vessels, which, even if made of thick, strong glass, break into a thousand pieces unless round in shape, whereas round vessels of glass, although very thin, do not break; nor is it necessary that they should be perfectly round, but it suffices if they do not depart very much from a true sphere.

In constructing the copper globes they could be built up from two halves and then connected by the usual process of soldering, or even built up of many parts and connected in the same way, in doing which there is not much difficulty.

Some difficulty may be experienced as to the height to which the vessel may ascend, because if it were to ascend above the air, which is commonly reckoned to have a height of fifty miles more or less, as we shall see further on, it would follow that men would not be able to breathe.

To which I would reply that the higher one ascends in the air so the more rarefied and lighter it is therefore there will be a certain height which the vessel may reach, but beyond which it will not be able to rise, because the air above will be lighter and unable to sustain it, so that it will stop at a point where the density of air will be so light as to equal the weight of the whole machine and the persons thereon. In order that it should not ascend too high, it will be well to add a greater or smaller weight, according

* Lucian (c. A.D. 120–180), Greek satirist.

to the height it is required to rise, but if even then it should continue to rise too high, that could easily be remedied by opening the taps, thus allowing a certain amount of air to enter the spheres so that, losing some of their lightness, they will descend and with them the ship; and if, on the contrary, it will not ascend as high as required, it could be made to rise by lightening it of any weight it was carrying. Similarly, wishing to descend to earth, it will only be necessary to open the taps so that the air entering slowly may cause the globes to lose their lightness and gradually descend until they bring the ship to earth.

Some may object that the ship could not be propelled by oars, seeing that they propel a ship through the water from the fact that the water offers resistance to the oars, whereas the air does not offer such a resistance.

To this I rejoin that, although air does not resist the thrust of the oars to such an extent as water, being lighter and more subtle, yet it offers an appreciable resistance and such as is sufficient to propel the ship; for the resistance of the air to the oars is exactly in the same proportion as its resistance to the motion of the ship, so that, although it offers little resistance to the oars, it will enable the ship to travel easily, also it will be rarely necessary to use the oars, as once up in the air there will be always a wind which, even if very feeble, will be sufficient to move it along with great speed; and if it were contrary to our intended course, I will give instructions elsewhere how to place the mast of the ship in such a manner as to enable it to travel by any wind, not only in the air, but also on the water.

Much greater is the difficulty of preventing the ship from being driven at too great a speed by a strong wind, whereby it runs the risk of hurling itself against the mountains, which are the rocks of the aerial oceans, and be wrecked or upset, but, as to the latter possibility, I contend it would be very difficult for the wind to upset the whole weight of the machine with many men standing on it. They would always counterbalance the lightness of the globes, so that the latter would always remain above the ship, neither could ever the ship be driven above them, nor could the ship fall to the ground if no air be allowed to enter the globes, nor can there be any peril of falling overboard and being drowned as at sea, as holding on to the ropes or to the woodwork the men would be secure. As to the first objection I confess that our aerial ship might run great perils, but not more than the ships on the seas are liable, because, as in their case, so could we be furnished with anchors, which would easily grapple to the trees. Besides, although our aerial ocean has no shores, it has this advantage, that there is no necessity for ports of refuge for the airships, they being able every time they are in danger to descend from the high air and land on the ground.

Other difficulties I do not foresee that could prevail against this invention, save one only, which to me seems the greatest of them all, and that is that God would never surely allow such a machine to be successful, since it would create many disturbances in the civil and political governments of mankind.

Where is the man who can fail to see that no city would be proof against surprise, as the ship could at any time be steered over its squares, or even over the courtyards of dwelling-houses, and brought to earth for the landing of its crew? And in the case of ships that sail the seas, by allowing the aerial ship to descend from the high air to the level of their sails, their cordage could be cut; or even without descending so low iron weights could be hurled to wreck the ships and kill their crews, or they could be set on fire by fireballs and bombs; not ships alone, but houses, fortresses, and cities could be thus destroyed, with the certainty that the airship could come to no harm as the missiles could be hurled from a vast height.

6

The Flight of Birds

By Giovanni Alphonso Borelli

Though the good Jesuit did chillingly predict the horrors of aerial warfare, Terzi's Aerial Ship was never built. Indeed, removing the air would have assured the collapse of its thin copper globes under atmospheric pressure. Not long after Terzi's work appeared, in 1680, a fellow scholar named Giovanni Alphonso Borelli had published posthumously his analysis of arm-flapping human flight and Terzi's Aerial Ship—using science and logic to shred both concepts.

Three principal points ought to be considered in flying: firstly, the motive power by which the body of the Animal may be sustained through the air; secondly, the suitable instruments, which are wings; thirdly, the resistance of the Animal's heavy body.

The degree of motive power is known by the strength and quantity of the muscles, which are designed to bend the arms or to flap the wings. And because the motive force in Birds' wings is apparently ten-thousand times greater than the resistance of their weight, and as Nature has endowed Birds with so great an excess of motive power, the Bird largely increases the strength of its pectoral muscles and skillfully decreases the weight of its body, as we have hinted above.

When, therefore, it is asked whether men may be able to fly by their own strength, it must be seen whether the motive power of the pectoral muscles (the strength of which is indicated and measured by their size), is proportionately great, as it is evident that it must exceed the resistance of the weight of the whole human body ten-thousand times, together with the weight of enormous wings which should be attached to the arms. And it is clear that the motive power of the pectoral muscles in men is much less than is necessary for flight, for in Birds the bulk and weight of the muscles for flapping the wings are not less than a sixth part of the entire weight of the body. Therefore, it would be necessary that the pectoral muscles of a man should weigh more than a sixth part of the entire weight of his body; so also the arms, by flapping with the wings attached, should be able to exert a power ten-thousand times greater than the weight of the human body itself. But they are far below such excess, for the aforesaid pectoral muscles do not equal a hundredth part of the entire weight of a man. Wherefore either the strength of the muscles ought to be increased or the weight of the human body must be decreased, so that the same proportion obtains in it as exists in Birds.

Hence it is deduced, that the Icarian invention is entirely mythical because impossible; for it is not possible either to increase a man's pectoral muscles or to diminish the weight of the human body; and whatever apparatus is used, although it is possible to increase the momentum, the velocity or the power employed can never equal the resistance; and therefore wing flapping by the contraction of muscles cannot give out enough power to carry up the heavy body of a man.

There only remains the diminution of the weight of the human body, not in itself, for this is impossible, its mechanism must remain intact, but especially and respectively to the aerial fluid in the same way as a strip of lead can float on water if a certain amount of cork be attached to it which causes the entire mass of lead and cork to float, being of like weight to the amount of water which it displaces, according to the law of Archimedes. And this device Nature uses in fishes. She places in their bellies a sack full of air by means of which they are able to maintain their equilibrium, so that they can remain in the same place as if they were part of the water itself.

By the same device some have lately persuaded themselves that the weight of the human body is able to be brought into equilibrium with the air, that is to say by the use of a large vessel, either a vacuum or very nearly so, of so great a size that it is possible to sustain a human body in the air together with the vessel.

But we easily perceive this to be a vain hope as it is necessary to construct the vessel of some hard metal such as brass or copper, and squeeze out and take away all the air from its interior, and it must also be of so great a size that when in the air it displaces a quantity of air of the same weight as itself, together with the man fastened to it; wherefore it would have to occupy a space of more than 22,000 cubic feet; moreover, the plates composing the sphere must be reduced to an extraordinary thinness. Furthermore, so thin a vessel of this size could not be constructed, or, if constructed, preserved intact, nor could it be exhausted by any pump, much less of mercury, of which so large a quantity is not to be found in the world, nor could be extracted from the earth, and if such a great vacuum were made the thin brass vessel could not resist the strong pressure of the air, which would break or crush it. I pass over the fact that so great a machine of the same weight as the air would not be able to keep itself in exact equilibrium with the air, and therefore would incontinently rise to the highest confines of the air like clouds, or would fall to the ground.

Again, such a large mass could not be moved in flight on account of the resistance of the air; in the same way feathers and soap bubbles can be moved only with difficulty through the air, even when they are blown by a light breeze, just as clouds, poised in the air, are driven by the wind.

At this point we cease to wonder that Nature, who is accustomed everywhere to imitate others' advantages, makes the swimming of fishes in water so easy and the flying of Birds through the air so difficult, for we see whereas fishes can remain in the midst of water, being of their own accord and without effort held up and poised, and can very easily descend and ascend, and are only moved by the strength of muscles placed transversely and obliquely to the direction of motion; on the other hand, Birds are not able to float in the air but owe their sustentation to the continual exertion of strength and a projectile force, not external, but natural and intrinsic, by contracting their pectoral muscles by which they make a series of bounds through the air; and this requires enormous strength, as they are not going upon feet supported on solid ground, but on wings supported by very fluid and greatly agitated air.

Nevertheless, I say that the act of flying is not difficult; indeed it is very simple and very easy in the various possible ways by which it can be accomplished. And the reason why flying is not performed in the same way as swimming is that Nature does not work miracles; fishes can easily float in heavy water, but it is impossible that Birds, made of bones, flesh, and blood two-thousand times heavier than the air, can float in the air.

7

"Some fire, my dear friend, some fire!"

Letter by the Marquis d'Arlandes, 1783

Joseph and Etienne Montgolfier, papermakers from the town of Annonay, near Lyon, France, stumbled into aeronautics sometime in 1782. One account says their inspiration was paper ashes rising in a column of smoke; another says the ascending object was a shirt hung to dry over a fire; a more picturesque third account, doubtlessly apocryphal, says it was the drying, billowing petticoats of Joseph's wife (the legend does not say whether she was in them at the time). Either way, the brothers were inspired to capture smoke in a paper bag, which they successfully launched skyward. A succession of ever-larger smoke balloons followed, including, on September 19, 1783, one containing the first living creatures: a cock, a sheep, and a duck. Just over two months later, November 21, the first two humans went aloft. Chosen by King Louis XVI himself—though at first he wanted to send up convicts—the hand-picked aeronauts were François Pilatre de Rozier and the Marquis d'Arlandes. The latter recalled the flight in a letter to a friend.

I wish to describe as well as I can the first journey which men have attempted through an element which, prior to the discovery of Messrs. Montgolfier, seemed so little fitted to support them.

We went up on the 21st of November, 1783, at near two o'clock, Monsieur Rozier on the west side of the balloon, I on the east. The wind was nearly northwest. The machine, say the public, rose with majesty; but really the position of the balloon altered so that M. Rozier was in the advance of our position, I in the rear.

I was surprised at the silence and the absence of movement which our departure caused among the spectators, and believed them to be astonished and perhaps awed at the strange spectacle; they might well have reassured themselves. I was still gazing, when M. Rozier cried to me—

"You are doing nothing, and the balloon is scarcely rising a fathom."

"Pardon me," I answered, as I placed a bundle of straw upon the fire and slightly stirred it. Then I turned quickly, but already we had passed out of sight of La Muette. Astonished I cast a glance toward the river. I perceived the confluence of the Oise. And naming the principle bends of the river by the places nearest them, I cried, "Passy, St. Germain, St. Denis, Sèvres!"

"If you look at the river in that fashion you will be likely to bathe in it soon," cried Rozier. "Some fire, my dear friend, some fire!"

We traveled on; but instead of crossing the river, as our direction seemed to indicate, we bore toward the Invalides, then returned upon the principle bend of the river, and traveled to above the barrier of La Conference, thus dodging about the river, but not crossing it.

"The river is very difficult to cross," I remarked to my companion.

"So it seems," he answered; "but you are doing nothing. I suppose it is because you are braver than I, and don't fear a tumble."

I stirred the fire, I seized a truss of straw with my fork; I raised it and threw it in the midst of the flames. An instant afterward I felt myself lifted as it were into the heavens.

"For once we move," said I.

"Yes, we move," answered my companion.

At the same instant I heard from the top of the balloon a sound which made me believe that it had burst. I watched, yet I saw nothing. My companion had gone into the interior, no doubt to make some observations. As my eyes were fixed on the top of the machine I experienced a shock, and it was the only one I had yet felt. The direction of the movement was from above downward. I then said,

"What are you doing? Are you having a dance to yourself?"

"I'm not moving."

"So much the better. It is only a new current which I hope will carry us from the river," I answered.

I turned to see where we were, and found we were between the Ecole Militaire and the Invalides.

"We are getting on," said Rozier.

"Yes, we are traveling."

"Let us work, let us work," said he.

I now heard another report in the machine, which I believed was produced by the cracking of a cord. This new intimation made me carefully examine the inside of our habitation. I saw that the part that was turned toward the south was full of holes, of which some were of a considerable size.

"It must descend," I then cried.

"Why?"

"Look!" I said. At the same time I took my sponge and quietly extinguished the little fire that was burning some of the holes within my reach; but at the same moment I perceived that the bottom of the cloth was coming away from the circle which surrounded it.

"We must descend," I repeated to my companion.

He looked below.

"We are upon Paris," he said.

"It does not matter," I answered. " Only look! Is there no danger? Are you holding on well?"

"Yes."

I examined from my side, and saw that we had nothing to fear. I then tried with my sponge the ropes which were within my reach. All of them held firm. Only two of the cords had broken.

I then said, "We can cross Paris."

During this operation we were rapidly getting down to the roofs. We made more fire, and rose again with the greatest ease. I looked down, and it seemed to me we were going toward the towers of St. Sulpice; but, on rising, a new current made us quit this direction and bear more to the south. I looked to the left, and beheld a wood, which I believed to be that of Luxembourg. We were traversing the boulevard, and I cried all at once,

"Get to ground!"

But the intrepid Rozier, who never lost his head, and who judged more surely than I, prevented me from attempting to descend. I then threw a bundle of straw on the fire. We rose again, and another current bore us to the left. We were now close to the ground, between two mills. As soon as we came near the earth I raised myself over the gallery, and leaning there with my two hands, I felt the balloon pressing softly against my head. I pushed it back, and leaped down to the ground. Looking around and ex-pecting to see the balloon still distended, I was astonished to find it quite empty and flattened. On looking for Rozier I saw him in his shirt sleeves creeping from under the mass of canvas that had fallen over him. Before attempting to descend he had put off his coat and placed it in the basket. After a deal of trouble we were at last all right.

As Rozier was without a coat I besought him to go to the nearest house. On his way thither he encountered the Duke of Chartres, who had fol-lowed us, as we saw, very closely, for I had had the honor of conversing with him the moment before we set out.

PART II

1799–1881

MANNED GLIDERS, POWERED MODELS

8

The Flight of the Sycamore Seed

From The Note-Book of Sir George Cayley, 1808

Sir George Cayley (1773–1857) was ten years old when the hot-air balloon was born, and there is little doubt that the invention made a profound impression on the baronet's mind. Encouraged by his mother, young Sir George kept a scientific journal in which he recorded his observations on everyday natural phenomenon, and the results of his experiments with heavier-than-air flight. This brief entry is a typical example.

Brompton, Octr. 9th. 1808. I was much struck with the beautiful contrivance of the chat of the sycamore seed. It is an oval seed furnished with one thin wing, which one would at first imagine would not impede its fall but only guide the seed downward, like the feathers upon an arrow. But it is so formed and balanced that it no sooner is blown from the tree than it instantly creates a rotative force preserving the seed for the centre, and the centrifugal force of the wing keeps it nearly horizontal, meeting the air in a very small angle like the bird's wing, and by this means the seed is supported till a moderate wind will carry it in a path not falling more than one in 6 from an horizontal one, so that from a moderately high tree it may fly 60 yards before it reaches the earth.

9

—»‣0‣«—

On Aerial Navigation

By Sir George Cayley, 1809

Around 1809 newspaper accounts began circulating about Viennese watchmaker Jacob Degen, reporting that he had risen to a height of fifty-four feet
by flapping the wings of his homebuilt ornithopter. Spurred by Degen's al-
leged success (the watchmaker had actually been lifted in the air with the
aid of a hydrogen balloon), Sir George Cayley decided to publish his findings before the watchmaker could publish his. Appearing in three parts between 1809 and 1810 in *Nicholson's Journal of Natural Philosophy, Chemistry,
and the Arts,* Cayley's *On Aerial Navigation* laid the foundation for the science of aeronautics.

—»‣0‣«—

I observed in your Journal for last month, that a watchmaker at Vienna,
of the name Degen, has succeeded in raising himself in the air by mechanical means. I waited to receive your present numbers, in expectation
of seeing some farther account of this experiment, before I commenced
transcribing the following essay upon aerial navigation, from a number of
memoranda which I have made at various times upon this subject. I am
induced to request your publication of this essay, because I conceive, that,
in stating the fundamental principles of this art, together with a considerable number of facts and practical observations that have arisen in the
course of much attention to this subject, I may be expediting the attainment of an object that will in time be found of great importance to
mankind, so much so, that a new aera [*sic*] in society will commence, from
the moment that aerial navigation is finally realized.

It appears to me, and I am more confirmed by the success of the ingenious Mr. Degen, that nothing more is necessary, in order to bring the following principles into common practical use, than the endeavours of skilful artificers, who may vary the means of execution, till those most
convenient are attained.

Since the days of Bishop Wilkins* the scheme of flying by artificial

---

* John Wilkins (1614–72), prelate and scientist, whose work included a review of several
ideas and suggestions about flight.

wings has been much ridiculed, and indeed the idea of attaching wings to the arms of a man is ridiculous enough, as the pectoral muscles of a bird occupy more than two-thirds of its whole muscular strength, whereas in man the muscles that could operate upon the wings thus attached would probably not exceed one-tenth of the whole mass. There is no proof that, weight for weight, a man is comparatively weaker than a bird; it is therefore probable, if he can be made to exert his whole strength advantageously upon a light surface similarly proportioned to his weight, as that of the wing to the bird, that he would fly like a bird. The flight of a strong man by great muscular exertion, though a curious and interesting circumstance, inasmuch as it will probably be the first means of ascertaining this power and supplying the basis whereon to improve it, would be of little use. I feel perfectly confident, however, that this noble art will soon be brought home to man's general convenience, and that we shall be able to transport ourselves and families, and their goods and chattels, more securely by air than by water, and with velocity of from 20 to 100 miles per hour. To produce this effect it is only necessary to have a first mover, which will generate more power in a given time, in proportion to its weight, than the animal system of muscles.

The consumption of coal in a Boulton & Watt's steam engine is only about 5½ lbs. per hour for the power of one horse. The heat produced by the combustion of this portion of inflammable matter is the sole cause of the power generated, but it is applied through the intervention of a weight of water expanded into steam, and a still greater weight of cold water to condense it again. The engine itself likewise must be massive enough to resist the whole external pressure of the atmosphere, and therefore is not applicable to the purpose proposed. Steam engines have lately been made to operate by expansion only, and these might be constructed so as to be light enough for this purpose, provided the usual plan of a large boiler be given up and the principle of injecting a proper charge of water into a mass of tubes, forming the cavity for the fire, be adopted in lieu of it. The strength of vessels to resist internal pressure being inversely as their diameters, very slight metallic tubes would be abundantly strong, whereas a large boiler must be of great substance to resist a strong pressure. . . .

I do not propose this statement in any other light than as a rude approximation to truth, for as the steam is operating under the disadvantage of atmospheric pressure it must be raised to a higher temperature than in Messrs. Boulton & Watt's engine, and this will require more fuel; but if it take twice as much still the engine would be sufficiently light, for it would be exerting a force equal to raising 550 lbs. one foot high per second, which is equivalent to the labour of six men, whereas the whole weight does not much exceed that of a man.

It may seem superfluous to enquire further relative to a first mover for aerial navigation, but lightness is of so much value in this instance that it is proper to notice the probability that exists of using the expansion of air, by the sudden combustion of inflammable powders or fluids, with great advantage. The French have lately shown the great power produced by igniting inflammable powders in close vessels, and several years ago an engine was made to work in this country in a similar manner by inflammation of spirit of tar. . . . Probably a much cheaper engine of this sort might be produced by a gas-light apparatus and by firing the inflammable air generated with a due portion of common air under a piston. Upon some of these principles it is perfectly clear that force can be obtained by a much lighter apparatus than the muscles of animals or birds, and therefore in such proportion may aerial vehicles be loaded with inactive matter. Even the expansion steam engine, doing the work of six men and only weighing equal to one, will as readily raise five men into the air as one man can elevate himself by his own exertions, but by increasing the magnitude of the engine 10, 50, or 500 men may be equally well conveyed, and convenience alone, regulated by the strength and size of materials, will point out the limit for the size of vessels in aerial navigation.

Having rendered the accomplishment of this object probable upon the general view of the subject, I shall proceed to point out the principles of the art itself. For the sake of perspicuity I shall, in the first instance, analyse the most simple action of the wing in birds, although it necessarily supposes many previous steps.

When large birds, that have a considerable extent of wing compared with their weight, have acquired their full velocity, it may frequently be observed that they extend their wings, and without waving them continue to skim for some time in a horizontal path. . . .

The whole problem is confined within these limits, viz.—To make a surface support a given weight by the application of power to the resistance of air. . . . It is perfectly indifferent whether the wind blow against the plane or the plane be driven with an equal velocity against the air. Hence if [a] machine were pulled along by a cord . . . it would be suspended in a horizontal path; and if, in lieu of this cord, any other propelling power were generated in this direction, with a like intensity, a similar effect would be produced. If therefore the waft of surfaces advantageously moved by any force generated within the machine took place to the extent required, aerial navigation would be accomplished. As the acuteness of the angle between the plane and current increases, the propelling power required is less and less. . . . In practice the extra resistance of the car and other parts of the machine, which consume a considerable portion of power, will regulate the limits to which this principle, which is the true basis of aerial navigation, can be carried; and the perfect ease with which some birds are suspended in long horizontal flights, without one waft of their wings, encourages the idea that a slight power only is required.

I have myself made a large machine on this principle, large enough for aerial navigation, but which I have not had an opportunity to try the effect of, excepting as to its proper balance and security. It was beautiful to see this noble white bird sail majestically from the top of a hill to any given point of the plane below it with perfect steadiness and safety, according to the set of its rudder, merely by its own weight descending in an angle of about 8 degrees with the horizon. . .

To render [a glider] perfectly steady, and likewise to enable it to ascend and descend in its path, it becomes necessary to add a rudder in a similar position to the tail in the bird. . . . From a variety of experiments upon this subject I find that when the machine is going forward, with a superabundant velocity, or that which would induce it to rise in its path, a very steady horizontal course is effected by a considerable depression of the rudder, which has the advantage of making use of this portion of sail in aiding the support of the weight. When the velocity is becoming less, as in the act of alighting, then the rudder must gradually recede from this position and even become elevated for the purpose of preventing the machine from sinking too much in front, owing to the combined effect of the want of projectile force sufficient to sustain the centre of gravity in its usual position, and of the centre of support approaching the centre of the sail.

The elevation and depression of the machine are not the only purposes for which the rudder is designed. This appendage must be furnished with a vertical sail and be capable of turning from side to side in addition to its other movements, which effects the complete steerage of the vessel.

All these principles upon which the support, steadiness, elevation, depression, and steerage of vessels for aerial navigation depend have been abundantly verified by experiments both upon a large and a small scale. I made a machine having a surface of 300 square feet, which was accidentally broken before there was an opportunity of trying the effect of the propelling apparatus, but its steerage and steadiness were perfectly proved, and it would sail obliquely downwards in any direction according to the set of the rudder. Its weight was 56 lbs., and it was loaded with 84 lbs., thus making a total of 140 lbs., about 2 square feet to 1 lb. Even in this state, when any person ran forward in it with his full speed, taking advantage of a gentle breeze in front, it would bear upward so strongly as scarcely to allow him to touch the ground, and would frequently lift him up and convey him several yards together.

The best mode of producing the propelling power is the only thing that remains yet untried towards the completion of the invention. I am preparing to resume my experiments upon this subject, and state the following observations in the hope that others may be induced to give their attention towards expediting the attainment of this art. . . .

Not having sufficient data to ascertain the exact degree of propelling power exerted by birds in the act of flying, it is uncertain what degree of energy may be required in this respect for vessels for aerial navigation; yet when we consider the many hundred miles of continued flight exerted by birds of passage, the idea of its being only a small effort is greatly corroborated. To apply the power of the first mover to the greatest advantage in producing this effect is a very material point. The mode universally adopted by Nature is the oblique waft of the wing. We have only to choose between the direct beat overtaking the velocity of the current, like the oar of a boat, or one applied like the wing, in some assigned degree of obliquity to it. . . .

In continuing the general principles of aerial navigation, for the practice of the art, many mechanical difficulties present themselves which require a considerable course of skilfully-applied experiments before they can be overcome; but, to a certain extent, the air has already been made navigable, and no one who has seen the steadiness with which weights, to the amount of ten stone (including four stone, the weight of the machine), hover in the air, can doubt of the ultimate accomplishment of this object.

The first impediment I shall take notice of is the great power that must be exerted previous to the machine's acquiring that velocity which gives support upon the principle of the inclined plane, together with the total want of all support during the return of any surface used like a wing. Many birds, and particularly water fowl, run and flap their wings for several yards before they gain support from the air. The swift is not able to elevate itself from level ground. The inconvenience under consideration arises from very different causes in these two instances. The supportive surface of most swimming birds does not exceed the ratio of four-tenths of a square foot to every lb. of their weight. The swift, though it scarcely weighs an ounce, measures 18 in. in extent of wing. The want of surface in the one case and the inconvenient length of wing in the other oblige these birds to aid the commencement of their flight by other expedients, yet they can both fly with great power when they have acquired this full velocity. . . .

The large surfaces that aerial navigation will probably require, though necessarily moved with the same velocity, will have a proportionately longer duration both of the beat and return of the wing, and hence a greater descent will take place during the latter action than can be overcome by the former.

There appear to be several ways of obviating this difficulty. There may be two surfaces, each capable of sustaining weight, and placed one above the other, having such a construction as to work up and down in opposition when they are moved, so that one is always ready to descend the moment the other ceases. These surfaces may be so made, by a valve-like structure, as to give no opposition in rising up, and only to resist in descent. The action may be considered either oblique, as in rotative flyers, alternately so, without any up-and-down waft as in the engine, . . . a number of small wings in lieu of large ones, upon the principle of the flight of birds, with small intervals of time between each waft, and, lastly, by making use of light wheels to preserve the propelling power, both of the beat and the return of the wings, till it accumulates sufficiently to elevate the machine upon the principle of those birds which run themselves up. This action might be aided by making choice of a descending ground like the swift.

With regard to another part of the first obstacle I have mentioned, viz.,—the absolute quantity of power demanded being so much greater at first than when the full velocity has been acquired,—it may be observed that, in the case of human muscular strength being made use of, a man can exert, for a few seconds, a surprising degree of force. . . . If expansive first movers be made use of they may be so constructed as to be capable of doing more than their constant work, or their power may be made to accumulate for a few moments by the formation of a vacuum or the condensation of air, so that these expedients may restore at one time, in addition to the working of the engine, that which they had previously absorbed from it.

With regard to the second obstacle in the way of aerial navigation, viz.,—the length of leverage to which large wing-like surfaces are exposed,—it may be observed that being a constant and invariable quality, arising from the degree of support such surfaces give, estimated at their centres of resistance, it may be balanced by an elastic agent that is so placed as to oppose it. . . .

Another principle that may be applied to obviate this leverage of a wing is that of using such a construction as will make the supporting power of the air counterbalance itself. It has been before observed that only about one-third of the wing in birds is applied in producing the propelling power, the remainder, not having velocity sufficient for this purpose, is employed in giving support both in the beat and return of the wing. . . .

A[nother] mode of avoiding leverage is by using the continued action of oblique horizontal flyers, or an alternate action of the same kind, with surfaces so constructed as to accommodate their position to such alternate motion, the hinge or joint being in these cases vertical. In the construction of large vessels for aerial navigation a considerable portion of fixed sail will probably be used, and no more surface will be allotted towards gaining the propelling power than what is barely necessary, with the extreme temporary exertion of the first mover, to elevate the machine and commence the flight. In this case the leverage of the fixed surface is done away. . . .

Avoiding direct resistance is the next general principle that it is necessary to discuss. Let it be remembered, as a maxim in the art of aerial navigation, that every lb. of direct resistance that is done away will support 30 lbs. of additional weight without any additional power. The figure of a man seems but ill calculated to pass with ease through the air, yet I hope to prove him to the full as well-made, in this respect, as the crow, which has hitherto been one standard of comparison, paradoxical as it may appear. . . .

It is of great importance to this art to ascertain the real solid of least resistance when the length or breadth is limited. Sir Isaac Newton's beautiful theorem upon this subject is of no practical use, as it supposes each particle of the fluid, after having struck the solid, to have free egress; making the angles of incidence and reflection equal. Particles of light seem to possess this power, and the theory will be true in that case; but in the air the action is more like an accumulation of particles, rushing up against each other in consequence of those in contact with the body being retarded. . .

It has been found by experiment that the shape of the hinder part of the spindle is of as much importance as that of the front in diminishing resistance. This arises from the partial vacuity created behind the obstructing body. If there be no solid to fill up this space a deficiency of hydrostatic pressure exists within it, and is transferred to the spindle. This is seen distinctly near the rudder of a ship in full sail, where the water is much below the level of the surrounding sea. The cause here being more evident and uniform in its nature may probably be obviated with better success, inasmuch as this portion of the spindle may not differ essentially from the simple cone. I fear, however, that the whole of this subject is of so dark a nature as to be more usefully investigated by experiment than by reasoning, and in the absence of any conclusive evidence from either, the only way that presents itself is to copy Nature.

10

"Certain Improvements in Locomotive Apparatus and Machinery for Conveying Letters, Goods, and Passengers from Place to Place through the Air, part of which Improvements are applicable to Locomotive and other Machinery to be used on Water and on Land"

Patent application No. 9478 of 1842 by William Henson

On Aerial Navigation received a cool reception among the scientific community, and over the next three decades Cayley had little to say publicly about heavier-than-air flight. But a pair of lacemakers named William Henson (1812–88) and John Stringfellow (1799–1883) from Chard, England, decided to try to apply Cayley's principles—and a few of their own—to the construction of a full-size, powered flying machine that they called an "Aerial Steam Carriage." Henson and Stringfellow's design was one of the most carefully thought-out up to its time, and quite prescient, as Henson's patent specifications show.

In order that the description hereafter given may be rendered clear, I will first shortly explain the principle on which the machine is constructed. If any light and flat or nearly flat article be projected or thrown edgewise in an slightly inclined position, the same will rise on the air till the force exerted is expended, when the article so thrown or projected will descend; and it will readily be conceived that, if the article so projected or thrown possessed in itself a continuous power or force equal to that used in throwing or projecting it, the article would continue to ascend so long as the forward part of the surface was upwards in respect to the hinder part, and that such article, when the power was stopped, or when the inclination was reversed, would descend by gravity only if the power was stopped, or by gravity aided by the force of the power contained in the article, if the power be continued, thus imitating the flight of a bird.

Now, the first part of my invention consists of an apparatus so constructed as to offer a very extended surface or plane of a light yet strong construction, which will have the same relation to the general machine which the extended wings of a bird have to the body when a bird is skimming in the air; but in place of the movement of the extended surface or plane, as in the case with the wings of birds, I apply suitable paddle-wheels or other proper mechanical propellers worked by a steam or sufficiently light engine, and thus obtain the requisite power for onward movement to the plane or extended surface; and in order to give control as to the upward and downward direction of such a machine I apply a tail to the extended surface which is capable of being inclined or raised, so that when the power is acting to propel the machine, by inclining the tail upwards the resistance offered by the air will cause the machine to rise on the air; and, on the contrary, when the inclination of the tail is greater or less; and in order to guide the machine as to the lateral direction which it shall take, I apply a vertical rudder or second tail, and, according as the same is inclined in one direction or the other, so will be the direction of the machine.

11

Proposal

By William Henson, 1842

But before this invention could be built they would need to raise some money.

For subscriptions of sums of £100, in furtherance of an Extraordinary Invention not at present safe to be developed by securing the necessary Patents, for which three times the sum advanced, namely, £300, is conditionally guaranteed for each subscription on February 1, 1844, in case of the anticipations being realised, with the option of the subscribers being shareholders for the large amount, if so desired, but not otherwise.

• • •

An invention has recently been discovered, which if ultimately successful will be without parallel even in the age which introduced to the world the wonderful effects of gas and of steam.

The discovery is of that peculiar nature, so simple in principle yet so perfect in all the ingredients required for complete and permanent success, that to promulgate it at present would wholly defeat its development by the immense competition which would ensue, and the views of the Originator be entirely frustrated.

This work, the result of years of labor and study, presents a wonderful instance of the adaptation of laws long since proved to the scientific world combined with established principles so judiciously and carefully arranged, as to produce a discovery perfect in all its parts and alike in harmony with the laws of Nature and science.

The Invention has been subjected to several tests and examinations and the results are most satisfactory, so much so that nothing but the completion of the undertaking is required to determine its practical operation, which being once established its utility is undoubted, as it would be a necessary possession of every empire, and it were hardly too much to say of every individual of competent means in the civilised world.

Its qualities and capabilities are so vast that it were impossible and, even if possible, unsafe to develop them further, but some idea may be formed from the fact that as a preliminary measure patents in Great Britain, Ireland, Scotland, the Colonies, France, Belgium, and the United States, and every other country where protection to the first discoveries of an Invention is granted, will of necessity be immediately obtained and by the time these are perfected, which it is estimated will be in the month of February, the Invention will be fit for Public Trial, but until the patents are sealed any further disclosure would be most dangerous to the principle on which it is based.

Under these circumstances, it is proposed to raise an immediate sum of £2,000 in furtherance of the Projector's views, and as some protection to the parties who may embark in the matter, that this is not a visionary plan for objects imperfectly considered, Mr. Colombine, to whom the secret has been confided, has allowed his name to be used on the occasion and who will if referred to corroborate this statement, and convince any inquirer of the reasonable prospects of large pecuniary results following the development of the Invention.

It is therefore intended to raise the sum of £2,000 in 20 sums of £100 each (of which any Subscriber may take one or more not exceeding five in number to be held by any individual) the amount of which is to be paid into the hands of Mr. Colombine as General Manager of the concern to be by him appropriated in procuring the several Patents, and providing the expense incidental to the works in progress. For each of which sums of £100 it is intended and agreed that 12 months after the 1st of February next, the several parties subscribing shall receive as an equivalent for the risk to be run the sum of £300 for each of the sums of £100 now subscribed provided when the time arrives the Patents shall be found to answer the purposes intended.

As full and complete success is alone looked to, no moderate or imperfect benefit is to be anticipated, but the work, if it once passes the necessary ordeal, to which inventions of every kind must be first subjected, will then be regarded by everyone as the most astonishing discovery of modern times; no half success can follow, and therefore the full nature of the risk is immediately ascertained.

The intention is to work and prove the Patent by collective instead of individual aid as less hazardous at first and more advantageous in the result of for the Inventor, as well as others, by having the interest of several engaged in aiding one common object—the development of a Great Plan. The failure is not feared, yet as perfect success might, by possibility, not ensue, it is necessary to provide for that result, and the parties concerned make it a condition that no return of the subscribed money shall be required, if the Patents shall by any unforeseen circumstances not be capable of being worked at all; against which, the first application of the money subscribed, that of securing the Patents, affords, a reasonable security, as no one without solid grounds would think of such an expenditure.

It is perfectly needless to state that no risk or responsibility of any kind can arise beyond the payment of the sum to be subscribed under any circumstances whatever.

As soon as the Patents shall be perfected and proved it is contemplated, so far as may be found practicable, to further the great object in view a Company shall be formed but respecting which it is unnecessary to state further details, than that a preference will be given to all those persons who now subscribe, and to whom shares shall be appropriated accordingly the larger amount (being three times the sum to be paid by each person) contemplated to be returned as soon as the success of the Invention shall have been established, at their option, or the money paid, whereby the Subscriber will have the means of either withdrawing with a large pecuniary benefit or by continuing his interest in the concern, lay the foundation for participating in the immense benefit which must follow the success of the plan.

It is not pretended to conceal that the project is a speculation—all parties believe that perfect success, and thence incalculable advantages of every kind, will follow to every individual joining in this great undertaking; but the Gentlemen engaged in it wish that no concealment of the consequences, perfect success, or possible failure, should in the slightest degree be inferred. They believe this will prove the germ of a mighty work, and in that belief call for the operation of others with no visionary object, but a legitimate one before them, to attain that point where perfect success will be secured from their combined exertions.

All applications to be made to D. E. Colombine, Esquire, 8, Carlton Chambers, Regent Street.

12

⎯⎯⎯➤•◆•◄⎯⎯⎯

"We feel very sanguine as to the results of our endeavour . . ."

A correspondence between Henson and Cayley, 1846

While the patent application produced a sarcastic hubbub in the press, William Henson quietly constructed a proof-of-concept model that he called *Ariel,* which he hoped to fly at London's Adelaide Gallery. The 14-pound, 40-square-foot-wing model firmly refused to fly off the end of its launch ramp. According to the August 4, 1843, *Morning Herald,* "A third, a fourth, and it is not likely known how many attempts were made, but with an invariable result. Directly the inclined plane was left the model came down flop. Up to the present time, therefore, the world is no nearer flying." Discouraged, Henson rejoined Stringfellow in Chard for another attempt with a model. This, too, failed. Now broke as well, Henson wrote to Cayley.

⎯⎯⎯➤•◆•◄⎯⎯⎯

Although I am personally unknown to you I have taken the liberty of addressing you this letter upon Aerial Navigation. . . . You probably imagined that I had long since given it up as a failure, but you will be pleased to hear that I have in conjunction with my friend Mr. Stringfellow been working more or less since 1843 towards the accomplishment of Aerial Navigation, and that we feel very sanguine as to the results of our endeavour and consider that we have arrived at that stage of proceedings which justifies us in obtaining that pecuniary assistance necessary to carry on our efforts upon an enlarged scale and with increased energy. We therefore resolved to apply to you as the Father of Aerial Navigation to ascertain whether you would like to have anything to do in the matter or not.

William Henson, September 28, 1846

I had thought that you had abandoned the subject, which tho' true in principle you had rushed upon with far too great confidence as to its practice some years ago. If you have been making experiments since that time you will have found how many difficulties you have to adjust and overcome before the results you wish can be accomplished. I think that Balloon Aerial

Navigation can be done readily and will probably come into use before Mechanical Flight can be rendered sufficiently safe and efficient for ordinary use. . . . As to new principles, there are none. Of practical expedience there will soon be an endless variety, and to select the best is the point at issue . . . when if you can show me any experimental proof of mechanical flight maintainable for a sufficient time by mechanical power, I shall be much gratified. Though I have not the weight of capital to apply to such matters, I perhaps might be able to aid you in some measure by my experience. . . . I do not however think that any money, except by exhibition of a novelty can be made by it.

Sir George Cayley, October 12, 1846

13

"Memoir of the Late John Stringfellow"

By Frederick W. Brearey, 1883

Thus rebuked, Henson left for America, and faded into history. His erstwhile partner, John Stringfellow, continued his experiments with flying models until his death, becoming the first person in history to achieve powered flight, with his 1846 model, which embodied the principles set forth in the Aerial Steam Carriage. Eventually England began believing in men like Stringfellow, Henson, and Cayley; in 1866 a few of them formed the Aeronautical Society of Great Britain, which continues to this day. The following article was written by the Society's first secretary, Frederick Brearey, on the death of Stringfellow in 1883.

On the 13th December, 1883, passed away the life of one whose later aspirations were fixed more upon the attainment of success in a special mechanical problem than upon the acquisition of wealth. Yet, though in comfortable circumstances, John Stringfellow, of Chard, in Somersetshire—like some of his Sheffield contemporaries, whose now familiar names we have heard him mention as schoolfellows—had his pursuit been wealth, might have vied with many in its attainment.

He was born at Attercliffe, near Sheffield, the 6th December, 1799.

He was in the foremost ranks of that army of observation which had studied the conditions of flight with a view to its imitation. But despairing apparently of accomplishing the end by the adaptation of wing action, he strove with Henson to obtain a bearing upon the air by the propulsion of a plane of dimensions deemed suitable to sustain a given weight per square foot of surface. The difficulty recorded in their experiments arose in the attempt, upon a large scale, to preserve a rigid plane surface. In 1844, he and Henson commenced the construction of a model, the former undertaking the manufacture of a steam engine for propelling purposes, whilst Henson constructed the model. Their combined efforts sufficed for its completion in 1845. The model measured 20 ft. from tip to tip of wing by 3½ ft. wide, giving about 70 square feet of sustaining surface in the wings, and about 10 more in the tail. The weight of the model, provided with its engine, fuel, and water, was from 25 to 28 pounds. This is a very large sustaining surface in proportion to weight, but in this respect all was tentative. Mr. Stringfellow, in his efforts to determine this question upon some well ascertained basis, had frequently availed himself of the express train, taking with him an arrangement for testing the resistance of various angles against the air at high speeds, but he said that those experiments only tended to prove that any guess work was better than the calculations made by writers upon the subject.

However, to give the model a fair trial, a tent was erected on the Downs two miles from Chard, and for seven weeks these two continued their experiments, though greatly annoyed by lookers on. As it was necessary to provide initial force, an inclined plane was constructed, down which the machine was to glide, and the velocity was to be maintained by the steam engine working two four-bladed propellers, each 3 ft. in diameter, at 300 revolutions per minute. It was found, however, that they could not maintain a rigid surface with the silk. Sometimes it was saturated with moisture, and the framework was altogether too weak. The steam engine was the best part. The absence of success was not for want of power, but for want of proper adaptation of the means to the end. Many trials by day showed a faulty construction, and its lightness proved an obstacle to its successfully contending with the ground currents.

Shortly after this Mr. Henson left for America, and Mr. Stringfellow, not disheartened, and in possession of his steam engine, renewed his experiments.

In 1846 his new model was shaped like the wings of a bird, 10 ft. from tip to tip, feathered at the posterior edge, and curved a little on the under side. The surface was two feet across at its widest part, and contained seventeen square feet. The propellers were 16 in. in diameter, with four blades three-fourths the area of circumference set at an angle of 60 degrees.

The cylinder of the steam engine was three-fourths of an inch in diameter; length of stroke 2 inches; level gear on crank-shaft giving three revolutions of the propellers to one stroke of the engine. The weight of the entire model and engine was 6 pounds; and with water and fuel it did not exceed 6½ pounds.

The room which he had available for experiments did not measure above 22 yards in length, and was rather contracted in height. In this room he fixed a horizontal wire down the centre for part of the distance, and so contrived that the model suspended whilst traversing it, should be released automatically upon reaching a certain point. He found upon setting his engine in motion, that in one-third the length of its run the machine was enabled to sustain itself, and upon reaching the point of self-detachment, it gradually rose until it reached the further end of the room where there was a canvas fixed to receive it. It frequently rose as much as one in seven.

The experiments were afterwards repeated at the solicitation of the manager, at Cremorne. There, when it reached its liberation point, it appeared to meet some obstruction, and threatened to come to the ground, but it soon recovered and darted in fair flight to a distance of about 40 yards, further than which it could not proceed. Finding but pecuniary loss and little honour attaching to these experiments, nothing further is heard of him until the year 1868. The announcement of the intention of the Aëronautical Society to hold an Exhibition at the Crystal Palace, of which he was informed by circular, aroused his old enthusiasm. In the meantime, by the perusal of an early number of the Society's Annual Report, he had become impressed with the value of Mr. Wenham's suggestion of superposed planes, conveyed in a Paper read at a General Meeting of the Society. It reads as follows:—"Having remarked how thin a stratum of air is displaced beneath the wings of a bird in rapid flight, it follows, that in order to obtain the necessary length of plane for supporting heavy weights, the surface may be superposed, or placed in parallel rows with an interval between them. A dozen pelicans may fly one above another without mutual impediment, as if framed together; and it is thus shown how two hundredweight may be supported in a transverse distance of only 10 ft."

This hint was sufficient for Mr. Stringfellow, and the result was seen at the Society's Exhibition in 1868, about which opinions differed. The effect of the superposed planes was certainly not overwhelming, but Mr. Stringfellow's opinion was given to the author in the following words:—

"With respect to the superposed planes, I consider they are the most practical arrangement hitherto proposed for machines on a large scale, but I had always my doubts if they would be effective in a small model on account of their nearness to each other."

Here then was the true reason. It contained in its three planes a sustaining surface of 28 square feet in addition to the tail.

Its weight with engine, boiler, fuel, and water was under 12 pounds. In its steam engine it possessed one-third the power of a horse, whilst its weight was only that of a goose.

The sustaining surface was more than 2 ft. to the pound, always supposing the limited space between the planes admitted of an independent effect of each plane upon the air. Whilst running suspended from the wire in the central transept at the Crystal Palace, its liberation was not permitted by the Company, but it had been observed by several Press Reporters to show a decided tendency to an upward course in its often repeated journeys.

However, in the basement afterwards, the author assisted to hold a canvas with which to break the fall of the model when liberated. When freed, it descended an incline with apparent lightness until caught in the canvas; but the impression conveyed was—that had there been sufficient fall, it would have recovered itself. In the author's experience, however, with every description of models, it is not sufficient to provide suitable surface to weight, even if accompanied with the motive power best calculated to convey it.

The balance must be found, and this means *repeated trials* under a condition of freedom of action. A model, especially in the air, is subject to varying conditions, which alter the equilibrium, and the balance can only be secured by intelligent control in the large machine which the model is constructed to represent. It was intended at the last to set this model free in the open country, when the requirements of the Exhibition were satisfied, but it was found that the engine, which had done much work, required repairs. Many months afterwards, in the presence of the author, an experiment was tried in a field at Chard, by means of wire stretched across it. The engine was fed with methylated spirits, and during some portion of its run under the wire, the draught occasioned thereby invariably extinguished the flames, and so these interesting trials were rendered abortive.

The best of Mr. Stringfellow's Exhibits at the Aëronautical Exhibition, and which gained him the prize of £100, was his light steam engine for aërial purposes.

It was entered in the Catalogue thus:—"Light Engine and Machinery for Aërial Purposes, about half-horse power. Cylinder 2 in. diameter, 3 in. stroke, generating surface of boiler 3½ ft., starts at 100 lbs. pressure in three minutes, works two propellers of 3 ft. diameter, about 300 revolutions per minute. With 3½ pints of water, and 10 ozs. of liquid fuel, works about ten minutes. Weight of engine, boiler, water, and fuel, 16¼ lbs.

The Council of the Aëronautical Society were announced as the adjudicators of the £100 prize for light engines, and upon this occasion it was represented by Mr. F. H. Wenham.

The following is taken from the Report of the Exhibition:—

"The Engine No. 4, by Stringfellow, from its size and power, may be considered something more than a mere model. The cylinder is 2 in. in diameter, stroke 3 in., and works with a boiler pressure of 100 lbs. per square inch; the engine making 300 revolutions per minute. The time of getting up steam was noted; in three minutes after lighting the fire, the pressure was 30 lbs., in five minutes 50 lbs., and in seven minutes there was the full working pressure of 100 lbs. When started, the engine had a fair amount of duty to perform in driving two four-bladed screw propellers 3 ft. in diameter, at 300 revolutions per minute.

"The data for estimating the power are taken as follows:—Area of piston 3 in., pressure in cylinder 80 lbs. per square inch, length of stroke 3 in., velocity of piston 150 ft. per minute, $3 \times 80 \times 150 = 36,000$ foot-pounds; this makes rather more than one-horse power (which is reckoned as 33,000 foot-pounds). The weight of the engine and boiler was only 13 lbs., and is probably the lightest steam engine that has ever been constructed. The engine, boiler, car, and propellers together were afterwards weighed, but without water and fuel, and were found to be 16 lbs.

"At a Meeting of Council, held at Stafford House on the 20th of July, it was agreed that this engine, as a complete working machine, met with the condition of the Society's award, for 'the lightest engine in proportion to its power from whatever source the power may be derived.' The Prize of £100 was accordingly allotted to Mr. Stringfellow."

Although for some time after this period, the subject of this Memoir pursued his experiments according to his expressed determination, for which purpose he erected, out of the prize-money, a building over 70 ft. long, he found his labour of love greatly aggravated by impaired sight, and it became painful for a looker-on to witness his distress when engaged in anything requiring minute investigation. It was easy to see that his work was done, and he knew it.

Three months before his death, he felt that the work he was executing for its improvement was a mistake, and to his son he said "I've hung it up, Fred, I shall touch it no more. I hope I have not spoiled it for you."

Had his cunning not departed from him, many a light engine would have been turned out in satisfaction of the enquiries and demands of Aëronautical Inventors. But in that case nearly all would have been manufactured with his own hands, because he would never allow a workman to prosecute any part of his mechanical labour without taking the tool from his hands and completing it himself. This was a perpetual source of amusement to his sons, who were all practical mechanics. This may be an answer to enquirers as to the utility of the prize awarded to Mr. Stringfellow for his light steam engine. As far as the author knows, none have followed his initiative.

We who survive to pass judgment upon the results of a man's life, should be very careful how we exercise that judgment. It is much too solemn a retrospect for the toleration of a flippant analysis. All that we are justified in concluding, is that John Stringfellow considered that aërial navigation was capable of accomplishment, and that he gave much of time and means to its elucidation. In the future years, when this end is accomplished—as it surely will—his name will be included in the roll of fame.

1. Although there were 77 exhibits on display at the 11-day Aeronautical Exhibition held in 1868 at the Crystal Palace—the world's first such event—Stringfellow's triplane was the focus. Its twice daily steam-powered "flights" gathered good-sized crowds, including royalty. And a steam engine designed by Stringfellow won a £100 prize for the engine with the greatest power-to-weight ratio. Reproduced with permission of the Royal Aeronautical Society, London.

14

≡》·●·《≡

The Artificial Bird of Captain Le Bris

From *Progress in Flying Machines* (1894), by Octave Chanute

Not all of the experimenting was confined to England, as this tale of an ancient mariner and his albatross shows. It was one of a number of fascinating stories published in the landmark *Progress in Flying Machines,* by engineer and aeronautical aficionado Octave Chanute.

≡》·●·《≡

The writer of this record of "Progress in Flying Machines" originally hesitated whether he should include therein the account of the experiments of Captain *Le Bris,* which is about to follow. Not because he deemed it incredible in itself, nor because, if correctly stated, the experiments were not most interesting and instructive, but because the only account of them which he had been able to procure was contained in a novel, in which the author, to make the book more attractive, had mixed up a love story with the record of the aerial experiments, which combination, in the present state of disbelief, the writer feared might be too much for the credulity of the reader. It is true that the author of the novel said that the account of the experiments was scrupulously correct, and that in this, the principal object of the book, he had endeavored to be very exact, even at the risk of detracting from his hero. It is also a fact that the *Aéronaute,* in reviewing the book, said:

> Throughout the novel are to be found absolutely historical data concerning the artificial bird of *Le Bris,* his experiments, his partial success, his mischances, and his deplorable final failure, the latter not through a radical defect, but through lack of method, steadiness in thought, and attention to details.

But still the writer hesitated to reproduce this tale of an ancient mariner.

Fortunately, after a year's seeking, he succeeded in getting a copy of an historical book, now quite out of print, by the same author which gives without any embellishments an account of Captain *Le Bris's* experiments and quite confirms that given in the novel, wherein it is said to have been related "with scrupulous exactness." From the historical work, therefore, of M. de la Landelle, supplemented by his novel, the following account has been compiled of what seems to have been a very remarkable series of experiments on "aspiration."

Captain *Le Bris* was a French mariner, who had in his younger days made several voyages around the Cape of Good Hope and Cape Horn, and whose imagination had been fired by the sight of the albatross, sporting in the tempest on rigid wings, and keeping up with the fleetest ships without exertion. He had killed one of these birds, and claimed to have observed a very remarkable phenomenon. In his own words, as quoted by M. de la Landelle:

> I took the wing of the albatross and exposed it to the breeze; and lo! in spite of me it drew forward into the wind; notwithstanding my resistance it tended to rise. Thus I had discovered the secret of the bird! I comprehended the whole mystery of flight.

Possessed with an ardent imagination, he early became smitten with the design of building an artificial bird capable of carrying him, whose wings should be controlled by means of levers and by a system of rigging; and when he returned to France, and had become the captain of a coasting vessel, sailing from Douarnenez (Finistère), where he was born, and where he had married, he designed and constructed with his own hands the artificial albatross shown in fig. 2.

This consisted of a body in the shape of a "sabot," or wooden shoe, the front portion being decked over, provided with two flexible wings and a tail. The body was built like a canoe, being 13½ ft. long and 4 ft. wide at its broadest point, made of light ash ribs well stayed, and covered on the outside with impermeable cloth, so it could float. A small inclined mast in front supported the pulleys and cords intended to work the wings. The latter were each 23 ft. long, so that the apparatus was 50 ft. across, and spread about 215 sq. ft. of supporting surface; the total weight, without the operator, being 92 lbs. The tail was hinged so as to steer both up and down and sideways, the whole apparatus being, as near as might be, proportioned like the albatross. The front edge of the wings was made of a flexible piece of wood, shaped like the front edge of the wing of the albatross, and to this, cross wands were fastened and covered with canton flannel, the flocculent side down. An ingenious arrangement, which *Le Bris* called his *rotules* (knee pans), worked by two powerful levers, imparted a rotary motion to the front edge of the wings, and also permitted of their adjustment to various angles of incidence with the wind. *Le Bris* was to stand upright in the canoe (an excellent position), his hands on the levers and cords, and his feet on a pedal to work the tail. His expectation was that, with a strong wind, he would rise into the air and reproduce all the evolutions of the soaring albatross, without any flapping whatever.

Le Bris's first experiment was conducted on a public road at Trefeuntec, near Douarnenez. Believing, like Count *D'Esterno*, that it was necessary that the apparatus should have an initial velocity of its own, in addition to that of the wind, he chose a Sunday morning, when there was a good 10-knot breeze from the right direction, and setting his artificial albatross horizontally on a cart, he started down the road against the brisk wind, the cart being driven by a peasant. The bird, with extended wings, 50 ft. across, was held down by a rope passing under the rails of the cart and terminating in a slip knot fastened to *Le Bris*'s wrist, so that with one jerk he could loosen the attachment and allow the rope to run. He stood upright in the canoe, unincumbered in his movements, his hands being on the levers and depressing the front edge of the wings, so that the wind should press upon the top only and hold them down, their position being, moreover, temporarily maintained by assistants walking along on each side.

When they came to the right turn in the road the assistants were directed to let go, and the driver was told to put his horse on a trot. Then *Le Bris,* pressing on his levers, slowly raised the front edge of the wings to a very slight angle of incidence; they fluttered a moment, and then took the wind like a sail on the under side, relieving the weight upon the cart so much that the horse began to gallop. With one jerk *Le Bris* loosened the fastening rope, but lo! it did not run, and the bird did not rise. Instead of this, its ascending power counterbalanced the weight of the cart, and the horse galloped as if at full liberty. It was afterward ascertained that the running rope had been caught on a concealed nail, and that the apparatus had remained firmly fastened to the cart. Finally the rails of the latter gave way, the machine rose into the air, and *Le Bris* said he found himself perfectly balanced, going up steadily to a height of nearly 300 ft., and sailing about twice that distance over the road.

But an accident had taken place. At the last moment the running rope had whipped and wound around the body of the driver, and lifted him from his seat, and carried him up into the air. He involuntarily performed the part of the tail of a kite; his weight, by an extraordinary chance, just balancing the apparatus properly at the assumed angle of incidence, and with the strength of the brisk wind then blowing. Up above, in the machine, *Le Bris* felt himself well poised in the breeze, and exulted that he was about to pass two hours in the air; but below, the driver was hanging on to the rope and howling with fright and anguish.

As soon as *Le Bris* became aware of this state of affairs, and this was doubtless in a very short time, he took measures to descend. He changed the angle of incidence of his wings, came down slowly, and manœuvred so well that the driver gently reached the soil, entirely unharmed, and ran off to catch his horse, who had stopped when he again felt the weight of the cart behind him; but the equilibrium of the artificial albatross was no longer the same, because part of the weight had been relieved, and *Le Bris* did not succeed in reascending. He managed with his levers to retard the descent, and came down entirely unhurt, but one wing struck the ground in advance of the other and was somewhat damaged.

This exploit naturally caused a great deal of local talk. Captain *Le Bris* was considered a visionary crank by most persons, and as a hero by others. He was poor, and had to earn his daily bread, so that it was some little time before, with the aid of some friends, he repaired his machine and was ready to try it again.

He determined this time to gain his initial velocity by dropping from a height, and for this purpose erected a mast, with a swinging yard, on the brink of a quarry, excavated in a sort of pocket, the bottom of which was well protected from the wind. In this quarry bottom he put his apparatus together, and standing in the canoe, it was suspended to a rope and hoisted up aloft to a height of some 30 ft. above the ridge, and nearly 100 ft. above the quarry bottom. A fresh breeze was blowing inland, and the yard was swung so that the apparatus should face both the wind and the quarry, while *Le Bris* adjusted his levers so that only the top surfaces of the wings should receive the wind. When he had, by trial, reached a proper balance, he raised upward the front edge of the wings, brought the tail into action through the pedal, and thought he felt himself well seated on the air, and, as it were, "aspired forward into the breeze." At this moment he tripped the hook suspending the apparatus, and the latter glided and sailed off toward the quarry.

Scarcely had it reached the middle of the pocket, when it met a stratum of wind inclined at a different angle from that prevailing at the starting-point—a vertical eddy, so to speak—probably caused by the reaction of the wind against the sides of the quarry. The apparatus then tilted forward; *Le Bris* pressed on his levers to alter the plane of the wings, but he was not quick enough. The accounts of the bystanders were conflicting, but it was thought that the apparatus next oscillated upward, and then took a second downward dip, but in any event it finally pitched forward, and fell toward the bottom of the quarry.

As soon as the apparatus become sheltered from the wind it righted up, and fell nearly vertically; but as it exposed rather less than 1 sq. ft. of surface to each pound of weight, it could scarcely act as a parachute, and it went down so violently that it was smashed all to pieces, and *Le Bris,* who at the last moment suspended himself to the mast of the canoe and sprang upward, nevertheless had a leg broken by the rebound of the levers.

This accident practically ruined him, and put an end for 12 or 13 years to any further attempt to prove the soundness of his theory. He had failed in both experiments for want of adequate equilibrium. He fairly provided for the transverse balance by making his wings flexible, but the longitudinal equilibrium was defective, as he could not adjust the fore-and-aft balance as instantly as the circumstances changed. The bird does this like a flash by instinct; the man was compelled to reason it out, and he could not act quickly enough.

M. de la Landelle makes the following comment:

> He was ... ingenious, persevering, and the most intrepid of men. He was entirely in the right in locating himself upright, both arms and legs quite free, in an apparatus which was besides exceedingly well designed. None was better fitted than he to succeed in *sailing flight* (*vol-à-voile*) in imitation of his model, the albatross.

In 1867 a public subscription at Brest enabled *Le Bris* to build a second artificial albatross ... much like the first, but a trifle lighter, although a movable counterweight was added, intended to produce automatic equilibrium. The apparatus when completed was publicly exhibited, and attracted much attention; but the inventor no longer had the audacity of youth, and he was influenced by numberless contradictory counsellors. He wanted to proceed as at Douarnenez, by giving an initial velocity to his apparatus, but he was dissuaded from this. He was also urged to test his machine with ballast, instead of riding in it himself, which at once changed all the conditions of equilibrium, as there was no longer command over a varying angle of incidence, and yet a first mischance led him to resort to the method of experimenting without riding in the machine.

M. de la Landelle relates the incident as follows:

> Once only did he obtain something like an ascension, by starting from a light wagon, which was not in motion. He as on the levee of the port of commerce at Brest, the breeze as light, and the gathered public was impatient, through failure to realize that success depended wholly on the intensity of the wind. *Le Bris* was hoping for a gust which should enable him to rise; he thought it had come, pulled on his levers, and thus threw his wings to the most favorable angle, but he only ascended a dozen yards, glided scarcely twice that distance, and after this brief demonstration came gently to the ground without any jerk.

This negative result occasioned a good many hostile comments, and so the inventor no longer experimented in public; but he had further bad luck; the machine was several times capsized at starting, and more or less injured, being repaired at the cost of *Le Bris,* whose means were nearly exhausted. Then he tried it in ballast with varying success, and on one occasion, the breeze being just right, it rose up some 50 yds., with a light line attached, and *advanced against the wind* as if gliding over it. Very soon the line became slack, and the assisting sailors were greatly astonished, for the bird, without waver, thus proceeded some 200 yds.; but at the approach of some rising ground, which undoubtedly altered the direction of the aerial current, the bird, shielded from the wind, began settling down, without jolt, very gently, and alighted so lightly that the grass was scarcely bruised.

Encouraged by this partial success, *Le Bris* tried to reproduce the same results, but he met many mishaps, in which the apparatus as upset and injured. At last, one day, by a stiff northeast breeze, he installed his bird on top of the rising ground near which it had performed so well a few weeks before, and this time he meant to ride in the machine himself. He was dissuaded by his friends, and probably made a serious mistake in yielding to them, for the uncontrolled apparatus was not intended to adjust itself to a gusty wind.

At any rate, the empty machine rose, but it did not sustain itself in the air. It gave a twist, a glide, and a plunge, and pitched forward to the ground, where it was shattered all to bits. The wings were broken, the covering cloth of the canoe was rent to pieces, while the bowsprit in front was broken and forced back like a dart into the canoe.

The friends claimed that if the operator had been aboard, he surely would have been spitted and killed, but *Le Bris* maintained that if he had been aboard he could, with his levers, have changed the angle of the wings in time to avoid the wreck; he blamed himself for having surrendered his better judgment, and he gave way to profound despair.

For this was the end. His second apparatus was smashed, his means and his credit were exhausted, his friends forsook him, and perhaps his own courage weakened, for he did not try again. He retired to his native place, where, after serving with honor in the war of 1870, he became a special constable, and was killed in 1872 by some ruffians whose enmity he had incurred.

2. Le Bris's Artificial Bird, 1867.

15

——◦◦◦◦◦——

"My apparatus, No. 3, the light, imperfect one"

Pierre Mouillard's description of a glide, from *Progress in Flying Machines,* by Octave Chanute

One of the more important researchers to emerge from that time was Pierre Mouillard, a farmer living in Algiers. His 1865 glider consisted solely of a single narrow wing.

——◦◦◦◦◦——

It was in my callow days, and on my farm in the plain of Mitidja, in Algeria, that I experimented with my apparatus, No. 3, the light, imperfect one, the one which I carried about like a feather.

I did not want to expose myself to possible ridicule, and I had succeeded by a series of profound combinations and pretexts in sending everybody away, so that I was left all alone on the farm. I had already tested approximately the working of my aeroplane by jumping down from the height of a few feet. I knew that it would carry my weight, but I was afraid to experiment in the wind before the home folks, and time dragged wearily with me until I knew just what the machine would do; so I finally sent everybody away—to promenade themselves in various directions—and as soon as their backs were turned, I strolled into the prairie with my apparatus upon my shoulders. I ran against the air and studied its sustaining power, for it was almost a dead calm; the wind had not yet risen, and I was waiting for it.

Nearby there was a wagon road, raised some 5 ft. above the plain. It had thus been raised with the soil from ditches about 10 ft. wide, dug on either side.

Then came a little puff of wind, and it also came into my head to jump over that ditch.

I used to leap across easily without my apparatus, but I thought that I might try it armed with my aeroplane; so I took a good run across the road, and jumped at the ditch as usual.

But, oh horrors! once across the ditch my feet did not come down to earth; I was gliding on the air and making vain efforts to land, for my aeroplane had set out on a cruise. I dangled only one foot from the soil, but, do what I would, I could not reach it, and I was skimming along without the power to stop.

At last my feet touched the earth, I fell forward on my hands, broke one of the wings, and all was over; but goodness! how frightened I had been! I was saying to myself that if even a light wind gust occurred, it would toss me up 30 to 40 ft. into the air, and then surely upset me backward, so that I would fall on my back. This I knew perfectly, for I understood the defects of my machine. I was poor, and I had not been able to treat myself to a more complete aeroplane. All's well that ends well. I then measured the distance between my toe marks, and found it to be 138 ft.

Here is the *rationale* of the thing. In making my jump I acquired a speed of 11 to 14 miles per hour, and just as I crossed the ditch I must have met a puff of the rising wind. It probably was traveling some 8 to 11 miles per hour, and the two speeds added together produced enough pressure to carry my weight.

I cannot say that on this occasion I appreciated the delights of traveling in the air. I was too much alarmed, and yet never will I forget the strange sensations produced by this gliding.

PART III

---⟫•⟪---

1883–1897

SUCCESSFUL GLIDING, AND THE FIRST POWERED, MANNED FLIGHTS

16

⇒•◦•⇐

"My Late Brother Otto"

The Evolution by Gustav Lilienthal, 1911

The most successful of the flying men of his time, Otto Lilienthal (1848–96) made 1,500 semi-controlled glides in his *Flugapparate* before he died in a crash. During much of his aeronautical work Lilienthal's younger brother Gustav worked alongside him. In the forword to this posthumous 1911 English-language edition of Otto's greatest and most influential work, *Birdflight as the Basis of Aviation,* originally released in 1889, Gustav wrote of his brother and his methods.

⇒•◦•⇐

An important work monopolizes a man and, besides many other sacrifices, claims the whole personality. It fires the imagination of the child, and softly approaches its elected disciple in an alluring, toying way, appropriate to the serenity of child life. But gradually it draws the soul more firmly into its golden nets.

It fascinates the youth, and never relaxes its hold on the adult.

The glory of a great discovery or an invention which is destined to benefit humanity, appears to him the more dazzling the closer he approaches it; he perceives not the thorns in that crown, he heeds not its weight, but his whole life is shaped to attain it.

My late brother Otto and I were amongst those upon whom enthusiasm seized at an early age. A story which was then much read powerfully stimulated our susceptible minds: "The travels of Count Zambeccay," an aeronaut, who finally lost his life on the occasion of one of his balloon journeys.

More particularly was our interest awakened by the detailed description and instruction which, in the language of an animal fable, the stork imparts to the willow wren.

The small willow wren happens to meet the stork, and complains of fatigue; the latter, in his generosity, offers him a seat on his back, and during the ensuing conversation the stork explains the method by which he sails without effort or wing-beats, and how he planes down in a straight line from a great altitude to a distant meadow:

This clear description of sailing flight impressed us with the possibility of attaining such by simple means.

Anklam, our native town, with its surrounding meadows, gave us ample opportunities for observation, since numerous families of storks had taken up their abode on the roofs of the barns, and we often watched the flight of the big, handsome birds. Our interest in the animal world also attracted us towards butterflies, and to complete our collection of these, which was the pride of our mother and ourselves, we did not shirk the weary miles to the "Karlsburgerheide," nor did we heed the gruesome nights spent in cemeteries, since there we found our rarest specimens. Still, very devoted the greater part of our immature nature studies to watching our friend the stork on the peaceful meadows of the "Karlsburgerheide." Often we would stalk him to within a very short distance and that with the wind, as his powers of scenting are but small, but on suddenly perceiving us he rose, hopping in our direction until sufficiently lifted by the force of his wings.

Even at that time it became obvious to us that rising against the wind must be easier than with the wind, because without some compelling cause the shy bird would not advance towards us.

In 1861 our father died; he had just prepared to emigrate to America, his mechanical aptitude finding no satisfaction in his business as a cloth merchant.

Our mother fostered in every way our mechanical proclivities, and never refused us the means to purchase the requisite materials for our experiments, however hard it may have been for her at times.

Well do I remember submitting to her our plans for our first flying machine, to the construction of which she readily consented.

Less encouraging was an apprehensive uncle, who constantly prophesied disaster.

Our first wings measured 2 metres [6 feet, 7 inches] by 1 metre [3 feet, 3 inches], and consisted of thin beach veneer with straps at the undersides, through which we pushed our arms. It was our intention to run down a hill and to rise against the wind like a stork. In order to escape the jibes of our schoolmates, we experimented at night time on the drill ground outside the town, but there being no wind on these clear star-lit summer nights, we met with no success.

We were then 13 and 14 years of age respectively, and our flying experiments rather interfered with the proper discharge of our school work. We were both not particularly strong on Latin, and our mother therefore placed me in the "Realschule," whilst Otto, my elder brother, was sent to the Provincial Technical School at Potsdam.

Here Otto was able to satisfy his thirst for technical knowledge, and after a lapse of two years he passed the final examination with the highest honours ever attained by any previous scholar.

We had no associate in our aviation experiments; we felt ourselves quite equal to the task. During the vacations we returned to our old hunting grounds; buzzards, hawks, rooks, and storks interested us most, and great was our delight when we saw a swarm of swans outlined against the sky on their migration to their northern breeding grounds.

My brother left Potsdam for Berlin, and for one year worked as mechanic at the machine works of Schwartzkopf. He soon proved his great skill in exact mechanical work of any kind with which he was entrusted. After that he was sent to the Technical Academy, but before the commencement of the first term, he paid us a month's visit at Anklam.

He brought with him a bundle of palisander sticks, which were intended for flying machine No. 2. I was at that time apprenticed to an architect, and took a holiday in order to assist my brother.

To work the hard palisander wood was no small matter; we pointed and rounded the sticks which served as quills for two wings, 3 metres [9 feet, 10 inches] long each. The feathers of these quills were represented by a series of large goose feathers which were sewn on tape.

For this purpose we had purchased all the feathers which were obtainable in our town, and this is no mean accomplishment in any Pomeranean town.

The sewing on of these quills was very troublesome and fatiguing for the fingers, and many a drop of blood upon the white feathers testified to the damage done to our finger tips.

The wings were fastened to two hoops, one of which was strapped round the chest, and the other round the hips, and by means of an angle lever and stirrup arrangement to the ropes we were enabled to beat the wings up and down by pushing out our legs. The single feathers were arranged to open and close on the up-and-down stroke, and the arrangement worked perfectly. We felt sure that this time failure was impossible. We believed that the lofty garret of our house in Anklam would be the most suitable experimenting room, a belief which was unfortunate, since we undertook to fly in a perfect calm, a method which presents difficulties even to the bird.

We did not heed the lesson taught by our storks, but suspended our apparatus from the beams of the roof and began to move the wings. The very first movement of our legs brought about a jumping at the suspension rope, and as our position was nearly horizontal we were most uncomfortable. When drawing up our legs, that is, when the wings moved upwards, the whole arrangement dropped down and hung on the taut rope. The lifting effect due to the beating down of the wings amounted to 20 cm [8 inches]. This was at least some success, but if our house had not possessed that high loft, we should have experimented in the open, and with a fresh wind would have recorded better results. But the holidays and leave were at an end, and flying machine No. 2 was relegated to the lumber room.

In October of 1867 my brother Otto entered the Technical Academy in order to study engineering. Unfortunately it was impossible for him to obtain a scholarship, not even our Family Scholarship, because, according to the idea then obtaining, the Technical Academy was not a high school, and it was therefore necessary to manage with very little.

In 1868 I joined my brother in Berlin, in order to devote myself to the building trade, and we attained a real proficiency in the "simple life." A pennyworth of cherries and about the same amount of bread was our favourite lunch, but when finally, through the recommendation of Director Reuleaux, my brother obtained a yearly scholarship of 300 Thalers, we were able to live like princes on this fabulous sum. The first thing which we afforded was a large bundle of willow canes with which to construct flying machine No. 3. We had abandoned the use of hard palisander wood, because experiments showed us that, weight for weight, the round willow canes possessed the greatest resistance against breakage so long as its surface was intact, and that even with the latter defective, it still held together.

This disagreeable descent while lifting the wings, we were going to eliminate by arranging two larger and four somewhat smaller wings, which alternately moved upwards and downwards, and instead of the expensive quills we employed a kind of valve between the separate canes made of shirting, sewn to the tips of willow canes. The whole apparatus had an area of 16 sq. m. [172 sq. ft.], and weighed only 15 kg. [33 lbs.].

When everything was prepared, since we could not mount the apparatus in our lodgings, we took it, during the holidays, to Demnitz, an estate near Anklam belonging to our uncle. . . .

The exigencies of our studies, for the time being, terminated our experiments. When the war of 1870 commenced, my brother Otto took the field; his comrades often spoke of their chum, who, even during the campaign never lost sight of the great object of his life, namely, the problem of flight. Full of plans he returned from the war, and I met him the day before the great entry of the troops in Berlin. His first words were, "Now we shall finish it," but matters did not develop quite so quickly. After he had left the service, we worked together in Berlin. We had now come to the conclusion that flight would be impossible without forward motion, and all the experiments which we made on small models were based upon the principle of forward motion. We possessed an apparatus which was fitted with beating wings, moved by spiral springs, and which was launched from an inclined plane out of the window of our lodging on the fourth floor, at 4 o'clock in the morning, so as to avoid being seen.

The centre of gravity of this apparatus was too low, and the resulting pendulum movements brought the wings almost into a vertical position and to rest; the apparatus swung back and in consequence of the oblique position of the feather-shaped valves it took a second and third start until the spring had run down. This experiment for the first time taught us the importance of the proper position of the centre of gravity.

The best of our various models was fitted with two pigeon's wings; it was able to make 20 wing-beats when the spring was wound up, and when pushed off gently, flew across two rooms.

Otto Lilienthal now commenced his business career. His first situation was in the engineering works of Weber, then under the management of the present Geheimrat Rathenau. After some time he took a position as designer in the engineering works of C. Hoppe.

There was now a longer interval in our flying experiments. In his spare time Otto took up the calculation of hot air motors and actually commenced a model without, however, finishing it. At this time, I was travelling in Austria and England, whilst Otto lived with our grandmother and sister; we lost our mother in 1872. In 1874, when I returned from England to Berlin, we again resumed our work on flight. In our loft we installed a regular workshop and laid the keel of a wing flyer. The wings were an exact copy of a bird's wings: the pinions consisting of willow canes with narrow front and wide back feathers. The latter we made of corrugated paper steeped in a solution of gum arabic, and after drying, it was covered with collodion. The whole apparatus was the size of a stork, and the propelling force was to be a light motor which, however, had first to be designed. It was on this occasion that my brother Otto, who was experienced in the designing of steam-engines, invented a system of tubular boilers, then quite new. The engine was provided with a high and low pressure cylinder, the former for the downstroke and the latter for the upstroke of the wings. I believe we should have succeeded in making the model fly, if the motor had not been too powerful, but at the very first trial both wings were broken, not being strong enough to withstand the increased air pressure due to the beating motion. Still we were not discouraged by this accident, which we considered as a success for the small motor. The latter with some water and a supply of spirit weighed 0.75 kg. [1.65 lb.] and had an output of 1/4 h.p. We also built kites in the form of birds, in order to study the behaviour of the apparatus in the wind; the surfaces of the wings being curved, in order to imitate a bird. Such a kite, which we flew on the high plain between the Spandau Road and the railway to Hamburg, showed some peculiar properties. It was held by three persons, one of whom took hold of the two lines which were fastened to the front cane and to the tail, respectively, whilst the other two persons each held the line which was fastened to each wing. In this way it was possible to regulate the floating kite, as regards its two axes. Once, in the autumn of 1874, during a very strong wind, we were able to so direct the kite that it moved against the wind. As soon as its long axis was approximately horizontal the kite did not come down but moved forward at the same level. I held the cords controlling the longitudinal axis, and my brother and my sister each one of the cords for the adjustment of the cross-axis. As the kite maintained its lateral equilibrium, they let go the cords; the kite then stood almost vertically above me and I also had to free it.

After another thirty steps forward my cords got entangled in some bushes, the kite lost its balance, and in coming down was destroyed. Yet, having gained another experience, we easily got over the loss of model No. 4. Our business duties as employees, with late office hours, prevented us from occupying ourselves with the subject more intensely. My brother Otto was then travelling frequently and for prolonged periods in order to introduce new machinery in mines. He had observed the slow method of bringing up coal and suggested to his chief an improvement which would facilitate the work of the miner. He constructed a special machine, and his firm, who could not take up this particular branch, gave him a prolonged leave to enable him to push the sale of this machine on his own account.

This brought him into the various mining centres of Saxony, Silesia, Tyrol, Hungary, and Galicia. He obtained some orders, especially from Austria, but as the coal trade was then bad, and whole mountains of coal were stored on the wharfs, there was little inducement to buy machines which were to expedite the work. His attempt to obtain an independent position was therefore a failure.

My brother made the acquaintance, during one of his journeys in Saxony, of his wife Agnes, née Fischer, the daughter of a mining official, and married her in 1878. Shortly before this, our grandmother was taken from us, and my sister had taken a position in England as a teacher. I lived for two years with the newly married couple, and during that time we invented the "Anchor" brick-boxes which became so well known in later years, and the joy of unnumerable children, but which caused us much annoyance, worry, and still more monetary loss.

Disappointed by all this trouble, I collected my belongings and emigrated to Australia, whilst my brother Otto developed a system of tubular boilers for which he obtained a German patent. The invention was a timely one, for at that period only very inferior small motors were in existence. The freedom from danger of these tubular boilers was soon recognized by the authorities, and my brother was able to give up his position at Hoppe's and to start for himself.

We kept up a regular correspondence and frequently ventilated the problem of flight. The report of my journey dated from Cape Town contained the detailed description of the flight of the Albatross: "the Albatross is exactly the same shape as that of our kite, but its wings are still more narrow." During this time (1881–1886) we made no experiments. I had, as similarly related of the brothers Wright, endeavoured to construct on a larger scale the small flyers moved by a rubber spring, then much patronized and known as Japanese flies. But the result of our experiments was as negative as that of the Americans.

Soon after my return from Australia in 1886, Otto's business had yielded him sufficient to permit his building a home of his own in Gross-Lichterfelde and we resumed our flight experiments, which were facilitated by a nice laboratory and a large lawn. We now commenced the fundamental experiments for the investigation of air pressure given in the present volume, and we continued them until the year 1893.

Whilst this book was still in the press, my brother Otto decided to compare the actual lifting power of larger curved surfaces with the values which we had determined by measurements. These supporting surfaces are here illustrated, and are now generally termed "Gliders." We were able to slowly glide downward against the wind from a height.

Our garden having many trees in it, was frequently without wind, and we therefore transferred the field of our experiments to the ground behind the Military Academy and later on to Gross-Kreuz on the line of the Madgeburg railway. Here we found that the wind was too changeable near the ground, so my brother built a shed on the brink of a gravel pit in Südende, and there was able to considerably extend his gliding flights.

In 1894, we had at considerable expense a special hill (15 metres [49 ft.] high) constructed, at the Heinersdorfer Brick-works near Gross-Lichterfelde. The summit of this hill was formed by a shed in which our gliders were stored. Several of our illustrations show the glides from this hill. In the meantime we had discovered a very suitably situated ground near Rinow and Stöllen between Neustadt on Dosse and Rathenow. There, there are a number of bare sandhills which rise up to a height of 50 metres [164 ft.] above the surrounding plain, and from this starting point my brother succeeded in making glides up to 350 metres [1,150 ft.] in length.

The starting point was only at half the height of the hill because at the summit the wind was generally too strong. According to my observations the drop of this gliding fight amounted to eighteen metres. On the occasion of one such flight one of the supports for the arm broke, so that the apparatus lost its balance and fell from a height of 15 metres, but the special shock absorber which was fitted to the apparatus, prevented my brother from betting seriously hurt. In 1896 we had three years of such flights behind us, and in my opinion we could not expect any better results. We therefore intended to take up experiments with an apparatus fitted with beating wings, the latter being moved by means of a carbonic acid motor. We had already tested the apparatus as a mere glider without a motor, the latter requiring some improvements; my brother Otto was of the opinion that these gliding flights would develop into a sport. He was therefore indefatigable, and always anxious, to obtain greater security, and also hoped to derive some pecuniary benefit from these glides. Our experiments at Stöllen imposed upon us great expense, and altogether we had spent more money on these flight experiments than, from a mere business point of view, we could afford. We had agreed that on Sunday the 9th August we should for the last time travel to Stöllen in order to pack up the apparatus. I was prevented from this by an accident with my cycle. Our families whom we intended to take with us remained at home and my brother drove out accompanied by a servant. He intended to make some change on the rudder, but at the very first glide, the wind being uncertain, the apparatus when at a considerable height lost its balance.

Unfortunately my brother had not fitted the shock-absorber and the full shock of the fall took effect, so that the apprehension of our uncle was fulfilled. My brother fell, a victim to the great idea, which—although at that time was so little recognized—is now acknowledged in its full bearing by the whole civilized world. Our work has already produced good results and, combined with the development of light motors, the lifting power of curved surfaces has been fully confirmed.

Therefore, whenever the laurels of success are attained by an aviator of the present day, let him remember with grateful acknowledgment the work of Otto Lilienthal!

3. Otto Lilienthal standing by his man-made hill outside Berlin,
in one of his biplane gliders.

4. Lilienthal caught in mid-glide on the same hill.

17

⟫•⟪

The Trials of the *Eole*

By Clément Ader, 1906

By now the leading French experimenter was Clément Ader (1841–1925), who invented a spate of devices, including a telephone. Ader is generally recognized for having, in 1890, become the first to achieve manned powered flight (albeit unsustained and uncontrolled, two important requisites—after all, going exactly where you want to go safely is a vital part of air travel). He tells of it—rather defensively, for the Wright brothers had usurped his glory—in this 1906 account, *La Premiere Etape de l'Aviation Militaire en France.*

⟫•⟪

Following lengthy researches on the flight of birds, in aerodynamics and the special mechanism of aerial navigation, the *Eole* was constructed in a laboratory located in rue Pajou, at Passy. It comprised two wings resembling those of bats; they folded themselves. The motive power was furnished by steam, and drove a propeller mounted forward. Two direct wheels carried the apparatus and a third one at the rear steered it on the ground. A rudder served for aerial guidance. After its completion one had to select, for its trial, a site closed off and tranquil; we found it in the Parc d'Armainvilliers, belonging to Madame Issac Pereire and which was placed at our disposal by her son, Gustave Pereire.

An area was laid out in a straight line, unturfed, smoothed, and leveled with a roller, so that one could see and record the traces of the wheels from the slightest lift to complete takeoff. At one of these trials, the 9th of October 1890, over a distance of about 50 meters [164 ft.] the *Eole* left the ground for the first time by the sole means of its motive power. This minor event was not officially recorded, but our foreman buried in the ground lumps of coal at the exact spot where we took off in our apparatus. What is certain is that these witnesses are still in the ground and that it would be possible to find them there if this should become necessary. The experiments were discontinued because of serious injury to the steam generator.

At that time the *Eole* was considered, by the initiate and by the scientific press, as the first aerial apparatus piloted by a man to have flown at a small height over a short distance.

18

⟶►◦◄⟵

Progress in Flying Machines: Introduction

By Octave Chanute, 1894

Despite admirable and growing progress, experimenters everywhere continued to work in obscurity, and, perhaps fearing ridicule, in anonymity. Often they wasted years on attempts that were doomed to failure, even muscle-powered ornithopters still. One man who hoped to change all that was Octave Chanute (1832–1910), a highly respected French-born civil engineer who, without formal education, was instrumental in building railroads and bridges from New York to Chicago to Kansas. In later life Chanute became intrigued by the way a not especially strong wind might lift a roof from a building; on a tour of Europe in 1875 he found many prominent men who believed that heavier-than-air flight was not only possible, it was inevitable. Upon his return to the States Chanute began organizing aeronautical meetings within the conventions of various engineering associations he led. Then, in 1891 a colleague at the *Railroad and Engineering Journal* asked him to write a series of articles, which Chanute collected into a single volume titled *Progress in Flying Machines,* published in 1894. He would go on to design and build a biplane glider that made a few successful flights in 1896. What follows are the opening and closing statements from *Progress,* summing up the advances in human flight, and its potential.

⟶►◦◄⟵

Having in a previous volume treated the general subject of "Aerial Navigation," in which a sketch was given of what has been accomplished with balloons, I propose in the following chapters to treat of Flying machines proper—that is to say, of forms of apparatus heavier than the air which they displace; deriving their support from and progressing through the air, like the birds, by purely dynamical means.

It is intended to give sketches of many machines, and to attempt to criticise them.

We know comparatively so little of the laws and principles which govern air resistances and reactions, and the subject will be so novel to most readers, that it would be difficult to follow the more rational plan of first laying down the general principles, to serve as a basis for discussing past attempts to effect artificial flight. The course will therefore be adopted of first stating a few general considerations and laws, and of postponing the statement of others until the discussion of some machines and past failures permits of showing at once the application of the principles.

The first inquiry in the mind of the reader will probably be as to whether we know just how birds fly and what power they consume. The answer must, unfortunately, be that we as yet know very little about it. Here is a phenomenon going on daily under our eyes, and it has not been reduced to the sway of mathematical law.

19

Progress in Flying Machines: Conclusion

By Octave Chanute, 1894

To the possible inquiry as to the probable character of a successful flying machine, the writer would answer that in his judgment two types of such machines may eventually be evolved: one, which may be termed the soaring type, and which will carry but a single operator, and another, likely to be developed somewhat later, which may be termed the journeying type, to carry several passengers, and to be provided with a motor.

The soaring type may or may not be provided with a motor of its own. If it has one this must be a very simple machine, probably capable of exerting power for a short time only, in order to meet emergencies, particularly in starting up and in alighting. For most of the time this type will have to rely upon the power of the wind, just as the soaring birds do, and whoever has observed such birds will appreciate how continuously they can remain in the air with no visible exertion. The utility of artificial machines availing of the same mechanical principles as the soaring birds will principally be confined to those regions in which the wind blows with such regularity, such force, and such frequency as to allow of almost daily use. These are the sub-tropical and the trade-wind regions, and the best conditions are generally found in the vicinity of mountains or of the sea.

This is the type of machine which experimenters with soaring devices heretofore mentioned have been endeavoring to work out. If unprovided with a motor, an apparatus for one man need not weigh more than 40 or 50 lbs., nor cost more than twice as much as a first-class bicycle. Such machines therefore are likely to serve for sport and for reaching otherwise inaccessible places, rather than as a means of regular travel, although it is not impossible that in trade-wind latitudes extended journeys and explorations may be accomplished with them; but if we are to judge by the performance of the soaring birds, the average speeds are not likely to be more than 20 to 30 miles per hour.

The other, or journeying type of flying machines, must invariably be provided with a powerful and light motor, but they will also utilize the wind at times. They will probably be as small as the character of the intended journey will admit of, for inasmuch as the weights will increase as the cube of the dimensions, while the sustaining power only grows as the square of those dimensions, the larger the machine the greater the difficulties of light construction and of safe operation. It seems probable, therefore, that such machines will seldom be built to carry more than from three to 10 passengers, and will never compete for heavy freights, for the useful weights, those carried in addition to the weight of the machine itself, will be very small in proportion to the power required. Thus M. *Maxim** provides his colossal aeroplane (5,500 sq. ft. of surface) with 300 horse power, and he hopes that it will sustain an aggregate of 7 tons, about one-half of which consists in its own dead weight, while the same horse power, applied to existing modes of transportation, would easily impel—at lesser speed, it is true—from 350 to 700 tons of weight either by rail or by water.

Although it by no means follows that the aggregate cost of transportation through the air will be in proportion to the power required, the latter being but a portion of the expense, it does not now seem probable that flying machines will ever compete economically with existing modes of transportation. It is premature, in advance of any positive success, to speculate upon the possible commercial uses and value of such a novel mode of transit, but we can already discern that its utility will spring from its possible high speeds, and from its giving access to otherwise unreachable points.

It seems to the writer quite certain that flying machines can never carry even light and valuable freights at anything like the present rates of water or land transportation, so that those who may apprehend that such machines will, when successful, abolish frontiers and tariffs are probably mistaken. Neither are passengers likely to be carried with the cheapness and regularity of railways, for although the wind may be utilized at times and thus reduce the cost, it will introduce uncertainty in the time required for a journey. If the wind be favorable, a trip may be made very quickly; but if it be adverse, the journey may be slow or even impracticable.

The actual speeds through the air will probably be great. It seems not unreasonable to expect that they will be 40 to 60 miles per hour soon after success is accomplished with machines provided with motors, and eventually perhaps from 100 to 150 miles per hour. Almost every element of the problem seems to favor high speeds, and, as repeatedly pointed out, high speeds will be (within certain limits) more economical than moderate speeds. This will eventually afford an extended range of journey—not at

---

* Hiram Maxim (1840–1916). His steam-powered biplane made a brief uncontrolled flight—accidentally—in 1894.

first probably, because of the limited amount of specially prepared fuel which can be carried, but later on if the weight of motors is still further reduced. Of course in civilized regions the supply of fuel can easily be replenished, but in crossing seas or in explorations there will be no such resource.

It seems difficult, therefore, to forecast in advance the commercial results of a successful evolution of a flying machine. Nor is this necessary; for we may be sure that such an untrammelled mode of transit will develop a usefulness of its own, differing from and supplementing the existing modes of transportation. It certainly must advance civilization in many ways, through the resulting access to all portions of the earth, and through the rapid communications which it will afford.

It has been suggested that the first practical application of a successful flying machine would be to the art of war, and this is possibly true; but the results may be far different from those which are generally conjectured. In the opinion of the writer such machines are not likely to prove efficient in attacks upon hostile ships and fortifications. They cannot be relied upon to drop explosives with any accuracy, because the speed will be too great for effective aim when the exact distance and height from the object to be hit cannot be accurately known. Any one who may have attempted to shoot at a mark from a rapidly moving railway train will probably appreciate how uncertain the shot must be.

For reconnoitring the enemy's positions and for quickly conveying information such machines will undoubtedly be of great use, but they will be very vulnerable when attacked with similar machines, and when injured they may quickly crash down to disaster. There is little question, however, that they may add greatly to the horrors of battle by the promiscuous dropping of explosives from overhead, although their limited capacity to carry weight will not enable them to take up a large quantity, nor to employ any heavy guns with which to secure better aim.

Upon the whole, the writer is glad to believe that when man succeeds in flying through the air the ultimate effect will be to diminish greatly the frequency of wars and to substitute some more rational methods of settling international misunderstandings. This may come to pass not only because of the additional horrors which will result in battle, but because no part of the field will be safe, no matter how distant from the actual scene of conflict. The effect must be to produce great uncertainty as to the results of manœuvres or of superior forces, by the removal of that comparative immunity from danger which is necessary to enable the commanding officers to carry out their plans, for a chance explosive dropped from a flying machine may destroy the chiefs, disorganize the plans, and bring confusion to the stronger or more skillfully led side. This uncertainty as to results must render nations and authorities still more unwilling to enter into contests than they are now, and perhaps in time make wars of extremely rare occurrence.

So may it be; let us hope that the advent of a successful flying machine, now only dimly foreseen and nevertheless thought to be possible, will bring nothing but good into the world; that it shall abridge distance, make all parts of the globe accessible, bring men into closer relation with each other, advance civilization, and hasten the promised era in which there shall be nothing but peace and good-will among all men.

PART IV

1898–1905

THE FIRST CONTROLLED, HEAVIER-THAN-AIR FLIGHT

20

"I have been afflicted with the belief that flight is possible to man"

Wilbur Wright's first letter to Chanute, 1900

The Wright brothers, Wilbur (1867–1912) and Orville (1872–1948), were moderately successful small-businessmen from Dayton, Ohio; they assembled and sold their own line of bicycles following the safety bicycle craze of the early 1890s. (Safety bicycles had two same-sized wheels, making them less hazardous than the old-style high-wheeler.) Though neither received any formal education beyond high school, the brothers were gifted tinkers with keen minds. The announcement of Lilienthal's death piqued their interest in flight, and after years of studying the problem and absorbing the works of Lilienthal, Langley, and Chanute, in 1899 they decided upon a plan and Wilbur contacted the retired engineer at his Chicago home. This letter was the first of some 1,500 exchanged between them over the next decade.

Dayton, May 13, 1900

For some years I have been afflicted with the belief that flight is possible to man. My disease has increased in severity and I feel that it will soon cost me an increased amount of money if not my life. I have been trying to arrange my affairs in such a way that I can devote my entire time for a few months to experiment in this field.

My general ideas of the subject are similar to those held by most practical experimenters, to wit: that what is chiefly needed is skill rather than machinery. The flight of the buzzard and similar sailers is a convincing demonstration of the value of skill, and the partial needlessness of motors. It is possible to fly without motors, but not without knowledge & skill. This I conceive to be fortunate, for man, by reason of his greater intellect, can more reasonably hope to equal birds in knowledge, than to equal nature in the perfection of her machinery.

Assuming then that Lilienthal was correct in his ideas of the principles on which man should proceed, I conceive that his failure was due chiefly to the inadequacy of his method, and of his apparatus. As to his method, the fact that in five years' time he spent only about five hours, altogether, in actual flight is sufficient to show that his method was inadequate. Even the simplest intellectual or acrobatic feats could never be learned with so short practice, and even Methuselah could never have become an expert stenographer with one hour per year for practice. I also conceive Lilienthal's apparatus to be inadequate not only from the fact that he failed, but my observations of the flight of birds convince me that birds use more positive and energetic methods of regaining equilibrium than that of shifting the center of gravity.

With this general statement of my principles and belief I will proceed to describe the plan and apparatus it is my intention to test. In explaining these, my object is to learn to what extent similar plans have been tested and found to be failures, and also to obtain such suggestions as your great knowledge and experience might enable you to give me. I make no secret of my plans for the reason that I believe no financial profit will accrue to the inventor of the first flying machine, and that only those who are willing to give as well as to receive suggestions can hope to link their names with the honor of its discovery. The problem is too great for one man alone and unaided to solve in secret.

My plan then is this. I shall in a suitable locality erect a light tower about one hundred and fifty feet high. A rope passing over a pulley at the top will serve as a sort of kite string. It will be so counterbalanced that when the rope is drawn out one hundred & fifty feet it will sustain a pull equal to the weight of the operator and apparatus or nearly so. The wind will blow the machine out from the base of the tower and the weight will be sustained partly by the upward pull of the rope and partly by the lift of the wind. The counterbalance will be so arranged that the pull decreases as the line becomes shorter and ceases entirely when its length has been decreased to one hundred feet. The aim will be to eventually practice in a wind capable of sustaining the operator at a height equal to the top of the tower. The pull of the rope will take the place of a motor in counteracting drift. I see, of course, that the pull of the rope will introduce complications which are not met in free flight, but if the plan will only enable me to remain in the air for practice by the hour instead of by the second, I hope to acquire skill sufficient to overcome both these difficulties and those inherent to flight.* Knowledge and skill in handling the machine are absolute essentials to flight and it is impossible to obtain them without extensive practice. The method employed by Mr. Pilcher of towing with horses in many respects is better than that I propose to employ, but offers no guarantee that the experimenter will escape accident long enough to acquire skill sufficient to prevent accident. In my plan I rely on the rope

---

* Chanute discouraged this scheme, and it was soon abandoned by the Wrights.

and counterbalance to at least break the force of a fall. My observation of the flight of buzzards leads me to believe that they regain their lateral balance, when partly overturned by a gust of wind, by a torsion of the tips of the wings. If the rear edge of the right wing tip is twisted upward and the left downward the bird becomes an animated windmill and instantly begins to turn, a line from its head to its tail being the axis. It thus regains its level even if thrown on its beam ends, so to speak, as I have frequently seen them. I think the bird also in general retains its lateral equilibrium, partly by presenting its two wings at different angles to the wind, and partly by drawing in one wing, thus reducing its area. I incline to the belief that the first is the more important and usual method. In the apparatus I intend to employ I make use of the torsion principle. In appearance it is very similar to the "double-check" machine with which the experiments of yourself and Mr. Herring were conducted in 1896–97. The point on which it differs in principle is that the cross-stays which prevent the upper plane from moving forward and backward are removed, and each end of the upper plane is independently moved forward or backward with respect to the lower plane by a suitable lever or other arrangement. By this plan the whole upper plane may be moved forward or backward, to attain longitudinal equilibrium, by moving both hands forward or backward together. Lateral equilibrium is gained by moving one end more than the other or my moving them in opposite directions. If you will make a square cardboard tube two inches in diameter and eight or ten long and choose two sides for your planes you will at once see the torsional effect of moving one end of the upper plane forward and the other backward, and how this effect is attained without sacrificing lateral stiffness. My plan is to attach the tail rigidly to the rear upright stays which connect the planes, the effect of which will be that when the upper plane is thrown forward the end of the tail is elevated, so that the tail assists gravity in restoring longitudinal balance. My experiments hitherto with this apparatus have been confined to machines spreading about fifteen square feet of surface, and have been sufficiently encouraging to induce me to lay plans for a trial with [a] full-sized machine.

My business requires that my experimental work be confined to the months between September and January and I would be particularly thankful for advice as to a suitable locality where I could depend on winds of about fifteen miles per hour without rain or too inclement weather. I am certain that such localities are rare.

I have your *Progress in Flying Machines* and your articles in the *Annuals* of '95, '96, & '97, as also your recent articles in the *Independent*. If you can give me information as to where an account of Pilcher's experiments can be obtained I would greatly appreciate your kindness.

21

———❧◦❧———

The First Journey to Kitty Hawk

Wilbur Wright, 1900

Upon Chanute's recommendation the Wrights investigated the possibility of beginning their gliding experiments along the Atlantic coast, for the necessary high, steady winds, for the soft sand dunes, and for the seclusion they preferred. After checking with the National Weather Bureau Wilbur found that a small village on North Carolina's Outer Banks reported the highest winds, and so he set out for there on September 6, 1900. The following was Wilbur's memorandum of the first difficult voyage to Kitty Hawk, written circa September 13, soon after he arrived.

———❧◦❧———

Left Dayton Thurs. eve. at 6:30 P.M. over Big Four and C. & O. Arrived at Old Point about six o'clock P.M. the next day, and went over to Norfolk via the steamer *Pennsylvania*. Put up at the Monticello Hotel. Spent Saturday morning trying to find some spruce for spars of machine, but was unsuccessful. Finally I bought some white pine and had it sawed up at J. E. Etheridge Co. mill. Cumpston Goffigon, the foreman, very accommodating. The weather was near 100 Fahr. and I nearly collapsed. At 4:30 left for Eliz. [Elizabeth] City and put up at the Arlington where I spent several days waiting for a boat to Kitty Hawk. No one seemed to know anything about the place or how to get there. At last on Tuesday left. I engaged passage with Israel Perry on his flat-bottom schooner fishing boat. As it was anchored about three miles down the river we started in his skiff which was loaded almost to the gunwale with three men, my heavy trunk and lumber. The boat leaked very badly and frequently dipped water, but by constant bailing we managed to reach the schooner in safety. The weather was very fine with a light west wind blowing. When I mounted the deck of the larger boat I discovered at a glance that it was in worse condition if possible than the skiff. The sails were rotten, the ropes badly worn and the rudderpost half rotted off, and the cabin so dirty and vermin-infested that I kept out of it from first to last. The wind became very light, making progress slow. Though we had started immediately after dinner it was almost dark when we passed out of the mouth of the Pasquotank and headed down the sound. The water was much rougher than the light wind would have led us to expect, and Israel spoke of it several times and seemed a little uneasy. After a time the breeze shifted to the south and east and gradually became stronger. The boat was quite unfitted for sailing against a head wind owing to the large size of the cabin, the lack of load, and its flat bottom. The waves which were now running quite high struck the boat from below with a heavy shock and threw it back about as fast as it went forward. The leeway was greater than the headway. The strain of rolling and pitching sprung a leak and this, together with what water came over the bow at times, made it necessary to bail frequently. At 11 o'clock the wind had increased to a gale and the boat was gradually being driven nearer and nearer the north shore, but as an attempt to turn round would probably have resulted in an upset there seemed nothing else to do but attempt to round the North River light and take refuge behind the point. In a severe gust the foresail was blown loose from the boom and fluttered to leeward with a terrible roar. The boy and I finally succeeded in taking it in though it was rather dangerous work in the dark with the boat rolling so badly. By the time we had reached a position even with the end of the point it became doubtful whether we would be able to round the light, which lay at the end of the bar extending out a quarter of a mile from the shore. The suspense was ended by another roaring of the canvas as the mainsail also tore loose from the boom, and shook fiercely in the gale. The only chance was to make a straight run over the bar under nothing but a jib, so we took in the mainsail and let the boat swing round stern to the wind. This was a very dangerous maneuver in such a sea but was in some way accomplished without capsizing. The waves were very high on the bar and broke over the stern very badly. Israel had been so long a stranger to the touch of water upon his skin that it affected him very much.

22

Life at Kitty Hawk, 1900

Orville Wright to Katharine Wright, October 14

Orville joined Wilbur at Kitty Hawk a few days later, after Wilbur had finished assembling their first man-carrying glider. Orville writes to his younger and only sister, Katharine.

I wrote you last Sunday, but maybe you have not got it yet. We have been having several big winds, and as the mail is carried out of Kitty Hawk in a small sailboat very likely letters have been slow in transportation this week. I got your letter of Monday last night.

We have been having a fine time, altogether we have had the machine out three different days, from 2 to 4 hours each time. Monday night and all day Tuesday we had a terrific wind blowing 36 miles an hour. Wednesday morning the Kitty Hawkers were out early peering around the edge of the woods and out of their upstairs windows to see whether our camp was still in existence. We were all right, however, and though wind continued up to 30 miles, got the machine out to give it another trial. The wind was too strong and unsteady for us to attempt an ascent in it, so we just flew it like a kite, running down a number of strings to the ground with which to work the steering apparatus. The machine seemed a rather docile thing, and we taught it to behave fairly well. Chains were hung on it to give it work to do, while we took measurements of the "drift" in pounds.

In the afternoon we took the machine to the hill just south of our camp, formerly known as "Look Out Hill," but now as the "Hill of the Wreck." (I have just stopped a minute to eat a spoonful of condensed milk. No one down here has any regular milk. The poor cows have such a hard time scraping up a living that they don't have any time for making milk. You never saw such poor pitiful-looking creatures as the horses, hogs and cows are down here. The only things that thrive and grow fat are the bedbugs, mosquitoes, and wood ticks. This condensed milk comes in a can and is just like the cream of our homemade chocolate creams. It is intended to be dissolved in water, but as we cannot down it that way, we just eat it out of the can with a spoon. It makes a pretty good but rather expensive dessert that way.)

Well, after erecting a derrick from which to swing our rope with which we fly the machine, we sent it up about 20 feet, at which height we attempt to keep it by the manipulation of the strings to the rudder. The greatest difficulty is in keeping it down. It naturally wants to go higher & higher. When it begins to get too high we give it a pretty strong pull on the ducking string, to which it responds by making a terrific dart for the ground. If nothing is broken we start it up again. This is all practice in the control of the machine. When it comes down we just lay it flat on the ground and the pressure of the wind on the upper surface holds it down so tightly that you can hardly raise it again.

After an hour or so of practice in steering, we laid it down on the ground to change some of the adjustments of the ropes, when without a sixteenth of a second's notice, the wind caught under one corner, and quicker than thought, it landed 20 feet away.

We had had a number of interesting experiences with it before, performing some feats which would almost seem an impossibility. We dragged the pieces back to camp and began to consider getting home. The next morning we had cheered up some and began to think there was some hope of repairing it. The next three days were spent in repairing, holding the tent down, and hunting; mostly the last, in which occupation we have succeeded in killing two large fish hawks each measuring over five feet from tip to tip, in chasing a lot of chicken hawks till we were pretty well winded, and in scaring several large bald eagles. Will saw a squirrel yesterday, but while he was crawling about over logs and through sand and brushes, trying to get a dead shot on it, it ate up several hickory nuts, licked chops, and departed, goodness knows where.

We did have a dinner of wild fowl the other day, but that was up to Tate's. He invited us up to help dispose of a wild goose which had been killed out of season by one of the neighboring farmers. The people about Kitty Hawk are all "game hogs" and pay little respect to what few game laws they have. But wild goose, whether due to its game flavor or not, tasted pretty good after a fast of several weeks in any kind of flesh except a mess or two of fish.

Kitty Hawk is a fishing village. The people make what little living they have in fishing. They ship tons & tons of fish away every year to Baltimore and other northern cities, yet like might be expected in a fishing village, the only meat they ever eat is fish flesh, and they never have any of that. You can buy fish in Dayton at any time, summer or winter, rain or shine; but you can't here. About the only way to get fish is to go and catch them yourself. It is just like in the north, where our carpenters never have their houses completed, nor the painters their houses painted; the fisherman never has any fish.

This is a great country for fishing and hunting. The fish are so thick you see dozens of them whenever you look down into the water. The woods are filled with wild game, they say; even a few "bars" are prowling about the woods not far away. At any time we look out of the tent door we can see an eagle flapping its way over head, buzzards by the dozen—till Will is 'most sick of them—soaring over the hills and bay, hen hawks making a raid on nearby chicken yards, or a fish hawk hovering over the bay looking for a poor little fish "whom he may devour." Looking off the other way to the sea, we find the seagulls skimming the waves, and the little sea chickens hopping about, as on one foot, on the beach, picking up the small animals washed in by the surf.

But the sand! The sand is the greatest thing in Kitty Hawk, and soon will be the only thing. The site of our tent was formerly a fertile valley, cultivated by some ancient Kitty Hawker. Now only a few rotten limbs, the topmost branches of trees that then grew in this valley, protrude from the sand. The sea has washed and the wind blown millions and millions of loads of sand up in heaps along the coast, completely covering houses and forest. Mr. Tate is now tearing down the nearest house to our camp to save it from the sand. . . .

You can't get dirty. Not enough to raise the least bit of color could be collected under a fingernail. We have a method of cleaning dishes that has made the dishrag and the tea towel a thing of the past. Poor Israel Perry was born and raised here. He never had to wash and consequently never learned to even perform the operation. No wonder that Will should find him in a foreign part in such an indescribable condition. You will hear more of Israel Perry when Will gets home. It was aboard his boat the Will passed through those "storms and terrors by day & by night, of privations of hunger & thirst, of bloodthirsty beasts, etc., etc.," that Will wrote us about. . . . A mockingbird lives in a tree that overhangs our tent, and sings to us the whole day long. He is very tame, and perches on the highest bough of the tree (which however is only about ten feet high) and calls us up every morning. I think he crows up especially early after every big storm to see whether we are still here; we often think of him in the night, when the wind is shaking the top and sides of the tent till they sound like thunder, and wonder how he is faring and whether his nest can stand the storm. The mockingbird is the most common about here. The redbird, brown thrasher, wren, sparrow, and dozens of birds which I do not know by name, are thick in the woods nearest our camp.

The sunsets here are the prettiest I have ever seen. The clouds light up in all colors in the background, with deep blue clouds of various shapes fringed with gold before. The moon rises in much the same style, and lights up this pile of sand almost like day. I read my watch at all hours of the night on moonless nights without the aid of any other light than that of the stars shining on the canvas of the tent.

I suspect you sometimes wonder what we eat, and how we get it. After I got down we decided to camp. There is no store in Kitty Hawk; that is, not anything that you would call a store. Our pantry in its most depleted state would be a mammoth affair compared with our Kitty Hawk stores. Our camp alone exhausts the output of all the henneries within a mile. What little canned goods, such as corn, etc., [there is,] is of such a nature that only a Kitty Hawker could down it. Mr. Calhoun, the groceryman, is striving to raise the tastes of the community to better goods, but all in vain. They never had anything good in their lives, and consequently are satisfied with what they have. In all other things they are the same way, satisfied in keeping soul and body together. Mr. Tate is probably the one exception. He gets interested in anything we have, wants to put acetylene gas in his house because he saw my bicycle gas lamp, has decided to buy our gasoline stove when we leave. Gasoline stoves are a curiosity in this neighborhood, and more feared by the natives than those "bars" up North River, where Israel Perry wouldn't land "for a thousand dollars." Mr. Tate would also like to spend his remaining days—which might be few—in experimenting with flying machines. He is already postmaster, farmer, fisherman, and political boss of Kitty Hawk. Doc. Cogswell, a man from N.Y. City, who married a sister of Tate's wife and who has settled down here, says Tate will be dead before Christmas from excitement if we don't get out. Tate can't afford to shirk his work to fool around with us, so he attempts to do a day's work in two or three hours so that he can spend the balance with us and the machine.

We need no introduction in Kitty Hawk. Every place we go we are called Mr. Wright. Our fame has spread far and wide up and down the beach. Will has even rescued the name of Israel Perry, a former Kitty Hawker, from oblivion, and it now is one of the most frequently spoken names about the place. Will admits that Israel meant well.

I believed I started to tell you what we eat. Well, part of the time we eat hot biscuits and eggs and tomatoes; part of the time eggs, and part tomatoes. Just now we are out of gasoline and coffee. Therefore no hot drink or break or crackers. The order sent off Tuesday has been delayed by the winds. Will is 'most starved. But he kept crying that when we were rolling in luxuries, such as butter, bacon, corn bread and coffee. I think he will survive. It is now suppertime. I must scratch around and see what I can get together. We still have half a can of condensed milk, which amounts to six or eight teaspoonfuls.

23

Life at Kitty Hawk, 1901

Orville Wright to Katharine Wright, July 28

The next year they returned to Kitty Hawk with a bigger glider, and an entourage including Octave Chanute and two assistants, Edward Huffaker, formerly of Smithsonian Secretary Samuel Langley's ongoing flying Aerodrome experiments, and George Spratt, a Pennsylvania doctor with an interest in aeronautics. Though their new glider flew better than any machine in history, it nonetheless flew with poorer results than the brothers had predicted. The 1901 season left them so discouraged, in fact, that Chanute feared they might abandon their work.

This is Sunday evening, six o'clock, and I am writing this letter while Will and Mr. Spratt are washing the dinner dishes. We did not get up this morning till half past seven, and had breakfast at a little after eleven, so that our dinner did not come till after five this evening. I have been so busy that I have not at any time had an opportunity to write, having had all the cooking to do besides the work on the machine. We completed it yesterday and spent the afternoon in gliding with some pretty exciting results which I will relate "after soon." Camping at Kill Devil is a different thing from that at Kitty Hawk. We haven't had a nor'easter yet, though we have been here over two weeks. In spite of the fact that I looked forward to nor'easters last year with some fear, nothing could have been more welcome this year, but it seems nature has been in a conspiracy with our enemy, the mosquito.

We landed at Kitty Hawk two weeks ago Thursday evening, one day after a 93-mile nor'easter which demolished the only remaining piece of our last year's machine.

. . . . The next morning we set out with all our baggage for Kill Devil Hills, selecting our site and pitching our tent in a drenching rain, which had come upon us unexpectedly but continued all day and night. After fooling around all day inside the tent, excepting on a few occasions when we rushed out to drive a few more tent pegs, our thirst became unbearable, and we decided upon driving the Webbert pump, no well where we could get water being within a mile's distance. Well (pun), we got no well; the point came loose down in the sand, and we lost it! Oh misery! Most dead for water and none within a mile! excepting what was coming from the skies. However, we decided to catch a little of this, and placed the dishpan where the water dripped down from the tent roof; and though it tasted somewhat of the soap which we had rubbed on the canvas to keep it from mildewing, it pretty well filled a longfelt want. These troubles were nothing in comparison to what was coming, so I will not relate them further.

We continued our well driving all day Saturday, and Sunday spent the day in making a trip to Kitty Hawk (four miles) and in reading. Sunday night I was taken sick and 'most died, that is, I felt as if I did; and managed to keep Will up the best part of the night. The next day I was all right, and we commenced work on our building. The work went along well and we had the building done in three days. The building is a grand institution, with awnings at both ends; that is, with big doors hinged at the top, which we swing open and prop up, making an awning the full length of the building at each end, and extending out a little over the distance of the porch around our house. We keep both ends open almost all the time and let the breezes have full sway. These breezes, by the way, are a little stronger than that big wind which blew the tops off the trees on our street a few days before we left—the night Ed Sines was over—and continue day and night, coming in turn from all points of the compass.

Mr. Huffaker arrived Thursday afternoon, and with him a swarm of mosquitoes which came in a mighty cloud, almost darkening the sun. This was the beginning of the most miserable existence I had ever passed through. The agonies of typhoid fever with its attending starvation are as nothing in comparison. But there was no escape. The sand and grass and trees and hills and everything was fairly covered with them. They chewed us clear through our underwear and socks. Lumps began swelling up all over my body like hen's eggs. We attempted to escape by going to bed, which we did at a little after five o'clock. We put our cots out under the awnings and wrapped up in our blankets with only our noses protruding from the folds, thus exposing the least possible surface to attack. Alas! Here nature's complicity in the conspiracy against us became evident. The wind, which until now had been blowing over twenty miles an hour, dropped off entirely. Our blankets then became unbearable. The perspiration would roll off of us in torrents. We would partly uncover and the mosquitoes would swoop down upon us in vast multitudes. We would make a few desperate and vain slaps, and again retire behind our blankets. Misery! Misery! The half can never be told. We passed the next ten hours in a state of hopeless desperation. Morning brought a little better condition, and we attempted on several occasions to begin work on our machine, but all attempts had to be abandoned. We now thought that surely our enemy had done its worst, and we could hope for something better soon. Alas, "how seldom do our dreams come true."

The next night we constructed mosquito frames and nets over our cots, thinking in our childish error we could fix the bloody beasts. We put our cots out on the sand twenty or thirty feet from the tent and house, and crawled in under the netting and bedclothes, Glen Osborn fashion, and lay there on our backs smiling at the way in which we had got the best of them. The tops of the canopies were covered with mosquitoes till there was hardly standing room for another one; the buzzing was like the buzzing of a mighty buzz saw. But what was our astonishment when in a few minutes we heard a terrific slap and a cry from Mr. Huffaker announcing that the enemy had gained the outer works and he was engaged in a hand-to-hand conflict with them. All our forces were put to complete rout. In our desperate attacks on the advancing foe our fortifications were almost entirely torn down, and in desperation, we fled from them, rushing all about the sand for several hundred feet around trying to find some place of safety. But it was of no use. We again took refuge in our blankets with the same results as in the previous night. Affairs had now become so desperate that it began to look as if camp would have to be abandoned or we perish in the attempt to maintain it.

Hope springs eternal; that is, it does the next morning when we begin to recover from the attack of the night before. Remembering the claim of the U.S. Army that safety is in "a superior fire," we proceeded to build big fires about camp, dragging in old tree stumps which are scattered about over the sands at about a quarter mile from camp, and keeping up such a smoke that the enemy could not find us. Mr. Spratt, after getting in bed with the smoke blowing over him, before long announced that he could no longer stand the fire, and dragged his cot out into the clear air. A few minutes later he returned, saying the mosquitoes were worse than the smoke. He spent the balance of the night in retreat from mosquito to smoke and from smoke to mosquito. However, the mosquitoes this night were small in number as compared with any previous night or even our fires would probably have been of no avail. Mr. Huffaker, Will, and I had passed the night in comparative comfort, but Mr. Spratt in the morning announced that this was the most miserable night he had ever passed through. Of course we explained to him what we had gone through, and that we were expecting a repetition of it every night. We nearly scared him off after the first night, but as every night since affairs have been improving, he is now a little less uneasy, and has hopes of enduring the agony a few weeks longer.

Yesterday most of the mosquitoes had disappeared and we had a fine day and wind for testing the new machine. We took it off to the Big Hill, about a thousand feet distant, and began our experiments. Our first experiments were rather disappointing. The machine refused to act like our machine last year and at times seemed to be entirely beyond control. On one occasion it began gliding off higher and higher (Will doing the gliding) until it finally came almost at a stop at a height variously estimated by Mr. Spratt and Huffaker at from 18 ft. to forty feet. This wound up in the most encouraging performance of the whole afternoon. This was the very fix Lilienthal got into when he was killed. His machine dropped head first to the ground and his neck was broken. Our machine made a flat descent to the ground with no injury to either operator or machine. On another occasion the machine made another similar performance and showed that in this respect it is entirely safe. These were the first descents ever made successfully after getting into the above-mentioned predicament. The adjustments of the machine are away off. We expect to get it in good shape in the morning and make more successful attempts. Mr. Huffaker was much pleased with a long glide we made, which he considered the longest ever made, but we think at least three or four better have been made before. Some of our glides were very encouraging.

It is now after bedtime and since very few mosquitoes have shown up we are going to get a good start on them. Tell Carrie* I will write to her in a few days, at least at the first opportunity. Tell Mr. Taylor† of what is going on, or give him our letters to read. I suspect it is a little tiresome running the shop all alone. I will write again in a few days.

[P.S.] That bill from the automobile company had been paid and we have receipt for same in letter file.

* The Wright's longtime housekeeper, Carrie Grumbach.
† Charlie Taylor, who helped at the Wright cycle shop, and assisted their aeronautical work.

24

Life at Kitty Hawk, 1902

Orville Wright to Katharine Wright, October 23

Chanute need not have worried. That next year the brothers returned to Kitty Hawk with a vengeance, bringing with them a superb new glider made possible in part by a wind tunnel they had built in the interim. On August 25, 1902, they headed back to Kitty Hawk for the third time.

Since Lorin* was here and has probably told you all the news from camp, I haven't thought it necessary to write very often, but I don't like the idea of that roaring big supper you are going to get up for us next Wednesday night getting cold before we get there Thursday, so I write to advise postponing it to Thursday, at least, for we might possibly not get home before Friday morning. We will leave here Tuesday morning on the *Lou Willis*, but Lorin has written us that the trains have changed time, so that we do not know exactly when we can reach Dayton. Lorin will know the time we ought to arrive.

Everybody is out of camp but Will and myself. Spratt left Monday. We had a good time last week after Chanute & Herring† left. The work about camp was so much easier, beside the fact that the fewer in camp the more there is for each one to eat, [and] that we had lots of time to go over to the woods botanizing and looking after birds. We went to the beach a number of times and have collected a whole bucketful of starfish besides a lot of shells and a couple of king crabs which we will bring home. Spratt is a fine fellow to be with in the woods, for he knows every bird, or bug, or plant that you are likely to run across. Lorin should have been here a little later—we didn't have a bit of time while Chanute and Herring were in camp—and the weather has been so much nicer since he left. We haven't had a rain since.

The past five days have been the most satisfactory for gliding that we

---

* Lorin Wright (1862–1939), the second of the four Wright brothers, after Reuchlin (1861–1920).

† Augustus Moore Herring, a sometime assistant to Chanute.

have had. In two days we made over 250 glides, or more than we had made all together up to the time Lorin left. We have gained considerable proficiency in the handling of the machine now, so that we are able to take it out in any kind of weather. Day before yesterday we had a wind of 16 meters per second or about 30 miles per hour, and glided in it without any trouble. That was the highest wind a gliding machine was ever in, so that we now hold all the records! The largest machine we handled in any kind [of weather, made the longest dis]tance glide (American), the longest time in the air, the smallest angle of descent, and the highest wind!!! Well, I'll leave the rest of the "blow" till we get home.

Rations are getting low again, and we are dropping back on beans. I'm cooking up a lot of them tonight, trying to do two things at once—cooking for tomorrow and writing letters. We are running a fire all night now so as to keep warm, and have managed to keep comfortable in bed, but on one or two mornings we found it a little chilly downstairs. Well, I can't think of anything else to say until I get home, so good-bye.

25

―――・◦・―――

Mr. Chanute in Paris

By Ernest Archdeacon

In April 1903, Chanute returned to his native France to speak on the current state of American aeronautical experiments before the Aéro-Club de France, emphasizing the work of the Wrights, distributing drawings of the brothers' successful 1902 glider, and even appearing to take some of the credit for himself. Hearing about all of this progress firsthand made French aviation leaders uneasy. In the April 11, 1903, edition of the journal *La Locomotion,* attorney Ernest Archdeacon called for all of France to respond to the Wrights' threat to France's aeronautical ascendancy.

―――・◦・―――

A great flurry in the "aerial" world was provoked in recent days, by the arrival in Paris, and reception at the Aéro-Club, of Mr. Chanute, the American inventor who, if not extremely well-known among ordinary mortals, is a veritable celebrity among "aviators."

For several years, Mr. Chanute has been working with indefatigable earnestness on the difficult problem of aerial navigation by heavier-than-air means.

A great German scientist, Lilienthal, was the first in this field to make lastingly memorable experiments. He built machines with stationary wings which were attached to the body and permitted him, by launching himself from the top of a small hill, to glide for a certain time in space, exactly like soaring birds. Lilienthal had dedicated several years of his life to this study and had attained very remarkable results. He had made over two thousand gliding experiments, succeeding at times in rising higher than the starting point, and covering by this means distances up to 300 meters.

Success seemed more and more to encourage his efforts; so that he constructed another machine, much more important than his preceding ones, which, it was his hope, would produce excellent results. Unfortunately at the first trials of his new apparatus, having risen to a good height, he, for some unexplained reason, crashed in full flight. The inventor, hurled violently to earth, died a few hours later.

Immediately after the death of Lilienthal, which occurred in 1896, Mr.

Chanute resumed his own experiments with tireless patience and precision of method, never allowing himself to swerve from the unalterable path he had laid out.

I shall not speak here of the innumerable apparatus built successively by Mr. Chanute, each new one marking a slight improvement over the former.

Moreover, Mr. Chanute, unlike most inventors who wish to keep for themselves alone the whole glory of their ideas, understood very well the necessity of helping one another in this tremendous task.

Admitting that he was no longer very young, he took pains to train young, intelligent, and daring pupils, capable of carrying on his researches by multiplying his gliding experiment to infinity.

Principal among them, certainly, is Mr. Wilbur Wright, of Dayton (Ohio), who for his part has made some extremely remarkable experiments, and whose most recently built machine now seems to be the model for its type. I shall therefore only describe this last one, lest my article become excessively long.

In Lilienthal's machines, the man was upright and obtained equilibrium by shifting the lower part of his body in the appropriate direction; in those of Mr. Wright, on the other hand, the man is placed in horizontal position on the machine.

In order to regulate the equilibrium in the transverse direction, he operates two cords which act, by means of warping, upon the right and left sides of the wing and, simultaneously, by the movement of the vertical rear rudder.

In order to steer the machine in the longitudinal direction, he can, in the same manner, using the cords, operate the horizontal forward rudder, which must be vigorously pointed vertically downward when the speed is to be killed for landing.

We know that, in order to benefit from the full supporting action of the wind, the "glide" is always made against the wind; it will be understood, then, that in pointing the horizontal rudder vertically downward, the machine turns up suddenly, presents an enormous surface to the opposing wind and finds itself stopped dead.

Mr. Wright's present machine weighs about 53 kilos.

The total supporting surface is about 28 square meters, divided into two surfaces, each about 10 by 1.40 m. each.

The distance between the two surfaces is 1.50 m.

The curvature of the wing is about $\frac{1}{20}$ of its chord, the point of deepest curvature being $\frac{1}{3}$ of the chord back from the front.

Here, in summary, are the results obtained at the present time:

The experimenters are launched from the top of a hill of about 30 meters, the slope of which is very gentle, not exceeding 10°.

Their longest "glides," to use Mr. Chanute's picturesque expression, have reached 200 meters, and they have several times risen higher than their starting point. Much longer flights could be made *with equal ease* by starting from a higher point.

In order to launch the machine, which the experimenter cannot himself do by running, as Lilienthal did, two assistants are sufficient: carrying the machine together, they take several steps against the wind and then let go when they feel the lifting action of the wind take effect.

With good conditions, a mean angle of descent of about 6° can be achieved, and this, according to Mr. Chanute, will diminish considerably with the incessant progress of the machines.

What is especially remarkable in these experiments is that they have been conducted with such prudence and so methodically that, from the beginning, Mr. Chanute has not had to report a single accident—except a pair of torn trousers! And this although a very large number of people, even but slightly initiated, have already attempted and accomplished "glides."

It is also true that the experimenters, with their extraordinary care, have marvelously chosen their ground, which is all of soft sand and like that of our dunes. A terribly violent shock would be necessary on such soil to lead to serious bruises.

Mr. Chanute is justly proud of this absence of accidents in his trials. Moreover, it is the only proud thing I know about him, for he is the most modest man in the world, always willing to attribute his own merits to others.

Finally, here is what Mr. Chanute said in closing:

"Our experiments, methodically conducted, will permit us, little by little, to learn completely 'the art of the bird'—an art which, without seeming so, is extremely difficult.

"In a year, then, or perhaps not for two, we will know it thoroughly.

"Until then, it is useless, and even dangerous, to burden oneself with a motor, and I much prefer to use such an untroublesome and simple motor as gravity.

"Besides," added Mr. Chanute, "these glides provide the most original and most enticing of sports; as proof of which, several of my friends, great sportsmen and hunters, have put aside their favorite sports to devote themselves with enthusiasm to aerial glides!"

Mr. Chanute, on his return to America, is to send us complete plans of his latest machines, so as to allow us to execute similar ones in France.

Moreover, I do not doubt that, before long, some of our dauntless automobile sportsmen will happen to make themselves some similar machines and seek out somewhere a favorable spot for competing in these exciting glides.

The machine fully equipped comes to about 350 francs. A little cheaper than an automobile!

If there are any orders, I will undertake to handle them. Let's go, gentlemen, take out your subscriptions. Just write me at *La Locomotion*.

26

——▷●◁——

Experiments with the Langley Aerodrome

By S. P. Langley

Samuel Langley had hoped to be the first in the air with his man-carrying *Great Aerodrome,* a scaled-up development of the successful powered, unmanned Aerodromes No. 5 and No. 6, which in 1896 became the first machines to sustain themselves in the air. Twice (in October and early December 1903) his manned machine failed. The newspapers called his invention a "buzzard," and said that it slid into the Potomac "like a handful of mortar." Here, on the other hand, is how Langley viewed his accomplishments, published in the 1904 *Smithsonian Annual Report.*

——▷●◁——

The experiments undertaken by the Smithsonian Institution upon an aerodrome, or flying machine, capable of carrying a man have been suspended from lack of funds to repair defects in the launching apparatus without the machine ever having been in the air at all. As these experiments have been popularly, and of late repeatedly, represented as having failed on the contrary, because the aerodrome could not sustain itself in the air I have decided to give this brief though late account, which may be accepted as the first authoritative statement of them.

It will be remembered that in 1896 wholly successful flights of between one-half and one mile by large steam-driven models, unsupported except by the mechanical effects of steam engines, had been made by me. In all these the machine was first launched into the air from "ways," somewhat as a ship is launched into the water, the machine resting on a car that ran forward on these ways, which fell down at the extremity of the car's motion, releasing the aerodrome for its free flight. I mention these details because they are essential to an understanding of what follows, and partly because their success led me to undertake the experiments on a much larger scale I now describe.

In the early part of 1898 a board, composed of officers of the Army and navy, was appointed to investigate these past experiments with a view to determining just what had been accomplished and what the possibilities were of developing a large-size man-carrying machine for war purposes.

The report of this board being favorable, the Board of Ordnance and Fortification of the War Department decided to take up the matter, and I having agreed to give without compensation what time I could spare from official duties, the Board allotted $50,000 for the development, construction, and test of a large aerodrome, half of which sum was to be available immediately and the remainder when required. The whole matter had previously been laid before the Board of Regents of the Smithsonian Institution, who had authorized me to take up the work and to use in connection with it such facilities of the Institution as were available.

Before consenting to undertake the construction of this large machine, I had fully appreciated that owing to theoretical considerations, into which I do not enter, it would need to be relatively lighter than the smaller one; and later it was so constructed, each foot of sustaining surface in the large machine carrying nearly the same weight as each foot in the model. The difficulties subsequently experienced with the larger machine were, then, due not to this cause, but to practical obstacles connected with the launching, and the like.

I had also fully appreciated the fact that one of the chief difficulties in its construction would lie in the procuring of a suitable engine of sufficient power and, at the same time, one which was light enough. (The models had been driven by steam engines whose water supply weighed too much for very long flights.) The construction of the steam engine is well understood, but now it would become necessary to replace this by gas engines, which for this purpose involve novel difficulties. I resolved not to attempt the task of constructing the engine myself, and had accordingly entered into negotiations with the best engine builders in this country, and after long delay had finally secured a contract with a builder who, of all persons engaged in such work, seemed most likely to achieve success. It was only after this contract for the engine had been signed that I felt willing to formally undertake the work of building the aerodrome.

The contract with the engine builder called for an engine developing 12 brake horsepower, and weighing not more than 100 pounds, including cooling water and all other accessories, and with the proviso that a second engine, exactly like this first one, would be furnished on the same terms. The first engine was to be delivered before the close of February, 1899, and the frame of the aerodrome with sustaining surfaces, propellers, shafting, rudders, etc., was immediately planned, and now that the engine was believed to be secured, their actual construction was pushed with the utmost speed. The previous experiments with steam-driven models, which had been so successful, had been conducted over the water, using a small houseboat having a cabin for storing the machine, appliances and tools, on top of which was mounted a track and car for use in launching. As full success in launching these working models had been achieved after several years spent in devising, testing, and improving this plan, I decided to follow the same method with the large machine, and accordingly designed and had built a house-boat, in which the machine could not only be stored, but which would also furnish space for workshops, and on the top of which was mounted a turntable and track for use in launching from whatever direction the wind might come.

Everything connected with the work was expedited as much as possible with the expectation of being able to have the first trial flight before the close of 1899, and time and money had been spent on the aerodrome, which was ready, except for its engine, when the time for the delivery of this arrived. But now the builder proved unable to complete his contract, and, after months of delay, it was necessary to decrease the force at work on the machine proper and its launching appliances until some assurance could be had of the final success of the engine. During the spring and summer of 1899, while these delays were being experienced in procuring suitable engines, former experiments on superposed wing surfaces were continued, time was found for overhauling the two steam-driven models which had been used in 1896, and the small houseboat was rebuilt so that further tests of these small machines might be made in order to study the effect of various changes in the balancing and the steering, equilibrium preserving and sustaining appliances, and the months of June, July, and a portion of August were spent in actual tests of these machines in free flight.

A new launching apparatus following the general plan of the former overhead one, but with the track underneath it, was built for the models, and it was used most successfully in these experiments, more than a dozen flights in succession being made with it, while in every case it worked without delay or accident. As soon as these tests with the models on this underneath launching apparatus were completed, that for the large machine was built as an exact duplicate, except for the enlargement, and with some natural confidence that what had worked so perfectly on a small scale would work fairly on a large one.

It was recognized from the very beginning that it would be desirable in a large machine to use "superposed" sustaining surfaces (that is, with one wing above another) on account of their superiority so far as the relation of strength to weight is concerned, and from their independence of guy wiring; and two sets of superposed sustaining surfaces of different patterns were built and experimented with in the early tests. These surfaces proved, on the whole, inferior in lifting power, though among compensating advantages are the strength of a "bridge" construction which dispenses with guy wires coming up from below, which, in fact, later were the cause of disaster in the launching.

It was finally decided to follow what experiment had shown to be successful, and to construct the sustaining surfaces for the large machine after the "single-tier" plan. This proved to be no easy task, since in the construction of the surfaces for the small machines the main and cross ribs of the framework had been made solid, and, after steaming, bent and dried to the proper curvature, while it was obvious that this plan could not be followed in the large surfaces on account of the necessity, already alluded to, of making them relatively lighter than the small ones, which were already very light. After the most painstaking construction, and tests of various sizes and thicknesses of hollow square, hollow round, I-beam, channel, and many other types of ribs, I finally devised a type which consisted of a hollow box form, having its sides of tapering thickness, with the thickest part at the point midway between contiguous sides and with small partitions placed inside every few inches in somewhat the same way that nature places them in the bamboo. These various parts of the rib (corresponding to the quill in a wing) were then glued and clamped together, and after drying were reduced to the proper dimensions and the ribs covered with several coats of a special marine varnish, which it had been found protected the glued joints from softening, even when they were immersed in water for twenty-four hours.

Comparative measurements were made between these large cross ribs, 11 feet long, and a large quill from the wing of a harpy eagle, which is probably one of the greatest wonders that nature has produced in the way of strength for weight. These measurements showed that the large, 11-foot ribs ("quills") for the sustaining surfaces of the large machine were equally as strong, weight for weight, as the quill of the eagle; but much time was consumed in various constructions and tests before such a result was finally obtained.

During this time a model of the large machine, one-fourth of its linear dimensions, was constructed, and a second contract was made for an engine for it. The delay with the large engine was repeated with the small one, and in the spring of 1900 it was found that both contract engines were failures for the purpose for which they were intended, as neither one developed half of the power required for the allotted weight.

I accordingly again searched all over this country, and, finally, accompanied by an engineer [Charles Manly], whose services I had engaged, went to Europe, and there personally visited large builders of engines for automobiles, and attempted to get them to undertake the construction of such an engine as was required. This search, however, was fruitless, as all of the foreign builders, as well as those of this country, believed it impossible to construct an engine of the necessary power and as light as I required (less than 10 pounds to the horsepower without fuel or water). I was therefore forced to return to this country and to consent most reluctantly, even at this late date, to have the work of constructing suitable engines undertaken in the shops of the Smithsonian Institution, since, as I have explained, the aerodrome frame and wings were already constructed. This work upon the engines began here in August, 1900, in the immediate care of Mr. Manly. These engines were to be of nearly double the power first estimated and of little more weight, but this increased power and the strain caused by it demanded a renewal of the frame as first built, in a stronger and consequently in a heavier form, and the following sixteen months were spent in such a reconstruction simultaneously with the work on the engines.

The flying weight of the machine complete, with that of the aeronaut, was 830 pounds; its sustaining surface, 1,040 square feet. It therefore was provided with slightly greater sustaining surface and materially greater relative horsepower than the model subsequently described which flew successfully. The brake horsepower of the engine was 52; the engine itself, without cooling water, or fuel, weighed approximately 1 kilogram to the horsepower. The entire power plant, including cooling water, carburetor, battery, etc., weighed materially less than 5 pounds to the horsepower. Engines for both the large machine and the quarter-size model were completed before the close of 1901, and they were immediately put in their respective frames and tests of them and their power-transmission appliances were begun.

It is well here to call attention to the fact that although an engine may develop sufficient power for the allotted weight, yet it is not at all certain that it will be suitable for use on a machine which is necessarily as light as one for traversing the air, for it would be impossible to use, for instance, a single cylinder gasoline engine in a flying machine unless it had connected to it prohibitively heavy flywheels. These facts being recognized, the engines built in the Smithsonian shops were provided with five cylinders, and it was found upon test that the turning effect received from them was most uniform, and that, by suitable balancing of rotating and reciprocating parts, they could be made to work so that there was practically no vibration, even when used in the very light frames of the aerodromes.

The engine is not all the apparatus connected with the development and delivery of power, for obviously there must be shafts, bearings, and in the present case there were also gears; and all of these parts must necessarily be phenomenally light, while all of the materials must be capable of withstanding repeated and constant strains far beyond their elastic limit. It is also evident to anyone having familiarity with such constructions that it is most difficult to keep the various bearings, shafts, gears, etc., in proper alignment without adding excessive weight, and also that when these various parts once get out of alignment when subject to strain, the disasters which are caused render them unfit for further use.

The engines themselves were successfully completed before the close of 1901, and were of much more power than those originally designed; but nearly a year and a half had been spent not only in their completion, but in properly coordinating the various parts of the frame carrying them, repairing the various breakages, assembling, dismounting, and reassembling the various parts of the appliances, and in general rebuilding the frame and appurtenances to correspond in strength to the new engines.

There are innumerable other details, for the whole question is one of details. I may, however, particularly mention the carburetors, which form an essential part of every gas engine, and such giving fair satisfaction for use in automobiles were on the market at the time, yet all of them failed to properly generate gas when used in the tests of the engine working in the aerodrome frame, chiefly because of the fact that the movement of the engine in this light frame must be constant and regular or the transmission appliances are certain of distortion. It was, therefore, necessary to devise carburetors for the aerodrome engines which would meet the required conditions, and more than half a dozen were constructed which were in advance of anything then on the market, and yet were not good enough to use in the aerodrome, before a satisfactory one was made. These experiments were made in the shop, but with an imitation of all the disturbing influences which would be met with in the actual use of the machine in the air, so as to make certain, as far as possible, that the first test of the machine in free flight would not be marred by mishaps or unseen contingencies in connection with the generation and use of power.

It is impossible for anyone who has not had experience with such matters to appreciate the great amount of delay which experience has shown is to be expected in such experiments. Only in the spring of 1903, and after two unforeseen years of assiduous labor, were these new engines and their appurtenances, weighing altogether less than 5 pounds to the horsepower and far lighter than any known to be then existing, so coordinated and adjusted that successive shop tests could be made without causing injury to the frame, its bearings, shafts, or propellers.

And now everything seemed to be as nearly ready for an experiment as could be, until the aerodrome was at the location at which the experiments were to take place. the large machine and its quarter-size counterpart were accordingly placed on board the large houseboat, which had been completed some time before and had been kept in Washington as an auxiliary shop for use in the construction work, and the whole outfit was towed to a point in the Potomac River, here 3 miles wide, directly opposite Widewater, Va., and about 40 miles below Washington and midway between the Maryland and Virginia shores, where the boat was made fast to moorings which had previously been placed in readiness for it.

Although extreme delays had already occurred, yet they were not so trying as the ones which began immediately after the work was thus transferred to the lower Potomac.

The object in constructing the quarter-size counterpart of the large machine was to duplicate in it the balancing and relative proportions of power, surface, etc., that had been arranged in the large one, so that a test of it might be made which would determine whether the large machine should be tried as arranged or the balancing and other arrangements modified. The launching apparatus, which had proved so eminently successful with the original steam-driven models in 1896, was considered a thing so well tested that it had, as I have stated, been duplicated on a suitable scale for use with the large aerodrome, and it was felt that if this apparatus were exactly similar to the smaller one it would be the one appliance least likely to mar the experiments.

In order to test the quarter-size model it was necessary to remove its launching track from the top of the small houseboat and place it upon the deck of the large boat, in order to have all the work go on at one place, as it was impossible, on account of its unseaworthiness, to moor the small houseboat in the middle of the river.

While this transfer of the launching apparatus from the small boat to the large one was being made, the changed atmospheric conditions incident to a large body of water over which tick fogs hung a great portion of the time, from those of a well-protected shop on the land, began to manifest themselves in such ways as the rusting of the metal parts and fittings, and the consequent disarrangement of the adjustment of the necessarily very accurate pieces of apparatus connected with the ignition system of the engine. These difficulties might have partly been anticipated, but there were others concerning which the cause of the deterioration and disarrangement of certain parts and adjustments was not immediately detected, and consequently when short preliminary shop tests of the small machine were attempted just prior to launching it, it was found that the apparatus did not work properly, necessitating repairs and new constructions and consequent delay. Although the large houseboat with the entire outfit had been moved down the river on July 14, 1903, it was not until the 8th of August that the test of the quarter-size model was made, and all of this delay was directly due to changed atmospheric conditions incident to the change in locality. This test of the model in actual flight was made on the 8th of August, 1903, when it worked most satisfactorily, the launching apparatus, as always heretofore, performing perfectly, while the model, being launched directly into the face of the wind, flew directly ahead on an even keel. The balancing proved to be perfect, and the power, supporting surface, guiding, and equilibrium-preserving effects of the rudder also. The weight of the model was 58 pounds, its sustaining surface 66 square feet, and the horsepower from 2½ to 3.

This was the first time in history, so far as I know, that a successful flight of a mechanically sustained flying machine was made in public.

The flight was not as long as had been expected, as it was found afterwards that one of the workmen, in his zeal to insure an especially good one, had overfilled the gasoline tank, which would otherwise have enabled a flight several times as long. However, as such a flight would have given absolutely no more data than the short one did, and as the delays in getting ready for testing the large machine had already far exceeded what was expected, it was thought best not to make any more tests with the small one, as all of the data which was desired had been procured, and it was accordingly stored away and every energy immediately concentrated in getting the large machine ready for its first test, which at that time seemed only a few days away.

During all these delays it may be remarked that we necessarily resided near the houseboat, and therefore in a region of malaria, from whose attacks a portion of us suffered.

I have spoken of the serious delays in the test of the small machine caused by changed atmospheric conditions, but they proved to be almost negligible compared with what was later experienced with the large one. I have also alluded to the fact that the necessarily light ribs of the large sustaining wing surfaces were covered with several coats of a special marine varnish which many tests had shown enabled the glue to withstand submersion in water for more than twenty-four hours without being affected. This water test was made with a view to guarding against the joints of the ribs being softened when the machine came down into the water, as it was planned for it to do at the close of its flight, and these submersions had apparently shown that no trouble need be anticipated from the effects of the sustaining surfaces getting wet. It is an instance of the unpredictable delays which present themselves, that when preparations had been begun for the immediate trial of the large machine, already down the river, it was found that every one of the cross ribs had been rendered almost useless by the damp, though under shelter. As it would take months to build new ones, a temporary means of repairing them was used. There were other delays too numerous to mention, but chiefly incident to working over the water, some of the principal of which were due to storms dragging the house-boat from its moorings and destroying auxiliary apparatus, such as launches, boats, rafts, etc., to say nothing of the time consumed in bringing workmen to and from the scene of the experiments. The propellers were even found to break under the strain of the actual engines in the open, though they had not done so in the shop, and this is mentioned as another instance of the numerous cases of trying delay which it was impossible to foresee.

Finally, however, on the 3d of September, everything seemed to be in readiness for the experiments, and the large aerodrome was accordingly placed in position and all orders given and arrangements made for a test that day. After stationing the various tugs, launches, etc., at their predetermined positions so that they might render any assistance necessary to the engineer or the aerodrome, in case it came down in the water at a point distant from the houseboat, and after the photographers, with special tele-photo cameras, had been stationed on the shore in order that photographs with their trigonometrical data might be obtained, from which speed, distance, etc., might be later determined, and when everyone was anxiously expecting the experiment, a delay occurred from one of the hardly predictable causes just mentioned in connection with the weather. An attempt was made to start the engine so that it might be running at its proper rate when the aerodrome was launched into free air after leaving the track, but the dry batteries used for sparking the engine, together with the entire lot of several dozen which were on hand as a reserve, had become useless from the dampness.

I have merely instanced some of these causes of failure when everything was apparently ready for the expected test, but only one who was on the spot and who had interest in the outcome could appreciate trials of this sort, and the delays of waiting for weather suitable for experiments.

It was found that every storm which came anywhere in the vicinity, immediately selected the river as its route of travel, and although a 10-mile wind on the land would not be an insurmountable obstacle during an experiment, yet the same wind on the river rendered it impossible to maintain the large houseboat on an even keel and free from pitching and tossing long enough to make a test.

While speaking of the difficulties imposed by the weather, it should also be understood that to take the aerodrome in parts from under the shelter of the roof and assemble and mount it upon the upper works was a task requiring four or five hours, and that during this time a change in the weather was altogether likely to occur, and did repeatedly occur, sufficient to render the experiment impossible. Experience has shown, then, that the aerodrome should be sheltered by a building, in which it shall be at all times ready for immediate launching. During all the delay resulting from this and other causes—since it was never known on what day the experiment might take place—a great expense for tug boats waiting at a distance of 40 miles from the city, was incurred, and this was a part of the continuous drain on the pecuniary resources, which proved ultimately more fatal than any mishap to the apparatus itself.

Following the 3d of September, and after procuring new batteries, short preliminary tests inside the boat were made in order to make sure that there would be no difficulty in the running of the engine the next time a fair opportunity arrived for making a test of the machine in free flight. Something of the same troubles which had been met with in the disarrangement of the adjustments of the small engine was experienced in the large one, although they occurred in such a different way that they were not detected until they had caused damage in the tests, and these dis-arrangements were responsible for broken propellers, twisted shafts, crushed bearings, distorted framework, etc., which were not finally overcome until the 1st of October. After again getting everything in apparent readiness, there then ensued a period of waiting on the weather until the 7th of October (1903), when it became sufficiently quiet for a test, which I was now beginning to fear could not be made before the following season. In this, the first test, the engineer took his seat, the engine started with ease and was working without vibration at its full power of over 50 horse, and the word being given to launch the machine, the car was released and the aerodrome sped along the track. Just as the machine left the track, those who were watching it, among whom were two representatives of the Board of Ordnance, noticed that the machine was jerked violently down at the front (being caught, as it subsequently appeared, by the falling ways), and under the full power of its engine was pulled into the water, carrying with it its engineer. When the aerodrome rose to the surface it was found, that while the front sustaining surfaces had been broken by their impact with the water, yet the rear ones were comparatively uninjured. As soon as a full examination of the launching mechanism had been made, it was found that the front portion of the machine had caught on the launching car, and that the guy post, to which were fastened the guy wires which are the main strength of the front surfaces, had been bent to a fatal extent.

The machine, then, had never been free in the air, but had been pulled down as stated.

The disaster just briefly described had indefinitely postponed the test, but this was not all. As has been said before, the weather had become very cold and the so-called equinoctial storms being near it was decided to remove the houseboat at the earliest time possible, but before it could be done, a storm came up and swept away all the launches, boats, rafts, etc., and in doing so completely demolished the greater part of them, so that when the houseboat was finally removed to Washington, on the 15th of October, these appurtenances had to be replaced. It is necessary to remember that these long series of delays worked other than mere scientific difficulties, for a more important and more vital one was the exhaustion of the financial means for the work.

Immediately upon getting the boat to Washington the labor of constructing new sustaining surfaces was begun, and they were completed about the close of November. It was proposed to make a second attempt near the city, though in the meantime the ice had formed in the river. However, on the 8th of December, 1903, the atmosphere became very quiet shortly before noon and an immediate attempt was made at Arsenal Point, quite near Washington, though the site was unfavorable. Shortly after arriving at the selected point everything was in readiness for the test. In the meantime the wind had arisen and darkness was fast approaching, but as the funds for continuing the work were exhausted, rendering it impossible to wait until spring for more suitable weather for making a test, it was decided to go on with it if possible. This time there were on hand to witness the test the writer, members of the Board of Ordnance, and a few other guests, to say nothing of the hundreds of spectators who were waiting on the various wharves and shores. It was found impossible to moor the boat without a delay which would mean that no test could be made on account of darkness, so that it was held as well as possible by a tug, and kept with the aerodrome pointing directly into the wind, though the tide, which was running very strong, and the wind, which was blowing 10 miles an hour, were together causing much difficulty. The engine being started and working most satisfactorily, the order was given by the engineer to release the machine, but just as it was leaving the track another disaster, again due to the launching ways, occurred. This time the rear of the machine, in some way still unexplained, was caught by a portion of the launching car, which caused the rear sustaining surfaces to break, leaving the rear entirely without support, and it came down almost vertically into the water. Darkness had come before the engineer, who had been in extreme danger, could aid in the recovery of the aerodrome, the boat and machine had drifted apart, and one of the tugs, in its zeal to render assistance, had fastened a rope to the frame of the machine in the reverse position from what it should have been attached and had broken the frame entirely in two. While the injury which had thus been caused seemed almost irreparable to one not acquainted with the work, yet it was found upon close examination that only a small amount of labor would be necessary in order to repair the frame, the engine itself being entirely uninjured. Had this accident occurred at an earlier period, when there were funds available for continuing the experiments, it would not have been so serious, for many accidents in shop tests had occurred which, while unknown to the general public, had yet caused greater damage and required more time for repair than in the present case. But the funds for continuing the work were exhausted, and it being found impossible to immediately secure others for continuing it, it was found necessary to discontinue the experiments for the present, though I decided to use, from a private fund, the small amount of money necessary to repair the frame so that it itself, together with its engine, which was entirely uninjured, might be available for further use if it should later prove possible, and that they themselves might be in proper condition to attest to what they really represent as an engineering accomplishment.

Entirely erroneous impressions have been given by the account of these experiments in the public press, from which they have been judged, even by experts; the impression being that the machine could not sustain itself in flight. It seems proper, then, to emphasize and to reiterate, with a view to what has just been said, that the machine has never had a chance to fly at all, but that the failure occurred on its launching ways; and the question of its ability to fly is consequently, as yet, an untried one.

There have, then, been no failures as far as the actual test of the flying capacity of the machine is concerned, for it has never been free in the air at all. The failure of the financial means for continuing these expensive experiments has left the question of their result where it stood before they were undertaken, except that it has been demonstrated that engines can be built, as they have been, of little over one-half the weight that was assigned as the possible minimum by the best builders of France and Germany; that the frame can be made strong enough to carry these engines, and that, so far as any possible prevision can extend, another flight would be successful if the launching were successful; for in this, and in this alone, as far as is known, all the trouble has come.

The experiments have also given necessary information about this launching. They have shown that the method which succeeded perfectly on a smaller scale is insufficient on a larger one, and they have indicated that it is desirable that the launching should take place nearer the surface of the water, either from a track upon the shore or from a houseboat large enough to enable the apparatus to be launched at any time with the wings

5. Langley's *Great Aerodrome* poised for launch from the houseboat in October 1903. For an indication of the machine's size, note the man standing just below the forward wing.

extended and perhaps with wings independent of support from guys. But the construction of this new launching apparatus would involve further considerable expenditures that there are no present means to meet; and this, and this alone, is the cause of their apparent failure.

Failure in the aerodrome itself or its engines there has been none; and it is believed that it is at the moment of success, and when the engineering problems have been solved, that a lack of means has prevented a continuance of the work.

6. Dramatic shot of the *Great Aerodrome* sliding tail-first
"like a handful of mortar" into the Potomac
after the December 8, 1903, launch.

27

⟹•◦•⟸

Life at Kitty Hawk, 1903

Orville Wright to Katharine and Milton Wright, November 15

Still, events were not always assured in the Wrights' Kitty Hawk camp.

⟹•◦•⟸

We are now alone again, the first time for about a month. Mr. Chanute came just as Dr. Spratt left. Spratt, by the way, left about two hours after the breaking of our propeller shafts, taking them along with him to express at Norfolk. We got Pop's letter yesterday saying that they had been received and were nearly ready to be sent back. We will not get them for three or four days yet. At the time they broke we were trying to get the engine in order. The strains on the shafts were enormous as a result of the sprockets being a little loose. The weight of our machine complete with man will be a little over 700 lbs. and we are now quite in doubt as to whether the engine will be able to pull it at all with the present gears, as we will not be able to use more than ¾ of our power in getting started. The screws came loose before we had time to either measure the speed of the engine or the thrust of the screws. Mr. Chanute says that no one before has ever tried to build a machine on such close margins as we have done to our calculations. He said that he nevertheless had more hope of our machine going than any of the others. He seems to think we are pursued by a blind fate from which we are unable to escape. He has been trying to purchase the Ader machine built by the French government at an expense of $100,000.00 which he was intending to have us fix and *run* for him. He thinks we could do it! He doesn't seem to think our machines are so much superior as the manner in which we handle them. We are of just the reverse opinion.

The past week and a half has just been a loaf, since we have almost nothing to do on the machine until the shafts come. The weather has been fairly cold at times but with a half cord of wood on hand we have not suffered any. Our carbide can is probably the best stove in Kitty Hawk.

We have had the old machine out only twice in the past three weeks. We took it out day before yesterday to test our starting truck and rails for the new machine. We succeeded in starting five times out of six. As we have no help at present one of us held the machine on the track until the other got on, when he would leave go. The machine of course would coast downhill on the wheels (bicycle hubs running on rails made of 2″ × 4″s) until enough speed was acquired to lift, when the one on board would turn up the rudder and sail off down the hill. We then experimented with one man taking hold of the front rudder (with the other on board) and starting by running a few steps backward till the machine supported. We had no trouble in getting started in this way either, but the fire in the building has so dried out the cloth and wood of the framework of the machine that it is now so rickety as to be unsafe for gliding in high winds. We have now probably made our last glides on it.

As long as we had company there was no chance to write or to do much of anything else. I am now taking up my German and French again, and am making some progress. The lack of a German dictionary prevents me, however, from reading much, the vocabulary in the grammar being quite limited. An article from a German paper, giving some account of our machine, has kept me guessing, as I have only been able to find a few of the words in the vocabulary I have. From what little I can read I would judge it to be about the same as that in the paper we had at home. Will is waiting to take this to station so I must close.

7. While the Wright brothers assembled their powered 1903 Flyer,
they practiced gliding from the Kill Devil Hills in their
highly successful aircraft from the previous year.
Note the two camp buildings in the distance.

28

"We tossed a coin to decide . . ."

Orville Wright's diary, December 14, 1903

After two and a half months in Kitty Hawk and numerous mechanical set-
backs, their powered "whopper flying machine" was finally ready to test. The
wind was too light to attempt a flight from level ground, so with the help of
locals the brothers pushed the machine up the side of the large sand dune
Kill Devil Hill.

We spent morning in making repairs on tail, and truck for starting. At half
past one o'clock we put out signal for station men, and started for hill,
which took us about 40 minutes. After testing engine, with help of men
(Bob Wescott, John T. Daniels, Tom Beacham, W. S. Dough, and Uncle
Benny O'Neal), we took machine 150 ft. uphill and laid track on 8° 50'
slope. A couple small boys, who had come with the men from the station,
made a hurried departure over the hill for home on hearing the engine
start. We tossed up coin to decide who should make first trial, and Will
won. After getting adjustments of engine ready I took right end of machine. Will got on. When all was ready Will attempted to release fastening to rail, but the pressure due to weight of machine and thrust of screws
was so great that he could not get it loose. We had to get a couple of the
men to help push machine back till rope was slipped loose. While I was
signaling man at other end to leave go, but before I myself was ready, Will
started machine. I grabbed the upright the best I could and off we went.
By the time we had reached the last quarter of the third rail (about 35 to
40 feet) the speed was so great I could stay with it no longer. I snapped
watch as machine passed end of track. (It had raised from track six or eight
feet from end.) The machine turned up in front and rose to a height of
about 15 feet from ground at a point somewhere in neighborhood of 60
feet from end of track. After thus losing most of its headway it gradually
sank to ground turned up at an angle of probably 20° incidence. The left
wing was lower than the right so that in landing it struck first. The machine swung around and scraped the front skids (bows running out to front

rudder) so deep in sand that one was broken, and twisted around until the main strut and brace were also broken, besides the rear spar to lower surface of front rudder. Will forgot to shut off engine for some time, so that the record of screw turns was mostly taken while the machine was on the ground. The engine made 602 rev. in 35½ s. Time of flight from end of track was 3½ sec. for a distance of 105 ft. Angle of descent for the 105 feet was 4° 55′. Speed of wind was between 4 and 8 miles.

8. Before attempting to launch the powered machine on December 14, the impromptu crew paused for a photograph.

29

"Success assured keep quiet"

Telegram from Orville Wright, December 15, 1903

That night Wilbur walked to the Kitty Hawk telegraph station (which was closed), and left this terse message to be wired back home the next day.

Misjudgment at start reduced flight one hundred twelve power and control ample rudder only injured success assured keep quiet.

30

"Mr. Daniels took a picture just as
it left the tracks"

Orville Wright's diary, December 17, 1903

With the flying machine repaired three days later, they tried again.

When we got up a wind of between 20 and 25 miles was blowing from the north. We got the machine out early and put out the signal for the men at the station. Before we were quite ready, John T. Daniels, W. S. Dough, A. D. Etheridge, W. C. Brinkley of Manteo, and Johnny Moore of Nags Head arrived. After running the engine and propellers a few minutes to get them in working order, I got on the machine at 10:35 for the first trial. The wind, according to our anemometers at this time, was blowing a little over 20 miles (corrected) 27 miles according to the Government anemometer at Kitty Hawk. On slipping the rope the machine started off increasing in speed to probably 7 or 8 miles. The machine lifted from the truck just as it was entering on the fourth rail. Mr. Daniels took a picture just as it left the tracks. I found the control of the front rudder quite difficult on account of its being balanced too near the center and thus had a tendency to turn itself when started so that the rudder was turned too far on one side and then too far on the other. As a result the machine would rise suddenly to about 10 ft. and then as suddenly, on turning the rudder, dart for the ground. A sudden dart when out about 100 feet from the end of the tracks ended the flight. Time about 12 seconds (not known exactly as watch was not promptly stopped). The lever for throwing off the engine was broken, and the skid under the rudder cracked. After repairs, at 20 min. after 11 o'clock Will made the second trial. The course was about like mine, up and down but a little longer over the ground though about the same in time. Dist. not measured but about 175 ft. Wind speed not quite so strong. With the aid of the station men present, we picked the machine up and carried it back to the starting ways. At about 20 minutes till 12 o'clock I made the third trial. When out about the same distance as Will's,

I met with a strong gust from the left which raised the left wing and sidled the machine off to the right in a lively manner. I immediately turned the rudder to bring the machine down and then worked the end control. Much to our surprise, on reaching the ground the left wing struck first, showing the lateral control of this machine much more effective than on any of our former ones. At the time of its sidling it had raised to a height of probably 12 to 14 feet. At just 12 o'clock Will started on the fourth and last trip. The machine started off with its ups and downs as it had before, but by the time he had gone over three or four hundred feet he had it under much better control, and was traveling on a fairly even course. It proceeded in this manner till it reached a small hummock out about 800 feet from the starting ways, when it began its pitching again and suddenly darted into the ground. The front rudder frame was badly broken up, but the main frame suffered none at all. The distance over the ground was 852 feet in 59 seconds. The engine turns was 1,071, but this included several seconds while on the starting ways and probably about a half second after landing. The jar of landing had set the watch on machine back so that we have no exact record for the 1,071 turns. Will took a picture of my third flight just before the gust struck the machine. The machine left the ways successfully at every trial, and the tail was never caught by the truck as we had feared.

After removing the front rudder, we carried the machine back to camp. We set the machine down a few feet west of the building, and while standing about discussing the last flight, a sudden gust of wind struck the machine and started to turn it over. All rushed to stop it. Will who was near one end ran to the front, but too late to do any good. Mr. Daniels and myself seized spars at the rear, but to no purpose. The machine gradually turned over on us. Mr. Daniels, having had no experience in handling a machine of this kind, hung on to it from the inside, and as a result was knocked down and turned over and over with it as it went. His escape was miraculous, as he was in with the engine and chains. The engine legs were all broken off, the chain guides badly bent, a number of uprights, and nearly all the rear ends of the ribs were broken. One spar only was broken.

After dinner we went to Kitty Hawk to send off telegram to M. W. While there we called on Capt. and Mrs. Hobbs, Dr. Cogswell and the station men.

9. December 17, 1903: One of the most famous photographs of the
twentieth century, taken by a man who had never before used a camera.

31

—————→•←—————

"Success four flights Thursday morning"

Telegram by Orville Wright, December 17, 1903

The following telegram was sent to Dayton that night.

—————→•←—————

Success four flights Thursday morning all against twenty-one mile wind started from level with engine power alone average speed through air thirty-one miles longest 57 seconds inform press home Christmas.

32

"Two Ohio Brothers Crowned with Success"

Item, *Norfolk Virginian-Pilot,* December 18, 1903

The Kitty Hawk telegraph operator had an acquaintance who worked for
the local newspaper, who fleshed out the "Success" telegram with reports
from Kitty Hawk in 1903. The result: This often-fantastic page-one-story,
which made its way onto the Associated Press newswire and into several
newspapers across the nation and overseas.

FLYING MACHINE SOARS 3 MILES IN TEETH
OF HIGH WIND OVER SAND HILLS AND
WAVES AT KITTY HAWK ON CAROLINA COAST

NO BALLOON ATTACHED TO AID IT

Three Years of Hard, Secret Work by Two Ohio Brothers Crowned
with Success

ACCOMPLISHED WHAT LANGLEY FAILED AT

With Man as Passenger, Huge Machine Flew Like Bird Under
Perfect Control

BOX KITE PRINCIPLE WITH TWO PROPELLERS

The problem of aerial navigation without the use of a balloon has been
solved at last.

Over the sand hills of the North Carolina Coast yesterday, near Kitty
Hawk, two Ohio men proved that they could soar through the air in a flying machine of their own construction, with ample power to steer it and
speed it along.

This, too, in the face of a wind blowing at the registered velocity of
twenty-one miles an hour.

Like a monster bird the invention hovered above the breakers and circled over the rolling sand hills at the command of its navigator and after soaring for three miles, it gracefully descended to earth again and rested lightly upon the spot selected by the man in the car as a suitable landing place.

While the United States government has been spending thousands of dollars in an effort to make practicable the ideas of Professor Langley of the Smithsonian Institute, Wilber [*sic*] and Orville Wright, two brothers, natives of Dayton, O., have, quietly, even secretly, perfected their invention, and put it to a successful test.

They are not yet ready that the world should know the methods they have adopted in conquering the air, but the *Virginian-Pilot* is able to state authentically the nature of their invention, its principles and its chief dimensions.

How Machine is Built.

The idea of the box kite has been adhered to strictly in the basic formation of the flying machine.

A huge framework of light timbers, 33 feet wide, five feet deep, and five feet across the top forms the machine proper.

This is covered with a tough, but light canvas.

In the center, and suspended just below the bottom plane, is the small gasoline engine which furnishes the motive power for the propelling and elevating wheels.

These are two six-bladed propellers, one arranged just below the center of the frame, so gauged as to exert an upward force when in motion, and the other extends horizontally to the rear from the center of the car, furnishing the forward impetus.

Protruding from the center of the car is a huge fan-shaped rudder of canvass, [*sic*] stretched upon a frame of wood. This rudder is controlled by the navigator and may be moved to each side, raised, or lowered.

Start Was a Success.

Wilber [*sic*] Wright, the chief inventor of the machine, sat in the operator's car and when all was ready his brother unfastened the catch which held the invention at the top of the slope.

The big box began to move slowly at first, acquiring velocity as it went, and when half way down the hundred feet the engine was started.

The propeller in the rear immediately began to revolve at a high rate of speed, and when the incline was reached the machine shot out into space without a perceptible fall.

By this time the elevating propeller was also in motion, and, keeping its altitude, the machine slowly began to go higher and higher until it finally soared sixty feet above the ground.

Maintaining this height by the action of the under wheel, the navigator increased the revolutions of the rear propeller, and the forward speed of the huge affair increased until a velocity of eight miles an hour was attained.

All this time the machine headed into a twenty-one mile wind.

Coast Folk Amazed.

The little crowd of fisher folk and coast guards, who have been watching the construction of the machine with unconcealed curiosity since September 1st, were amazed.

They endeavored to race over the sand and keep up with the thing of the air, but it soon distanced them and continued its flight alone, save the man in the car.

Steadily it pursued its way, first tacking to port, then to starboard, and then driving straight ahead.

"It is a success," declared Orville Wright to the crowd on the beach after the first mile had been covered.

But the inventor waited. Not until he had accomplished three miles, putting the machine through all sorts of maneuvers en route, was he satisfied.

Then he selected a suitable place to land, and gracefully circling drew his invention slowly to the earth, where it settled, like some big bird, in the chosen spot.

"Eureka," he cried, as did the alchemists of old.

Success After Failure.

The success of the Wright brothers in their invention is the result of three years of hard work. Experiment after experiment has been made and failure resulted, but each experiment had its lesson, and finally, when the two reappeared at Kitty Hawk last fall they felt more confident than ever.

The spot selected for the building and perfecting of the machine is one of the most desolate upon the Atlantic seaboard. Just on the southern extremity of that coast stretch known as the graveyard of American shipping, cut off from civilization by a wide expanse of sound water and seldom in touch with the outer world save when a steamer once or twice a week touches at the little wharf to take and leave government mail, no better place could scarcely have been selected to maintain secrecy.

And this is where the failures have grown into success.

The machine which made yesterday's flight easily carried the weight of a man of 150 pounds, and is nothing like so large as the ill-fated "Buzzard" of Potomac river fame.

It is said the Wright brothers intend constructing now a much larger machine, but before this they will go back to their homes for the holidays.

WHO INVENTORS ARE.

Wilber [*sic*] Wright, the inventor, is a well-groomed man of prepossessing appearance. He is about five feet, six inches tall, weighs about 150 pounds and is of swarthy complexion. His hair is raven hued and straight, but a piercing pair of deep blue eyes peer at you over a nose of extreme length and sharpness.

His brother, Orville, on the other hand, is a blonde, with sandy hair and fair complexion, even features and sparkling black eyes. He is not quite so large as Wilber [*sic*] but is of magnificent physique.

The pair htve [*sic*] spent almost the entire fall and winter and early spring months of the past three years at Kitty Mawk [*sic*] working upon their invention, leaving when the weather began to grow warm and returning in the early fall to work.

Their last appearance was on September 1st, and since then they have been actively engaged upon the construction of the machine which made ysterday's [*sic*] successful flight.

There was no apparatus used in yesterday's test to give the machine a starting velocity. From the top of an inclined plane, constructed upon a hill of sand the start was made.

33

The Wright Boys Are Coming Home

Brief item, *Dayton Daily News*

The "Success" telegram was the signal for brother Lorin to deliver a notice to the local newspapers. According to their official biographer, Fred C. Kelly, the editor of the *Dayton Journal* said, "Fifty-seven seconds, hey? If it had been fifty-seven minutes then it might have been a news item." This short item did appear in another paper, the Saturday, December 19, 1903, *Dayton Daily News*.

THE WRIGHT BOYS ARE COMING HOME

Norfolk, Va., Dec. 19—Orville and Wilbur Wright, inventors and builders of the *Wright Flyer,* which made several successful flights near here Thursday, left today for their home in Dayton, O., to spend Christmas with their parents.

34

Statement to the Associated Press

The Wright brothers

In order to correct the erroneous AP account, the brothers issued the following press release on January 5, 1904.

It had not been our intention to make any detailed public statement concerning the private trials of our power "Flyer" on the 17th of December last; but since the contents of a private telegram, announcing to our folks at home the success of our trials, was dishonestly communicated to the newspapermen at the Norfolk office, and led to the imposition upon the public, by persons who never saw the "Flyer" or its flights, of a fictitious story incorrect in almost every detail; and since this story together with several pretended interviews or statements, which were fakes pure and simple, have been very widely disseminated, we feel impelled to make some correction. The real facts were as follows:

On the morning of December 17th, between the hours of 10:30 o'clock and noon, four flights were made, two by Orville Wright and two by Wilbur Wright. The starts were all made from a point on the level sand about two hundred feet west of our camp, which is located a quarter of a mile north of the Kill Devil sand hill, in Dare County, North Carolina. The wind at the time of the flights had a velocity of 27 miles an hour at ten o'clock, and 24 miles an hour at noon, as recorded by the anemometer at the Kitty Hawk Weather Bureau Station. This anemometer is thirty feet from the ground. Our own measurements, made with a hand anemometer at a height of four feet from the ground, showed a velocity of about 22 miles when the first flight was made, and 20½ miles at the time of the last one. The flights were directly against the wind. Each time the machine started from the level ground by its own power alone with no assistance from gravity, or any other source whatever. After a run of about 40 feet along a monorail track, which held the machine eight inches from the ground, it rose from the track and under the direction of the operator climbed upward on an inclined course till a height of eight or ten feet from the ground was reached, after which the course was kept as near horizontal as the wind gusts and the limited skill of the operator would permit. Into the teeth of a December gale the "Flyer" made its way forward with a speed of ten miles an hour over the ground and thirty to thirty-five miles an hour through the air. It had previously been decided that for reasons of personal safety these first trials should be made as close to the ground as possible. The height chosen was scarcely sufficient for maneuvering in so gusty a wind and with no previous acquaintance with the conduct of the machine and its controlling mechanisms. Consequently the first flight was short. The succeeding flights rapidly increased in length and at the fourth trial a flight of fifty-nine seconds was made, in which time the machine flew a little more than a half mile through the air, and a distance of 852 feet over the ground. The landing was due to a slight error of judgment on the part of the aviator. After passing over a little hummock of sand, in attempting to bring the machine down to the desired height, the operator turned the rudder too far; and the machine turned downward more quickly than had been expected. The reverse movement of the rudder was a fraction of a second too late to prevent the machine from touching the ground and thus ending the flight. The whole occurrence occupied little, if any, more than one second of time.

Only those who are acquainted with practical aeronautics can appreciate the difficulties of attempting the first trials of a flying machine in a twenty-five mile gale. As winter was already well set in, we should have postponed our trials to a more favorable season, but for the fact that we were determined, before returning home, to know whether the machine possessed sufficient power to fly, sufficient strength to withstand the shocks of landings, and sufficient capacity of control to make flight safe in boisterous winds, as well as in calm air. When these points had been definitely established, we at once packed our goods and returned home, knowing that the age of the flying machine had come at last.

From the beginning we have employed entirely new principles of control; and as all the experiments have been conducted at our own expense without assistance from any individual or institution, we do not feel ready at present to give out any pictures or detailed description of the machine.

35

Fall Wrecks Airship

The New York Times, 1904

The Wrights decided to move their experiments to a cow pasture outside of Dayton. They built a second, slightly more refined *Flyer* in the spring of 1904, and owing to the interest that had been building since December, they offered to demonstrate the new machine publicly when trials commenced in late May. A handful of newspapers sent representatives. This is how the flight appeared to a *New York Times* reporter in attendance.

FALL WRECKS AIRSHIP

On Trial Trip It Went Thirty Feet and Dropped—
Inventors Satisfied, Though.

Special to the New York Times—

DAYTON, Ohio, May 26.—The Wright flying machine, invented by Orville and Wilbur Wright, brothers, of this city, which made its successful flight at Kitty Hawk, N.C., last December had another trial near this city to-day, which the brothers say was successful. Great secrecy was maintained about the test, and but few witnessed it.

The machine after being propelled along a track for a distance of a hundred feet, rose twelve feet in the air, and flew a distance of thirty feet, when it dropped. This was due, the inventors say, to a derangement of the gasoline engine that furnishes the power. In the fall the propellers were broken and the test could not be repeated.

36

"What Hath God Wrought?"

From *Gleanings in Bee Culture*, by Amos Root

None too sure that the age of flight had actually arrived, reporters stayed away from the Wright's field after that, and soon the brothers were all but forgotten. In late 1904 an apiculturist and Sunday-school teacher named Amos Root heard of the Wrights, and in September he drove two hundred miles across bad roads in a shaky newfangled automobile just to see them fly. He wrote of it in the January 1905 issue of his own small beekeeping journal, *Gleanings in Bee Culture*. The first eyewitness account of an airplane in flight was titled "What Hath God Wrought?"

Dear friends, I have a wonderful story to tell you—a story that, in some respects, outrivals the Arabian Nights fables—a story, too, with a moral that I think many of the younger ones need, and perhaps some of the older ones too if they will heed it. God in his great mercy has permitted me to be, at least somewhat, instrumental in ushering in and introducing to the great wide world an invention that may outrank the electric cars, the automobiles, and all other methods of travel, and one which may fairly take a place beside the telephone and wireless telegraphy. Am I claiming a good deal? Well, I will tell my story. . . .

It was my privilege, on the 20th day of September, 1904, to see the first successful trip of an airship, without a balloon to sustain it, that the world has ever made, that is, to turn the corners and come back to the starting-point. . . .

At first there was considerable trouble about getting the machine up in the air and the engine well up to speed. They did this by running along a single-rail track perhaps 200 feet long. . . . The operator takes his place lying flat on his face. This position offers less resistance to the wind. The engine is started and got up to speed. The machine is held until ready to start by a sort of trap to be sprung when all is ready; then with a tremendous flapping and snapping of the four-cylinder engine, the huge machine springs aloft. When it first turned that circle, and came near the starting-point, I was right in front of it; and I said then, and I believe still, it was one of the grandest sights, if not the grandest sight, of my life. Imagine a locomotive that has left its track, and is climbing up in the air right toward you—a locomotive without any wheels, we will say, but with white wings instead. . . . Well, now, imagine this white locomotive, with wings that spread 20 feet each way, coming right toward you with a tremendous flap of its propellers, and you will have something like what I saw. The younger brother bade me move to one side for fear it might come down suddenly; but I tell you, friends, the sensation that one feels in such a crisis is something hard to describe.

When Columbus discovered America he did not know what the outcome would be, and no one at that time knew; and I doubt if the wildest enthusiast caught a glimpse of what really did come from his discovery. In a like manner these two brothers have probably not even a faint glimpse of what their discovery is going to bring to the children of men. No one living can give a guess of what is coming along this line, much better than any one living could conjecture the final outcome of Columbus' experiment when he pushed off through the trackless waters.

10. Orville (*left*) and Wilbur confer before the wing
of their 1904 machine.

37

⟶•◦•⟵

"We are prepared to furnish a machine
on contract . . ."

Correspondence between the Wrights and the War Department

By the completion of trials with their second *Flyer* the brothers had perfected the airplane to the extent that they now felt they could sell it. Their first customer, they hoped, would be the U.S. Government, which would quickly understand its obvious benefits as a military observation platform.

⟶•◦•⟵

*To Congressman Robert M. Nevin**

January 18, 1905

The series of aeronautical experiments upon which we have been engaged for the past five years has ended in the production of a flying-machine of a type fitted for practical use. It not only flies through the air at high speed, but it also lands without being wrecked. During the year 1904 one hundred and five flights were made at our experimenting station, on the Huffman prairie, east of the city; and though our experience in handling the machine has been too short to give any high degree of skill, we nevertheless succeeded, toward the end of the season, in making two flights of five minutes each, in which we sailed round and round the field until a distance of about three miles had been covered, at a speed of thirty-five miles an hour. The first of these record flights was made on November 9th, in celebration of the phenomenal political victory of the preceding day,[†] and the second, on December 1st, in honor of the one hundredth flight of the season.

The numerous flights in straight lines, in circles, and over "S"-shaped courses, in calms and in winds, have made it quite certain that flying has been brought to a point where it can be made of great practical use in various ways, one of which is that of scouting and carrying messages in time of war. If the latter features are of interest to our own government, we shall

---

* Their local representative.
† Theodore Roosevelt won the presidential election.

be pleased to take up the matter either on a basis of providing machines of agreed specification, at a contract price, or of furnishing all the scientific and practical information we have accumulated in these years of experimenting, together with a license to use our patents; thus putting the government in a position to operate on its own account.

If you can find it convenient to ascertain whether this is a subject of interest to our own government, it would oblige us greatly, as early information on this point will aid us in making our plans for the future.

Wilbur and Orville Wright

To Congressman Nevin

I have the honor to inform you that, as many requests have been made for financial assistance in the development of designs for flying-machines, the Board has found it necessary to decline to make allotments for the experimental development of devices for mechanical flight, and has determined that, before suggestions with that object in view will be considered, the device must have been brought to the stage of practical operation without expense to the United States.

It appears from the letter of Messrs. Wilbur and Orville Wright that their machine has not yet been brought to the stage of practical operation, but as soon as it shall have been perfected, this Board would be pleased to receive further representations from them in regard to it.

The Board of Ordnance and Fortification, signed
by Major General G. L. Gillespie

To Secretary of War William H. Taft

Dayton, October 9, 1905

Some months ago we made an informal offer to furnish to the War Department practical flying-machines suitable for scouting purposes. The matter was referred to the Board of Ordnance and Fortification, which seems to have given it scant consideration. We do not wish to take this invention abroad, unless we find it necessary to do so, and therefore write again, renewing the offer.

We are prepared to furnish a machine on contract, to be accepted only after trial trips in which the conditions of the contract have been fulfilled; the machine to carry an operator and supplies of fuel, etc., sufficient for a flight of one hundred miles; the price of the machine to be regulated according to a sliding scale based on the performance of the machine in the trial trips, the minimum performance to be a flight of at least twenty-five miles at a speed of not less than thirty miles an hour.

We are also willing to take contracts to build machines carrying more than one man.

Wilbur and Orville Wright

To Wilbur and Orville Wright

Washington, October 16, 1905

I have the honor to inform you that, as many requests have been made for financial assistance in the development of designs for flying-machines, the Board has found it necessary to decline to make allotments for the experimental development of devices for mechanical flight, and has determined that, before suggestions with that object in view will be considered, the device must have been brought to the stage of practical operation without expense to the United States.

Before the question of making a contract with you for the furnishing of a flying-machine is considered it will be necessary for you to furnish this Board with the approximate cost of the completed machine, the date upon which it would be delivered, and with such drawings and descriptions thereof as are necessary to enable its construction to be understood and a definite conclusion as to its practicability to be arrived at. Upon receipt of this information, the matter will receive the careful consideration of the Board.

Major General J. C. Bates, Board of
Ordnance and Fortification

To the President of the Board of Ordnance and Fortification,
War Department

Dayton, October 19, 1906

Your communication of October 16th has been received. We have no thought of asking financial assistance from the government. We propose to sell the results of experiments finished at our own expense.

In order that we may submit a proposition conforming as nearly as possible to the ideas of your Board, it is desirable that we be informed what conditions you would wish to lay down as to the performance of the machine in the official trials, prior to the acceptance of the machine. We cannot well fix a price, nor a time for delivery, till we have your idea of the qualifications necessary to such a machine. We ought also to know whether you would wish to reserve a monopoly on the use of the invention, or whether you would permit us to accept orders for similar machines from other governments, and give public exhibitions, etc.

Proof of our ability to execute an undertaking of the nature proposed will be furnished whenever desired.

Wilbur and Orville Wright

Minutes from Board of Ordnance and Fortification meeting, October 24, 1905.

The Board then considered a letter, dated October 19, 1905, from Wilbur and Orville Wright requesting the requirements prescribed by the Board that a flying-machine would have to fulfill before it would be accepted.

It is recommended that the Messrs. Wright be informed that the Board does not care to formulate any requirements for the performance of a flying-machine or take any further action on the subject until a machine is produced which by actual operation is shown to be able to produce horizontal flight and to carry an operator.

Finally, however, word got out of their success, and 19 months later the board inquired of them.

＊＊＊

To the Board of Ordnance and Fortification, War Department
Dayton, May 17, 1907

Your communication of May 11th has been received.

We have some flyers in course of construction, and would be pleased to sell one or more of them to the War Department, if an agreement as to terms can be reached.

These machines will carry two men, an operator and an observer, and a sufficient supply of fuel for a flight of two hundred kilometers. We are willing to make it a condition of a contract that the machine must make a trial trip before Government representatives of not less than fifty kilometers at a speed of not less than fifty kilometers an hour, before its acceptance by the Department, and before any part of the purchase price is paid to us.

If the War Department is in a position to purchase at this time, we will be pleased to have a conference for the purpose of discussing the matter in detail, or we are willing to submit a formal proposition, if that is preferred.

Orville Wright

PART V

———⋗•⋖———

1906–1908

THE SPREAD OF POWERED FLIGHT

38

"Like everybody else, I cried: 'Bravo! Bravo!'"

The first flight of *14 bis*, witnessed by Antoinette Gastambide.
Originally published in *O Cruzeiro* magazine, April 7, 1971

In Europe, a wealthy Brazilian named Alberto Santos-Dumont had built
quite a reputation since the turn of the century for taking to the air in a series of dirigibles. By 1906 he and his mechanics had built what was ostensi-
bly a heavier-than-air companion to his Dirigible No. 14, and he called it *14
bis*. It was in this odd, duck-shaped biplane that Santos-Dumont made what
is generally recognized as the first two flights in Europe: a hop of 162 feet on
October 23, 1906, and a longer leap of 720 feet on November 12. Among the
witnesses to that second flight was Antoinette Gastambide. And too, her de-
fensive posture toward the end was because Santos-Dumont's public flight
preceded the Wrights' first such demonstration by several months. That was
understood to be proof that others like Santos-Dumont and even Ader had
been the first to fly.

We [Antoinette, her father Robert Gastambide, and marine engineer
Leon Levavasseur] were talking about birds' flight and said: "Man should
fly also." I got very excited at that idea, and said: "Papa, you must do something about it!" Then, my father encouraged Engineer Levavasseur and
promised to help him financially. . .

That was, no doubt, the starting point of aviation. . .

My father, who knew Mr. Levavasseur's workmanship and ability very
well, said: "I will help you, my friend. I will give you all the money you may
need to make the engine."

Engineer Levavasseur said to my father: "Your daughter must be the engine sponsoress. She will bring us luck!"

"Very well," said my father, "she will."

There was no ceremony.

It was Mr. Santos-Dumont himself who constructed his own first airplane, the engine of which was made by Levavasseur, using an Antoinette
engine on an airplane for the first time.

But it was Santos-Dumont who made his own first bird. Antoinette engines were used for ships. Then came the idea to make lighter engines for airplanes.

Santos-Dumont had said: "I declare for everyone to know that today I am testing my mechanical bird for the first time. I beg the public's forbearance, and thank you for your moral support. I am going to glide on the grass, and I wish you to clear the lawn by going toward the polo field during my take-off. I would also like you to keep very quiet so that my orders may be heard and repeated by my assistants. Upon sensing the engine is turning at 1,700 revolutions, I will raise my arm. This will be the signal to let go."

Then, the bystanders cleared a space 100 meters long and as wide as the runway. Aéro-Club members, aided by Bagatelle Park security guards, kept order tactfully but earnestly.

The usual take-off orders were heard. The propeller was turned through, and the engine started. Quickly, Santos-Dumont advances the throttle, raises his arm; the airplane is released and runs on the grass like an enormous, white butterfly.

The airplane was white in color, being made of white fabric.

At 200 meters from its starting point, the airplane, having reached enough speed, left the ground and rose in the air so that its two wheels were at a height of about three meters above the ground.

It was the first time that was accomplished.

An Ah! full of admiration was suddenly exclaimed in unison by the bystanders.

It was an Ah! full of surprise and wonder at that miracle, a cry full of respect for a man that had dared and won, a cry full of pride at that unbelievable conquest, and a cry full of adoration, too, from the hearts of the faithful giving thanks to God.

But suddenly the Ah! uttered by the crowd changed in tone, became almost savage, a cry of fear, of dread, of guilt for that feat, a cry of anguish, of panic, from people afraid of punishment from heaven for having violated Nature.

Then, there was a sigh of relief, when they saw that Man had returned to Earth.

Then the crowd, in a delirious state, rushed the *14 bis* airplane, wrested Santos-Dumont out of it, and carried him off triumphantly.

Taking advantage of the tumult, Montmartre bohemians surrounded the *14 bis* and one of them tore off one piece of the fuselage fabric. This piece of fabric was to become a historical one later.

[The date was] November 12, 1906. The recorded flight of that day covered 200 meters. I attended that flight.

I was present then, that is why I can tell it. Like everybody else, I cried:

"Bravo! Bravo!" Then we went and took the hero from his airplane and then went and celebrated his victory together.

I attended other *14 bis* flights too. Since then, many people started flying, but the first man to rise above the ground using a Levavasseur engine was Santos-Dumont. He was who inaugurated aviation!

Levavasseur made the engine, my father supplied the money, but it was Santos-Dumont who made the first formally witnessed flight.

39

⎯⎯⎯≫•◦•≪⎯⎯⎯

Competition

By Gabriel Voison, in *Men, Women and 10,000 Kites,*
translated by Oliver Stewart (1963)

The middling initial success of Santos-Dumont aside, much greater
progress in French aviation came through the recently established shop of
the Voisin brothers, Charles and the rather egotistical Gabriel.

⎯⎯⎯≫•◦•≪⎯⎯⎯

[A] new client presented himself at the rue de la Ferme in May 1907. He
was a former racing cyclist, a racing car driver whose name was well known
among sportsmen. He was called Henry Farman. He had visited Archdeacon a few days before and our friend had given him our address, telling
him that we were well placed to complete an order for a powered aeroplane
with a flight guarantee. In 1907 Henry Farman had not the slightest
knowledge of anything to do with aviation, but, to make up for that, he
was adroit, sporting and skilled at the control of the internal combustion
engine. On 1 June 1907 he gave us an order for a Voisin aeroplane fitted
with an Antoinette engine of fifty horsepower, completion of the contract
to be after a successful flight of one kilometre.

The terms of his order are clear; they show in indisputable manner that
the machine ordered was indeed a Voisin and that Henry Farman gave us
no sort of instructions as to its construction. I give these details because,
for forty years, people have believed that Henry Farman was the "engineer" who created the 1907–1908 machine with which he not only won the
Deutsch-Archdeacon prize, but also obtained most of the prizes offered
at this time and achieved, eventually, in August 1908, the first city-to-city
aerial voyage, Mourmelon-Reims.

Ordered on 1 June 1907, the machine was delivered to Henry Farman in
August 1907. The speed with which this machine was built is proof of the
confidence we had in our design and construction.

Henry Farman had realised that he must not lose a moment in training. He ordered from us, in July 1907, a hangar able to house his machine
fully assembled and ready to fly. This hangar was erected alongside the ma-

noeuvre ground at Issy-les-Moulineaux, from which it was separated by a six-foot wall. A mobile bridge gave us access to the ground. Farman, armed with certain information we had been able to give him on piloting, taxied for the first time on 30 August 1907 and our machine was so easy to control that on 7 October, thirty-seven days after it first emerged, it made its first flight.

To sum up: Henry Farman, after entering our works to order a Voisin on 1 June 1907, flew on 7 October the same year. It took us four months to build the aircraft and to obtain the first results in the hands of the buyer. I do not think, now, fifty years later, as I write these words, that any firm, however great, would be capable of a similar achievement. It is true that for ten years previously my brother and I had to go through a great deal of work and effort to obtain this result.

Delagrange had, of course, been present when Henry Farman was training. He ordered from us in September 1907 a hangar similar to the one we had already built in which his machine could, in turn, be housed.

So in October 1907 we had two pilots, with two identical machines, but with very different personal abilities. Delagrange was not the sporting type. He knew nothing about running an engine. Henry Farman, on the other hand, was manipulative skill personified and his mechanical gifts were to give him a distinct advantage over his competitor.

On 5 November 1907, during a flight of 1,000 ft., Delagrange succeeded in making his first turn and at the end of November our two clients, piloting exactly the same kind of machine, were both capable of the same level of performance.

Bad weather now troubled us. The manoeuvre ground was muddy and huge puddles of water splashed over our machine and dented the blades of our propellers which were mounted behind the wheels. Obviously good weather was needed for training. Yet the wind held us cooped up in our hangars for weeks on end. Precious time went by with ground running and useless tests. Finally we noticed that our competitors were hard on our heels and that they were working energetically.

Santos-Dumont, who had not flown since his 722-ft. flight of 12 November 1906, had successively given up the two or three biplanes which he had built, without result, in 1906 and 1907. In December 1907 he completed his little monoplane, the *Demoiselle*, whose obvious good qualities caused us some anxiety.

Ferber was working at Chalais-Meudon, under the War Minister. This official position displeased him because he appreciated that we were going to get ahead of him. I often saw him, tied up with volumes of the paper work which goes with the administrative services. On his own, he ought to have achieved the magic kilometre by the end of 1907. But he did not cause us anxiety, not because we were unaware of his ability, but because we knew the difficulties which he would have to contend with and the delays that would result.

Blériot, in 1907, had taken the wrong direction with a "canard," or tail-first aircraft, badly balanced, which he gave up in order to build a Langley* which proved satisfactory on trial. These trials were to end with the famous monoplane which he used to cross the Channel in 1909. Esnault-Pelterie was not wasting a moment at Buc. He ought to have got ahead of us because he combined profound technical knowledge with financial resources. But he had tackled together the problems of the wings and of the engine and this allowed us to get ahead of him in our turn. Louis Breguet had chosen the most difficult way at this time. He was building a helicopter, with great courage and with technical means of the first order. He turned too late to wing-borne craft and did not worry us. Vuia, on his side, was working on an ingenious machine worked by a compressed air engine, but despite its mechanical interest, he was making no progress. Finally de Pischoff had built a small, light aeroplane which had started taxying but which did not do its first take-off until December 1907.

As can be seen, we only had an advantage of a few weeks over the bulk of our competitors and this advantage was constantly imperilled by their efforts. Our trials, moreover, were made in public and the results were commented upon with an incredible mass of detail. The press followed us about and the most fantastic statements found a place in the columns of the sporting papers. The unbelievers had a large place there. We were now attacked, now supported. I answered the attacks as well as I could and we made steady progress.

On 31 December 1907 the official aviation records stood as follows:

12 November 1906. Santos-Dumont . . . 722 ft. (220 metres)

26 October 1907. H. Farman in a Voisin . . . 2,530 ft. (771 metres).

As I have emphasised, these performances were official; that is, they were observed and controlled by an organisation which set up special committees for the purpose.

It goes without saying that our competitors also flew, but over shorter distances. It was only necessary for one of their machines to be especially well tuned for the Deutsch-Archdeacon prize for the first closed circuit kilometre to be snatched from us. This risk caused us to redouble our efforts. Everything that was humanly possible we did without counting the cost, working by day and by night.

I am not able, fifty years later, to set out or classify the work we accomplished during the later part of this year of 1907. There were constant adjustments and often major modifications. These allowed us to make

* As the tandem-wing configuration was generally known.

progress. Thus I changed the empennage for Farman for a smaller and lighter one. The first had been intended to correct the pilot's errors automatically, but our most favoured client was becoming more skilful every day and his quick reflexes enabled him to dispense with the primitive stabilising vane which I had mounted on his machine's empennage. This modification gave our champion considerable help towards the final result. In January 1908 Henry Farman was capable of turning correctly. His Antoinette engine was working admirably and allowed us to hope for the best. The hour was approaching when we were to obtain our reward.

At the beginning of 1908 Henry Farman was ready to compete for the Deutsch-Archdeacon prize.

At the end of December 1907, Delagrange came to me to suggest an advantageous arrangement. He would agree, if I enabled him to win the kilometre prize, to pass over to me the 50,000 francs.

It would have been easy for me to favour one or the other of our two clients. Henry Farman spent all his time on his engine and left us to deal with his wings in our own manner. A small defect would have held him to the ground for six weeks and Delagrange, who was in full pursuit, would have taken this famous prize.

I must admit that I had a moment of hesitation. But Delagrange was inaccurate and inconstant. Santos-Dumont, Blériot, Esnault-Pelterie were hot on our heels and were making progress every day.

We decidedly preferred to back Henry Farman and when, on 11 January 1908, our client summoned the Aéro-Club committee for an attempt on the prize, we were ready for a final supreme effort to aid the one whom we regarded as a loyal friend.

. . . On 13 January 1908 the Voisin personnel left the rue de la Ferme for Issy-les-Moulineaux and there opened the doors of Farman's hangar. . . .

We had fashioned a few days earlier the three markers which were to indicate the course. My brother, accompanied by one of our men, placed the starter markers near the Paris fortifications. The turning pylon was hardly visible 1,640 feet (500 metres) away to the west of the Issy ground.

At seven o'clock in the morning we were ready. Our machine was manhandled to the starting line to await the arrival of the special committee members of the Aéro-Club. I was anxious because the west wind might get up at any moment and we should have been obliged to postpone the attempt. Towards ten minutes past eight, Blériot, then M. Fournier and finally Kapferer, Delagrange, and E. Archdeacon arrived by car. The wind was blowing lightly from the west but it should not trouble our pilot.

Henry Farman climbed into the fuselage of the aircraft which, at the moment of the start, was at the extreme north-east point of the military manoeuvre ground, near the ditch of the fortifications. This part is not occupied by the Air Ministry. I myself started the engine, swinging the propeller by hand . . . two of our men held the machine at the starting point for the official timing.

Mechanically everything was working admirably. Henry Farman gave a hand signal, the aeroplane started and left the ground in a few yards. It was as high as the markers when it crossed the starting line. The turn was accomplished with consummate skill and the return was completed without incident. Henry Farman landed at the point which he had left one minute twenty-eight seconds earlier.

The magic circle of the first closed circuit kilometre, officially timed and observed, was ours. The heroic era had ended. Aviation was about to enter the commercial era. For the first time in the world, under official observation, that is in a manner whose exactitude cannot be challenged, a machine, carrying on board the power needed for its flight and the man piloting it, had left the ground under its own power and, on a predetermined course, had accomplished a flight over a closed circuit with return to the point of departure. It had thus demonstrated the possibility of voyaging by a heavier-than-air craft and of manoeuvring in altitude and in azimuth, a thing which nobody, until that day, had been able to do.

Some will say that the Wrights had achieved this at least two years earlier. The reply to that is simple:

(a) the Wrights' performances were not officially observed;
(b) their courses were not marked out;
(c) the Wright aircraft—and this is of capital importance—*did not leave the ground under its own power;*
(d) the Wrights were incapable of giving a demonstration on a day and at an hour fixed in advance because they were dependent upon the wind, their machine, until 1908, being nothing other than a motorised glider.

News of our exploit spread at once to Paris. The machine was not back in its hangar before journalists invaded the ground.

Archdeacon asked us to check the distance separating the pylons. My brother borrowed a bicycle from one of the spectators who were all around us and, under observation by the committee, counted the revolutions of the wheels. The starting posts were at the place determined, 82 ft. (25 metres) apart, and the turning pylon was at 1,653 ft. (554 metres) from the starting line. No objection could be raised. The Deutsch-Archdeacon prize had been won in accordance with the rules.

Henry Farman disappeared in the middle of the crowd. I remained . . . near my machine. The pilot was collecting his trophies. He did so with the greatest calmness. At that instant I knew the meaning of indifference.

40

——⬥◦⬥——

Beginning to Fly

By Glenn Curtiss (with Augustus M. Post)

Though Samuel Langley died in 1906, his good friend, telephone inventor Alexander Graham Bell, assembled a group of bright young men into the Aerial Experiment Association with the intent of succeeding where Langley had failed. Bell's protégé in this venture was a famous motorcycle racer named Glenn Curtiss, a thin, serious-looking man in his thirties with an ability to build lightweight V-8 engines. Curtiss described the AEA's early days in *The Curtiss Aviation Book* (1912).

——⬥◦⬥——

BEGINNING TO FLY

In 1905, while in New York City, I first met Dr. Alexander Graham Bell, the inventor of the telephone. Dr. Bell had learned of our lightweight motors, used with success on the Baldwin dirigibles, and wanted to secure one for use in his experiments with kites. We had a very interesting talk on these experiments, and he asked me to visit him at Bienn Bhreagh, his summer home near Baddeck, Nova Scotia. Dr. Bell had developed some wonderfully light and strong tetrahedral kites which possessed great inherent stability, and he wanted a motor to install in one of them for purposes of experimentation. This kite was a very large one. The Doctor called it an "aerodrome." The surfaces not being planes, it could not properly be described as an aeroplane. He believed that the time would come when the framework of the aeroplane would have to be so large in proportion to its surface that it would be too heavy to fly. Consequently, he evolved the tetrahedral or cellular form of structure, which would allow of the size being increased indefinitely, while the weight would be increased only in the same ratio.

Dr. Bell had invited two young Canadian engineers, F. W. Baldwin and J.A.D. McCurdy, to assist him, and they were at Baddeck when I first visited there in the summer of 1907. Lieutenant Thomas Selfridge, of the United States Army, was also there. Naturally, there was a wide discussion on the subject of aeronautics, and so numerous were the suggestions made and so many theories advanced, that Mrs. Bell suggested the formation of a scientific organisation, to be known as the "Aerial Experiment Association." This met with a prompt and hearty agreement and the association was created very much in the same manner as Dr. Bell had previously formed the "Volta Association" at Washington for developing the phonograph. Mrs. Bell, who was most enthusiastic and helpful, generously offered to furnish the necessary funds for experimental work, and the object of the Association was officially set forth as "to build a practical aeroplane which will carry a man and be driven through the air by its own power."

Dr. Alexander Graham Bell was made chairman; F. W. Baldwin, chief engineer; J.A.D. McCurdy, assistant engineer and treasurer; and Lieut. Thomas Selfridge, secretary; while I was honored with the title of Director of Experiments and Chief Executive Officer. Both Baldwin and McCurdy were fresh from Toronto University, where they had graduated as mechanical engineers, and Baldwin later earned the distinction of making the first public flight in a motor-driven, heavier-than-air machine. This was accomplished at Hammondsport, N. Y., March 12, 1908, over the ice on Lake Keuka. The machine used was Number One, built by the Aerial Experiment Association, designed by Lieutenant Selfridge, and known as the *Red Wing.* The experiments carried on at Baddeck during the summer and fall of 1907 covered a wide range. There were trials and tests with Dr. Bell's tetrahedral kites, with motors, and with aerial propellers mounted on boats. Finally, at the suggestion of Lieutenant Selfridge, it was decided to move the scene of further experiments to Hammondsport, N. Y., where my factory is located, and there to build a glider. I had preceded the other members of the Association from Baddeck to Hammondsport in order to prepare for the continuance of our work. A few days after my return I was in my office, talking to Mr. Augustus Post, then the Secretary of the Aero Club of America, when a telegram came from Dr. Bell, saying: "Start building. The boys will be down next week." As no plans had been outlined, and nothing definite settled upon in the way of immediate experiments, I was somewhat undecided as to just what to build. We then discussed the subject of gliders for some time and I finally decided that the thing to do was to build a glider at the factory and to take advantage of the very abrupt and convenient hills at Hammondsport to try it out. We therefore built a double-surface glider of the Chanute type.

As almost every schoolboy knows in this day of advanced information on aviation, a glider is, roughly speaking, an aeroplane without a motor. Usually it has practically the same surfaces as a modern aeroplane, and may be made to support a passenger by launching it from the top of a hill in order to give it sufficient impetus to sustain its own weight and that of a rider. If the hill is steep the glider will descend at a smaller angle than the slope of the hill, and thus glides of a considerable distance may be made with ease and comparative safety.

Our first trials of the glider, which we built on the arrival of the members of the Experiment Association, were made in the dead of winter, when the snow lay deep over the hillsides. This made very hard work for everybody. It was a case of trudging laboriously up the steep hillsides and hauling or carrying the glider to the top by slow stages. It was easy enough going down, but slow work going up; but we continued our trials with varied success until we considered ourselves skilful enough to undertake a motor-driven machine, which we mounted on runners.

FIRST FLIGHTS

It was my desire to build a machine and install a motor at once, and thus take advantage of the opportunity furnished by the thick, smooth ice over Lake Keuka at that season of the year. But Lieutenant Selfridge, who had read a great deal about gliders and who had studied them from every angle, believed we should continue experimenting with the glider. However, we decided to build a machine which we believed would fly, and in due time a motor was installed and it was taken down on Lake Keuka to be tried out. We called it the *Red Wing,* and to Lieutenant Selfridge belongs the honour of designing it, though all the members of the Aerial Experiment Association had some hand in its construction. We all had our own ideas about the design of this first machine, but to Lieutenant Selfridge was left the privilege of accepting or rejecting the many suggestions made from time to time, in order that greater progress might be made. A number of our suggestions were accepted, and while the machine as completed cannot properly be described as the result of one man's ideas, the honour of being the final arbiter of all the problems of its design certainly belongs to Lieutenant Selfridge.

Now that the machine was completed and the motor installed, we waited for favourable weather to make the first trial. Winter weather around Lake Keuka is a very uncertain element, and we had a long, tiresome wait until the wintry gales that blew out of the north gave way to an intensely cold spell. Our opportunity came on March 12, 1908. There was scarcely a bit of wind, but it was bitterly cold. Unfortunately, Lieutenant Selfridge was absent, having left Hammondsport on business, and "Casey" Baldwin was selected to make the first trial. We were all on edge with eagerness to see what the machine would do. Some of us were confident, others sceptical.

Baldwin climbed into the seat, took the control in hand, and we cranked the motor. When we released our hold of the machine, it sped over the ice like a scared rabbit for two or three hundred feet, and then, much to our joy, it jumped into the air. This was what we had worked for through many long months, and naturally we watched the brief and uncertain course of Baldwin with a good deal of emotion. Rising to a height of six or eight feet, Baldwin flew the unheard-of distance of three hundred and eighteen feet, eleven inches! Then he came down ingloriously on one wing. As we learned afterward, the frail framework of the tail had bent and the machine had flopped over on its side and dropped on the wing, which gave way and caused the machine to turn completely around.

But it had been a successful flight—and we took no toll of the damage to the machine or the cost. We had succeeded! that was the main thing. We had actually flown the *Red Wing* three hundred and eighteen feet and eleven inches! We knew now we could build a machine that would fly longer and come down at the direction of the operator with safety to both.

It had taken just seven weeks to build the machine and to get it ready for the trial; it had taken just about twenty seconds to smash it.

But a great thing had been accomplished. We had achieved the first public flight of a heavier-than-air machine in America!

As our original plans provided for the building of one machine designed by each member of the Association, with the assistance of all the others, the building of the next one fell to Mr. Baldwin, and it was called the *White Wing*. The design of the *Red Wing* was followed in many details, but several things were added which we believed would give increased stability and greater flying power. The construction of the *White Wing* was begun at once, but before we could complete it the ice on the lake had yielded to the spring winds and we were therefore obliged to transfer our future trials to land. This required wheels for starting and alighting in the place of the ice runners used on the *Red Wing*. An old half-mile race track a short distance up the valley from the Lake was rented and put in shape for flights. The place was called "Stony Brook Farm," and it was for a long time afterward the scene of our flying exploits at Hammondsport.

It would be tiresome to the reader to be told of all the discouragements we met with; of the disheartening smashes we suffered; how almost every time we managed to get the new machine off the ground for brief but encouraging flights, it would come down so hard that something would give way and we would have to set about the task of building it up again. We soon learned that it was comparatively easy to get the machine up in the air, but it was most difficult to get it back to earth without smashing something. The fact was, we had not learned the art of landing an aeroplane with ease and safety—an absolutely necessary art for every successful aviator to know. It seemed one day that the limit of hard luck had been reached, when, after a brief flight and a somewhat rough landing, the machine folded up and sank down on its side, like a wounded bird, just as we were feeling pretty good over a successful landing without breakage.

Changes in the details of the machine were many and frequent, and after each change there was a flight or an attempted flight. Sometimes we managed to make quite a flight, and others—and more numerous—merely short "jumps" that would land the machine in a potato patch or a cornfield, where, in the yielding ground, the wheels would crumple up and let the whole thing down. Up to this time we had always used silk to cover the planes, but this proved very expensive and we decided to try a substitute. An entirely new set of planes were made and the new covering put on them. They looked very pretty and white as we took the rebuilt machine out with every expectation that it would fly. Great was our surprise, however, when it refused absolutely to make even an encouraging jump. Then the reason became as plain as day; we had used cotton to cover the planes, and, being porous, it would not furnish the sustaining power in flight. This was quickly remedied by coating the cotton covering with varnish, rendering it impervious to the air. After that it flew all right. I believe this was the first instance of the use of a liquid filler to coat the surface cloth. It is now used widely, both in this country and in Europe.

We had a great many minor misfortunes with the *White Wing*, but each one taught us a lesson. We gradually learned where the stresses and strains lay, and overcame them. Thus, little by little, the machine was reduced in weight, simplified in detail, and finally took on some semblance to the standard Curtiss aeroplane of today.

All the members of the Aerial Experiment Association were in Hammondsport at this time, including Dr. Alexander Graham Bell. We had established an office in the annex which had been built on the Curtiss homestead, and here took place nightly discussions on the work of the day past and the plans for the day to follow. Some of the boys named the office the "thinkorium." Every night the minutes of the previous meeting would be read and discussed. These minutes, by the way, were religiously kept by Lieutenant Selfridge and later published in the form of a bulletin and sent to each member. Marvellous in range were the subjects brought up and talked over at these meetings! Dr. Bell was the source of the most unusual suggestions for discussion. Usually these were things he had given a great deal of thought and time to, and, therefore, his opinions on any of his hobbies were most interesting. For instance, he had collected a great deal of information on the genealogy of the Hyde family, comprising some seven thousand individuals. These he had arranged in his card index system, in order to determine the proportion of male and female individuals, their relative length of life, and other characteristics. Or, perhaps, the Doctor would talk about his scheme to influence the sex of sheep by a certain

method of feeding; his early experiences with the telephone, the phonograph, the harmonic telegraph, and multiple telegraphy. At other times we
would do a jig-saw puzzle with pictures of aeroplanes, or listen to lectures
on physical culture by Dr. Alden, of the village. Then, for a change, we
would discuss, with great interest and sincerity, the various methods of
making sounds to accompany the action of a picture, behind the curtain
of the moving-picture show, which we all had attended. Motorcycle construction and operation were studied at the factory and on the roads
around Hammondsport. McCurdy used to give us daily demonstrations
of how to fall off a motorcycle scientifically. He fell off so often, in fact,
that we feared he would never make an aviator. In this opinion, of course,
we were very much in error, as he became one of the first, and also one of
the best aviators in the country. Atmospheric pressure, the vacuum motor,
Dr. Bell's tetrahedral construction, and even astronomical subjects—all
found a place in the nightly discussions at the "thinkorium."

Of course there were many important things that took up our attention,
but we could not always be grave and dignified. I recall one evening somebody started a discussion on the idea of elevating Trinity Church, in New
York City, on the top of a skyscraper, and using the revenue from the
ground rental to convert the heathen. This gave a decided shock to a min-
isterial visitor who happened to be present.

When summer came on there were frequent motorcycle trips when the
weather did not permit of flying, or when the shop was at work repairing
one of our frequent smashes. "Casey" Baldwin and McCurdy furnished a
surprise one day by a rather unusual long-distance trip on motorcycles.
"Let's go up to Hamilton, Ontario," said Baldwin, probably choosing
Hamilton as the destination because he was charged with having a sweet-
heart there.

"All right," answered McCurdy.

Without a moment's hesitation the two mounted their wheels, not even
stopping to get their caps, and rode through to Hamilton, a hundred and
fifty miles distant, buying everything they required along the way. They
were gone a week and came back by the same route.

A favourite subject of talk at the "thinkorium," at least between Mc-
Curdy and Selfridge, was on some of the effects of the "torque" of a propeller and whenever this arose we would expect the argument to keep up
until one or the other would fall asleep.

After the nightly formal sessions of the members of the Association the
courtesy of the floor was extended to any one who might be present for
the discussion of anything he might see fit to bring up. Later we would ad-
journ to Dr. Bell's room, where he would put himself into a comfortable
position, light his inevitable pipe, and produce his note books. In these
note books Dr. Bell would write down everything—his thoughts on every

subject imaginable, his ideas about many things, sketches, computations. All these he would sign, date, and have witnessed. It was Dr. Bell's custom to work at night when there were no distracting noises, though there were few of these at Hammondsport even during the daylight hours; at night it is quiet enough for the most exacting victim of insomnia. Dr. Bell often sat up until long after midnight, but he made up for the lost time by sleeping until noon. No one was allowed to wake him for any reason. The rest of us were up early in order to take advantage of the favourable flying conditions during the early morning hours. Dr. Bell had a strong aversion to the ringing of the telephone bell—the great invention for which he is responsible. I occasionally went into his room and found the bell stuffed with paper, or wound around with towels.

"Little did I think when I invented this thing," said Dr. Bell, one day when he had been awakened by the jingling of the bell, "that it would rise up to mock and annoy me."

While the Doctor enjoyed his morning sleep we were out on "Stony Brook Farm" trying to fly. We had put up a tent against the side of an old sheep barn, and out of this we would haul the machine while the grass was still wet with dew. One never knew what to expect of it. Sometimes a short flight would be made; at others, something would break. Or, maybe, the wind would come up and this would force us to abandon all further trials for the day. Then it was back to the shop to work on some new device, or to repair damages until the wind died out with the setting of the sun. Early in the morning and late in the evening were the best periods of the day for our experimental work because of the absence of wind.

On May 22, 1908, our second machine, the *White Wing*, was brought to such a state of perfection that I flew it a distance of one thousand and seventeen feet in nineteen seconds, and landed without damage in a ploughed field outside the old race track. It was regarded as a remarkable flight at that time, and naturally, I felt very much elated.

41

The *June Bug*

By Glenn Curtiss (with Augustus M. Post),
in *The Curtiss Aviation Book* (1912)

Scientific American offered the first prize in America for a heavier-than-air flying machine: $2,500 and a silver trophy for the first to fly one kilometer, taking off and landing on wheels. Since the Wrights used a catapult and landed on skids, and because they refused to demonstrate their machine publicly until they had a firm sale, Wilbur and Orville declined the contest. Glenn Curtiss announced that he would try for the prize on July 4, 1908.

Following the success of the *White Wing*, we started in to build another machine, embodying all that we had learned from our experience with the two previous ones. Following our custom of giving each machine a name to distinguish it from the preceding one, we called this third aeroplane the *June Bug*. The name was aptly chosen, for it was a success from the very beginning. Indeed, it flew so well that we soon decided it was good enough to win the trophy which had been offered by *The Scientific American* for the first public flight of one kilometer, or five-eights of a mile, straight-away. This trophy, by the way, was the first to be offered in this country for an aeroplane flight, and the conditions specified that it should become the property of the person winning it three years in succession. The *June Bug* was given a thorough try-out before we made arrangements to fly for the trophy, and we were confident it would fulfill the requirements.

The Fourth of July, 1908, was the day set for the trial. A large delegation of aero-club members came on from New York and Washington, among whom were Stanley Y. Beach, Allan R. Hawley, Augustus Post, David Fairchild, Chas. M. Manly, Christopher J. Lake, A. M. Herring, George H. Guy, E. L. Jones, Wilbur R. Kimball, Captain Thomas S. Baldwin, and many other personal friends. The excitement among the citizens of Hammondsport in general was little less than that existing among the members of the Aerial Experiment Association, and seldom had the Fourth of July been awaited with greater impatience.

When Independence Day finally dawned it did not look auspicious for the first official aeroplane flight for a trophy. Clouds boded rain and there was some wind. This did not deter the entire population of Hammondsport from gathering on the heights around the flying field, under the trees in the valley and, in fact, at every point of vantage. Some were on the scene as early as five o'clock in the morning, and many brought along baskets of food and made a picnic of it. The rain came along toward noon, but the crowd hoisted its umbrellas or sought shelter under the trees and stayed on. Late in the afternoon the sky cleared and it began to look as if we were to have the chance to fly after all. The *June Bug* was brought out of its tent and the motor given a tryout. It worked all right. The course was measured and a flag put up to mark the end. Everything was ready and about seven o'clock in the evening the motor was started and I climbed into the seat. When I gave the word to "let go" the *June Bug* skimmed along over the old race track for perhaps two hundred feet and then rose gracefully into the air. The crowd set up a hearty cheer, as I was told later—for I could hear nothing but the roar of the motor and I saw nothing except the course and the flag marking a distance of one kilometer. The flag was quickly reached and passed and still I kept the aeroplane up, flying as far as the open fields would permit, and finally coming down safely in a meadow, fully a mile from the starting place. I had thus exceeded the requirements and had won the Scientific American Trophy for the first time. I might have gone a great deal farther, as the motor was working beautifully and I had the machine under perfect control, but to have prolonged the flight would have meant a turn in the air or passing over a number of large trees. The speed of this first official flight was closely computed at thirty-nine miles an hour.

Dr. Bell had gone to Nova Scotia, unfortunately, and, therefore, did not witness the Fourth of July flight of the *June Bug*. The other members, however, were all present. It was a great day for all of us and we were more confident than ever that we had evolved, out of our long and costly experiments, a machine that would fly successfully and with safety to the operator. Lieutenant Selfridge was particularly enthusiastic, and I recall when Mr. Holcomb, special agent for a life insurance company, visited the field one day and heard Selfridge talk about flying.

"You must be careful, Selfridge," said Mr. Holcomb, "or we will need a bed for you in the hospital of which I am a trustee."

"Oh, I am careful, all right," replied Selfridge, but it was only a few days later when he left Hammondsport for Washington, and was killed while flying as a passenger with Orville Wright at Fort Myer.

11. The AEA *June Bug* lifts off from a field outside Hammondsport
with Glenn Curtiss at the controls, July 4, 1908.

42

<hr/>

"We would be glad to take up the matter of a license. . ."

Letter from Orville Wright to Glenn Curtiss

Sixteen days later, Orville Wright sent Curtiss this letter. It was a sign of things to come, for eventually the Wrights sued Curtiss and anyone anywhere who flew using a system of lateral control.

<hr/>

To Glenn H. Curtiss

Dayton, July 20, 1908

I learn from the *Scientific American* that your *June Bug* has movable surfaces at the tips of the wings, adjustable to different angles on the right and left sides for maintaining the lateral balance. In our letter to Lieutenant Selfridge of January 18th, replying to his of the 15th, in which he asked for information on the construction of flyers, we referred him to several publications containing descriptions of the structural features of our machines, and to our U.S. patent No. 821,393. We did not intend, of course, to give permission to use the patented features of our machine for exhibitions or in a commercial way.

This patent broadly covers the combination of sustaining surfaces to the right and left of the center of a flying machine adjustable to different angles, with vertical surfaces adjustable to correct inequalities in the horizontal resistances of the differently adjusted wings. Claim 14 of our patent No. 821,393, specifically covers the combination which we are informed you are using. We believe it will be very difficult to develop a successful machine without the use of some of the features covered in this patent.

The commercial part of our business is taking so much of our time that we have not been able to undertake public exhibitions. If it is your desire to enter the exhibition business, we would be glad to take up the matter of a license to operate under our patents for that purpose.

Please give to Capt. Baldwin* my best wishes for his success in the coming government tests.

Orville Wright

---

* Dirigiblist Thomas Baldwin (no relation to the AEA's chief engineer) whom the Wrights met accompanied by Curtiss in Dayton in 1904, and who would be demonstrating one of his rigid airships in the Ft. Myer tests along with the Wrights' military *Flyer*.

PART VI

1908–1914

THE EARLY GREAT FLIGHTS

43

⟫•◦•⟪

The Pioneers of Flight

By Claude Grahame-White, in *The Aeroplane—Past, Present,*
Future (1911)

In 1908 the Wrights almost simultaneously sold a machine to both France
and the United States, requiring them to demonstrate their *Flyers* in each
place at the same time—Orville in the U.S. and Wilbur in Europe. Previously fearing that the mere sight of their flying machine flying would reveal
its secrets to all and thus undercut the profitability of their invention, they
had remained mysteriously groundbound for nearly three years, and were
roundly castigated as bluffers. Yet when they finally took to the air, and flew
with a finesse previously unseen in flying machines, there was widespread
jubilation. In America reporters rushed Orville's machine in tears; the population of all of Europe, it seemed, would turn out to watch Wilbur fly.
Soon-to-be aviator Claude Grahame-White met the now-famous Day-
tonan during one flight in France.

⟫•◦•⟪

One day in December, 1908, at the Aéro-Club of France, I assisted in wel-
coming Colonel Massy, and a deputation of Britishers interested in aeronautics, amongst whom were Alec Ogilvie and T. P. Searight.

The rumour was circulated that Wilbur Wright would make a flight on
December 16th; so it was decided that a pilgrimage should be made to the
Camp d'Auvours. I crossed over to the other side of the Champs Elysees,
and called on Mr. Hart O. Berg, who most courteously gave me all the requisite information regarding Wilbur Wright's proposed flight.

Colonel Massy, the leader of the little British contingent, decided that
we should leave for Le Mans by an early train to be in good time for the
flights, which were expected to take place about 10 o'clock in the morning. It *was* early—5:55 A.M. from the Gare de Montparnasse, to be precise.

Travelling by a slow train in France is not enjoyable. The journey, which
should have lasted about three hours, took nearly seven. We experienced
the extreme annoyance of being shunted into a siding to allow a train to
pass us which had left Paris three hours and a half later than our own. But
the truth of the old saying, "A merry heart goes all the way," was proved

by the state of good humour in which we were kept by Colonel Massy, who possesses, together with the qualities of a soldier, and sportsman, all the charm of the cheery and ready-witted Irishman.

Champagne, at last! The town, I mean, not the wine. Here we found the motor-cars for which we had wired overnight, waiting to take us to the flying ground. Here, upon our arrival, we learned that Wilbur Wright most probably would not fly, as, through the neglect of someone, alcohol had been poured into his tank in mistake for petrol.

Messages reached Mr. Wright, however, that a party of Britishers had travelled down specially from Paris to see him fly; so, with the generous instinct of the sportsman, which is one of the principal characteristics of this truly exceptional man, he decided that we should not go back disappointed. He ordered his tank to be emptied of its undesirable contents; and we were told that Mr. Wright, who was lunching at the moment, would make a flight during the afternoon.

I learned afterwards that it had been his intention to make an attempt for the altitude prize that morning; so, had it not been for the mistake above mentioned, I should have been deprived, through the delay of our train, of witnessing the most impressive and fascinating experience in my life.

By this time the tank was empty. We readily followed our guide over to Wright's hangar. It was a simple shed, built of boards, one corner partitioned off like a loose box, furnished only by a truckle-bed in the corner, a bicycle, two chairs, and a common little deal table.

When I asked, afterwards, why Wilbur Wright slept there, under conditions minus all the comforts of modern life, I was told that he had to keep an eye on his beloved aeroplane. I believe that his affection for his aeroplane resembled that of a parent for his child.

Afterwards, we strolled across to where the aeroplane rested on the rail, and examined Wright's great inanimate bird, the achievements of which have been sung in the four quarters of the globe.

I think that what struck me most was the apparently simple mechanism, the crudeness of the materials employed in its construction, and the rough-and-ready way in which they had been put together.

I had always taken it as a *sine qua non* that the surfaces of the plane should be absolutely airproof to ensure resistance, but that this idea was a fallacy was proved by a rent in the under plane, large enough to put your hand through; and, here and there, the loops employed to attach the canvas of the planes to the framework were missing.

In fact, in one place, a portion of the canvas was attached by what looked suspiciously like a bootlace. I mention these facts about the appearance of the greatest mechanical contrivance of the age to show that Wilbur Wright was above the considerations of the showman—and this is a proof of true greatness in an inventor.

Presently someone remarked, "*Voila qu'il vient!*" and a minute or two after we were joined by the great man himself, with his gaunt form, weather-beaten face, and piercing, hawk-like eyes.

Everybody has read descriptions of Mr. Wright's modesty, and so forth, and I need not, therefore, dilate upon it. I will content myself with repeating an utterance of his, which is an excellent indication of his character: "The only birds that talk are parrots, and they are not birds of high flight."

I was greatly struck with the extreme caution exercised by Wilbur Wright to insure every part of his machinery being in working order. For instance, before mounting the seat, he personally inspected the vulnerable points of his aeroplane. Then, being already seated, I heard him inquire of one of his mechanicians—"Is that tap shut off? Are you sure that tap is shut off?"

And then, to make assurance doubly sure, he dismounted and personally satisfied himself that the tap *was* shut off. I mention this as a proof of his thoroughness, and that Wilbur Wright was a man who took no unnecessary risks.

He again mounted to the pilot's seat, taking hold of the levers working the rudders. The motor was set in motion, the two propellers, revolving in opposite directions, were started. He called out the word "Go!"

The lever of the starting derrick was pulled, the weight dropped, and the aeroplane glided forward, rapidly gaining momentum from the action of the propellers. The pilot, having reached the end of the rail, detached the runner, raised the elevator, and the aeroplane buzzed into the air.

The first flight I saw him make, he flew round the ground at a height of about from 25 to 30 metres [80–100 ft.], rising, falling and turning at will, and returning to earth with the greatest ease. Whereupon, we all gathered round him and expressed our congratulations, to which I believe he was utterly indifferent—only he was too good-natured to show it.

On the second flight, which I witnessed, a successful start was made, and the aeroplane gradually rose to a height of 70 metres [230 ft.], gazed on with ever-increasing admiration by the enthusiastic crowd.

The scenic conditions under which this flight was made left a most delightful impression in my mind. It was past 4 o'clock; a darkening veil was falling on the wintry landscape, which one of our companions, the Tika of Kapurthala, said reminded him of an Indian jungle scene.

The rays of the setting sun tinged the western sky with shafts of purple, red, and gold. The outline of the great man-eagle, circling round above our heads, stood out black against the sky.

Suddenly he soared to an altitude of 300 feet, and poised for a moment; then, like a hawk, he swooped down to a level of about 200 feet. Again he soared; then, amidst the enthusiastic applause of the spectators, he glided gracefully to earth.

44

Blériot Tells of His Flight—Dropped Crutches to Do It

By Louis Blériot, in the *New York Times,* July 26, 1909

After Lord Northcliffe offered £1,000 in his newspaper, the London *Daily Mail,* to the first flier to cross the English Channel, the dark horse in the race that developed was Louis Blériot, who flew a diminutive monoplane of his own design, the *Blériot XI.* Crippled by burns sustained in previous flights, with an underpowered machine covered in paper whose engine sprayed hot oil all over him, Blériot hardly had a chance compared with the privileged few who owned the well-tested Wright machines, or against Hubert Latham, a handsome playboy who was everybody's favorite to win. Storms kept the contenders on the ground till May 25, 1909. Blériot was the first to rise that morning, and took advantage of reports that the storm had cleared. Here is his description of the flight, written soon after landing safely at Dover.

BLÉRIOT TELLS OF HIS FLIGHT

First Man to Cross English Channel in Aeroplane Dropped Crutches to Do It

PASSAGE MADE IN 23 MINUTES

Ten Minutes Out of Sight of Land with No Guide But Machine's Direction

SWEPT OUT OF HIS COURSE

When He Caught Sight of Dover Castle Was Headed for Goodwin Sands

BROKE PROPELLER LANDING

Stole March on Rivals, Surprised Dover, Disappointed Photographers, and Won Daily Mail Prize

Special Cable to The New York Times
Dispatch to The London Daily Mail
By Louis Blériot
Dover, England, July 25

I rose at 2:30 this (Sunday) morning, and finding that the conditions were favorable, ordered the torpedo boat destroyer, *Escopette,* which had been placed at my disposal by the French Government, to start. Then I went to the garage at Sangatte and found that the motor worked well. At 4 A.M. I took my seat in the aeroplane and made a trial flight around Calais of some fifteen kilometers (over nine miles), descending at the spot chosen for the start across the Channel.

Here I waited for the sun to come out, the conditions of *The Daily Mail* prize requiring that I fly between sunrise and sunset. At 4:30 daylight has come, but it was impossible to see the coast. A light breeze from the southwest was blowing the air clear, however, and everything was prepared.

I was dressed in a khaki jacket lined with wool for warmth over my tweed clothes and beneath my engineer's suit of blue cotton overalls. A close-fitting cap was fastened over my head and ears. I had neither eaten nor drunk anything since I rose. My thoughts were only upon the flight and my determination to accomplish it this morning.

"All Ready" at 4:35

At 4:35 "All's ready." My friend Leblanc gives the signal, and in an instant I am in the air, my engine making 1,200 revolutions, almost its highest speed, In order that I may get quickly over the telegraph wires along the edge of the cliff.

As soon as I am over the cliff I reduce speed. There is now no need to force the engine. I begin my flight, steady and sure, toward the coast of England. I have no apprehensions, no sensation—pas du tout—none at all.

"The Escopette*" Follows*

The *Escopette* has seen me. She is driving ahead at full speed. She makes perhaps 42 kilometers (26 miles) an hour. What matters it? I am making at least 68 kilometers (over 42 miles). Rapidly I overtake her traveling at a height of 80 meters (260 feet). Below me is the surface of the sea, disturbed by the wind, which is now freshening. The motion of the waves beneath me is not pleasant. I drive on.

Ten minutes are gone. I have passed the destroyer, and I turn my head to see whether I am proceeding in the right direction. I am amazed. There is nothing to be seen—neither the torpedo boat destroyer nor France nor England. I am alone; I can see nothing at all.

For ten minutes I am lost; it is a strange position to be in—alone, guided without a compass in the air over the middle of the Channel.

I touch nothing; my hands and feet rest lightly on the levers. I let the aeroplane take its own course. I care not wither it goes.

Sees England's Cliffs

For ten minutes I continue, neither rising nor falling nor turning, and then twenty minutes after I have left the French coast, I see green cliffs and Dover Castle, and away to the west the spot where I had intended to land.

What can I do? It is evident the wind has taken me out of my course. I am almost at St. Margaret's Bay, going in the direction of Goodwin Sands.

Now it is time to attend to the steering. I press a lever with my foot and turn easily toward the west, reversing the direction in which I am traveling. Now I am in difficulties, for the wind here by the cliffs is much stronger and my speed is reduced as I fight against it, yet my beautiful aeroplane responds still steadily.

Flies Over Dover Harbor

I fly westward, chopping across the harbor, and reach Shakespeare Cliff. I see an opening in the cliff. Although I am confident I can continue for an hour and a half, that I might, indeed, return to Calais, I cannot resist the opportunity to make a landing upon this green spot.

Once more I turn my aeroplane, and, describing a half circle, I enter the opening and find myself again over dry land. Avoiding the red buildings on my right, I attempt a landing, but the wind catches me and whirls me around two or three times. At once I stop my motor, and instantly my machine falls straight upon the ground from a height of twenty meters (seventy-five feet). In two or three seconds I am safe upon your shore.

Soldiers in khaki run up, and policemen. Two of my compatriots are on the spot. They kiss my cheeks. The conclusion of my flight overwhelms me.

Thus ended my flight across the Channel—a flight which could easily be done again. Shall I do it? I think not. I have promised my wife that after a race for which I have already entered I will fly no more.

Louis Blériot

12. Louis Blériot departs France for England in his monoplane, *Blériot XI*.

45

⇒•◦•⇐

The First Air Meet

By Glenn Curtiss, in *The Curtiss Aviation Book* (1912)

Blériot's Channel crossing captured the public imagination as few feats had before. Flushed with success, he went on to compete against his fellow aviators in the first international flying competition, held in Reims, France, later that summer, and sponsored by Gordon Bennett, owner of the Paris *Herald*. Nearly two hundred thousand spectators paid to see thirty-five aviators—mostly French—competing for numerous prizes. The lone American competing was Glenn Curtiss. The following is Curtiss's account of the event.

⇒•◦•⇐

In the try-outs it became evident to the Frenchman that my aeroplane was very fast and it was conceded that the race for the Gordon Bennett Cup would lie between Blériot and myself, barring accidents. After a carefully timed trial circuit of the course, which, much to my surprise, I made in a few seconds less than M. Blériot's time, and that too with my motor throttled down slightly, I gained more confidence. I removed the large gasoline tank from my machine and put on a smaller one in order to lessen the weight and the head-resistance. I then selected the best of my three propellers, which, by the way, were objects of curiosity to the French aviators, who were familiar only with the metal blades used on the Antoinette machine, and the Chauvière, which was being used by M. Blériot. M. Chauvière was kind enough to make a propeller especially fitted to my aeroplane, notwithstanding the fact that a better propeller on my machine would lessen the chances of the French flyers for the cup. However, I decided later to use my own propeller, and did use it—and won.

August 28 dawned hot and clear. It was agreed at a meeting of the Committee, at which all the contestants were present, that each contestant should be allowed to make one trial flight over the course and that he might choose his own time for making it, between the hours of ten o'clock in the morning and six o'clock in the evening. The other starters were Blériot, Lefèbvre, and Latham for France, and Cockburn for England. As I have already stated, Blériot was the favorite because of his trip across the

English Channel and because of his records made in flights at various places prior to the Reims meet.

As conditions were apparently good, I decided to make my trial flight shortly after ten o'clock. The machine was brought out, the engine given a preliminary run, and at half past ten I was in the air. Everything had looked good from the ground, but after the first turn of the course I began to pitch violently. This was caused by the heat waves rising and falling as the cooler air rushed in. The up and down motion was not at all pleasant and I confess that I eased off on the throttle several times on the first circuit. I had not then become accustomed to the feeling an aviator gets when the machine takes a sudden drop. On the second round I got my nerve back and pulled the throttle wide open and kept it open. This accounts for the fact that the second lap was made in faster time than the first. The two circuits were made safely, and I crossed the finish line in seven minutes, 55 seconds, a new record for the course.

Now was my chance! I felt that the time to make the start for the cup was then, in spite of the boiling air conditions, which I had found existed all over the course and made flying difficult if not actually dangerous. We hurriedly refilled the gasoline tank, sent official notice to the judges, carefully tested the wiring of the machine by lifting it at the corners, spun the propeller, and the official trial was on. I climbed as high as I thought I might without protest, before crossing the starting line—probably five hundred feet—so that I might take advantage of a gradual descent throughout the race and thus gain additional speed. The sun was hot and the air rough, but I had resolved to keep the throttle wide open. I cut the corner as close as I dared and banked the machine high on the turns. I remember I caused great commotion among a big flock of birds which did not seem to be able to get out of the wash of my propeller. In front of the tribunes the machine flew steadily, but when I got around on the back stretch, as we would call it, I found remarkable air conditions. There was no wind, but the air seemed fairly to boil. The machine pitched considerably, and when I passed above the "graveyard," where so many machines had gone down and were smashed during the previous days of the meet, the air seemed literally to drop from under me. It was so bad at one point that I made up my mind that if I got over it safely I would avoid that particular spot thereafter.

Finally, however, I finished the 20 kilometers in safety and crossed the line in 15 minutes, 50 seconds, having averaged 46½ miles an hour. When the time was announced there was great enthusiasm among the Americans present, and everyone rushed over to offer congratulations. Some of them thought that I would surely be the winner, but of this I was by no means certain. I had great respect for Blériot's ability, and besides, Latham and his Antoinette might be able to make better speed than they had thus

far shown. In a contest of this sort it is never safe to cheer until all the re-
turns are in. I confess that I felt a good deal like a prisoner awaiting the
decision of a jury. I had done my best, and had got the limit of speed out
of the machine; still I felt that if I could do it all over again, I would be
able to improve on the time. Meantime, Cockburn, for England, had made
a start but had come down and run into a haystack. He was only able to
finish the course in 20 minutes, 47⅗ seconds. This put him out of the
contest.

Latham made his trial during the afternoon but his speed was five or six
miles an hour slower than my record. The other contestants were flying
about 35 miles an hour and were, therefore, not really serious factors in the
race.

It was all up to M. Blériot. All day long he tinkered and tested, first
with one machine and then another; trying different propellers and making changes here and there. It was not until late in the afternoon that he
brought out his big machine, Number 22, equipped with an eight-
cylinder water-cooled motor, mounted beneath the planes (wings), and
driving by chain a four-bladed propeller, geared to run at a speed somewhat less than that of the engine. He started off at what seemed to be a
terrific burst of speed. It looked to me as if he must be going twice as
fast as my machine had flown; but it must be remembered that I was very
anxious to have him go slow. The fear that he was beating me was father
to the belief.

As soon as Blériot was off, Mr. Cortlandt Field Bishop and Mr. David
Wolfe Bishop, his brother, took me in their automobile over to the judges'
stand. Blériot made the first lap in faster time than I had made it, and our
hearts sank. Then and there I resolved that if we lost the cup I would build
a faster aeroplane and come back next year to win it.

Again Blériot dashed past the stand and it seemed to me that he was
going even faster than the first time. Great was my surprise, therefore,
when, as he landed, there was no outburst of cheers from the great crowd.
I had expected a scene of wild enthusiasm, but there was nothing of the
sort. I sat in Mr. Bishop's automobile a short distance from the judges'
stand, wondering why there was no shouting, when I was startled by a
shout of joy from my friend, Mr. Bishop, who had gone over to the judges'
stand.

"You win! You win!" he cried, all excitement as he ran toward the automobile. "Blériot is beaten by six seconds!"

A few moments later, just at half past five o'clock, the Stars and Stripes
were slowly hoisted to the top of the flagpole and we stood uncovered
while the flag went up. There was scarcely a response from the crowded
grand stands; no true Frenchman had the heart to cheer.

46

⟶•⟨—

An Exchange between Two Old Friends

By Wilbur Wright and Octave Chanute

Meanwhile, the Wrights had decided to bring suit against all aviators flying with anything resembling their revolutionary wingwarping control. The Wright Company would grant licenses on an individual basis for each manufacturer; for promoters of aeroplane meets, it granted licenses for 20 percent of the total amount of prize money and 10 percent of the gross gate and grandstand receipts. Sometimes the company would grant licenses for a lump sum based on estimated receipts. Many of the leaders in aviation—especially those who had refused to pay such fees—were not too sanguine about the action. Surprisingly, one of the Wright's detractors was their old friend Octave Chanute. In the December 12, 1909, edition of the *New York World,* he said, "I admire the Wrights."

"I feel friendly toward them for the marvels they have achieved; but you can easily gauge how I feel concerning their attitude at present by the remark I made to Wilbur Wright recently. I told him I was sorry to see they were suing other experimenters and abstaining from entering the contests and competitions in which other men are brilliantly winning laurels. I told him that in my opinion they are wasting valuable time over lawsuits which they ought to concentrate in their work. Personally, I do not think that the courts will hold that the principle underlying the warping tips can be patented. They may win on the application of their particular mechanism.

"The fundamental principle underlying the warping of tips for the purposes of balance was understood even before the suggestion contained in d'Esterno's* pamphlet fifty years ago. In modern times the warping tips were actually used in flight by Pierre Mouillard . . . the idea is protected in a patent granted him by the United States Government in 1901.

"The Wrights I am told, are making their strongest attack upon the point that they warp the tips in connection with the turning of their rudder. Even this is covered by a patent granted to an American in 1901.

"There is no question that the fundamental principle underlying was well known before the Wrights incorporated it in their machine."

Wilbur Wright was shocked when he read the article. That interview led to this exchange of letters between him and Chanute.

⟶•⟨—

* Count Honoré Phillipe d'Esterno, whose 1864 pamphlet, titled "Des Vols des Oiseaux," stated that flight had three distinct requirements: equilibrium, guidance, and propulsion.

January 20, 1910

To Octave Chanute

[You] are represented as saying that our claim to have been the first to maintain lateral balance by adjusting the wing tips to different angles of incidence cannot be maintained, as this idea was well known in the art when we began our experiments. As this opinion is quite different from that which you expressed in 1901 when you became acquainted with our methods, I do not know whether it is mere newspaper talk or whether it really represents your present views. So far as we are aware the originality of this system of control with us was universally conceded when our machine was first made known, and the questioning of it is a matter of recent growth springing from a desire to escape the legal consequences of awarding it to us. In our affidavits we said that when we invented this system we were not aware that such an idea had ever suggested itself to any other person, and that we were the first to make a machine embodying it, and also that we were the first to demonstrate its value to the world, and that the world owed the invention to us and to no one else. The patent of Mouillard was cited as an anticipation by the Germans and the English patent offices, and also by the defendants' attorneys in the recent trial at Buffalo, and in each case it was decided that it did not constitute an anticipation. I have also seen Le Bris and d'Esterno mentioned as having anticipated us, but the accounts in your book regarding the works and writings of these men do not contain any explanation of such a system of lateral control. Do the French documents from which you derived your information contain it, and if so can you give information as to where such documents can be obtained? It is our view that morally the world owes its almost universal use of our system of lateral control entirely to us. It is also our opinion that legally it owes it to us. If however there is anything in print which might invalidate our legal rights, it will be to our advantage to know it before spending too much on lawyers, and any assistance you may be able to give us in this respect will be much appreciated, even though it may show that legally our labors of many years to provide a system of lateral control were of no benefit to the world and a mere waste of time, and the world already possesses the system without us.

Wilbur Wright

January 23, 1910

This [newspaper] interview, which was entirely unsought by me, is about as accurate as such things usually are. Instead of discussing it I prefer to take up the main principles at issue.

I did tell you in 1901 that the mechanism by which your surfaces were

warped was originally with yourselves. This I adhere to, but it does not follow that it covers the general principle of warping or twisting wings, the
proposals for doing this being ancient. . . . The original sources of information are indicated in the footnotes [of *Progress in Flying Machines*]. I
did not explain the mechanism because I had not the data.

When I gave you a copy of the Mouillard patent in 1901 I think I called
your attention to his method of twisting the rear of the wings. If the courts
will decide that the purpose and results were entirely different and that you
were the first to conceive the twisting of the wings, so much the better for
you, but my judgment is that you will be restricted to the particular method
by which you do it. Therefore it was that I told you in New York that you
were making a mistake by abstaining from prize-winning contests while
public curiosity is yet so keen, and by bringing suits to prevent others from
doing so. This is still my opinion and I am afraid, my friend, that your usually sound judgment has been warped by the desire for great wealth.

If, as I infer from your letter, my opinions form a grievance in your mind,
I am sorry, but this brings me to say that I also have a little grievance
against you.

In your speech at the Boston dinner, you began by saying that I "turned
up" at your shop in Dayton in 1901 and that you invited me to your camp.
This conveyed the impression that I thrust myself upon you at that time
and it omitted to state that you were the first to write me, in 1900, asking
for information which was gladly furnished, that many letters passed between us, and that both in 1900 and 1901 you had written me to invite me
to visit you, before I "turned up" in 1901. This, coming subsequently to
some somewhat disparaging remarks concerning the helpfulness I may
have been to you, attributed to you by a number of French papers, which
I, of course disregarded as newspaper talk, has grated upon me since that
dinner, and I hope, that, in future, you will not give out the impression that
I was the first to seek your acquaintance, or pay me left-handed compli-
ments, such as saying that "sometimes an experienced person's advice was
of great value to younger men."

Octave Chanute

January 29, 1910

Until confirmed by you the interview in the *New York World* . . . seemed
incredible. We never had the slightest ground for suspecting that when you
repeatedly spoke to us in 1901 of the originality of our methods, you referred only to our methods of driving tacks, fastening wires, etc., and not
to the novelty of our general systems. Neither in 1901, nor in the five years
following, did you in any way intimate to us that our general system of lateral control had long been part of the art, and strangely enough, neither

your books, addresses or articles, nor the writings of Lilienthal, Langley, Maxim, Hargrave,* etc., made any mention whatever of such a system. . . . If the idea was really old in the art, it is somewhat remarkable that a system so important that the individual ownership of it is considered to threaten strangulation of the art was not considered worth mentioning then, nor embodied in any machine built prior to ours.

The patent of Mouillard, to which you refer, does not even mention the control of the lateral balance, nor disclose a system by which it is possible to attain it. I have read . . . what your book says on . . . d'Esterno, Le Bris, etc., but I do not find . . . any mention whatever of controlling balance by adjustments of wings to respectively different angles of incidence on the right and left sides. Have you ever found such mention? It is not disputed that every person who is using this system today owes it to us and to us alone. The French aviators freely admit it. No legal disclosure of the system prior to us has yet been produced. Unless something as yet unknown to anybody is brought to light to prove the invention technically known to everybody prior to 1900, our warped judgment will probably continue to be confirmed by the other judges as it was by Judge Hazel at Buffalo.

As to inordinate desire for wealth, you are the only person acquainted with us who has ever made such an accusation. We believed that the physical and financial risks which we took, and the value of the service to the world, justified sufficient compensation to enable us to live modestly with enough surplus income to permit the devotion of our future time to scientific experimenting instead of business. We spent several years of valuable time trying to work out plans which would have made us independent without hampering the invention by the commercial exploitation of the patents. These efforts would have succeeded but for jealousy and envy. It was only when we found that the sale of the patents offered the only way to obtain compensation for our labors of 1900–1906 that we finally permitted the chance of making the invention free to the world to pass from our hands. You apparently concede to us no right to compensate for the solution of a problem ages old except such as is granted to persons who had no part in producing the invention. That is to say, we may compete with mountebanks for a chance to earn money in the mountebank business, but are entitled to nothing whatever for past work as inventors. If holding a different view constitutes us almost criminal, as some seem to think, we are not ashamed. We honestly think that our work of 1900–1906 has been and will be of value to the world, and that the world owes us something as inventors, regardless of whether we personally make Roman holidays for accident-loving crowds.

You mention as a grievance . . . some disparaging remarks concerning

---

* Lawrence Hargrave (1850–1915), inventor of the box kite (1893).

your helpfulness to us . . . we also have a grievance extending back to as far as 1902, and on one occasion several years ago we complained to you that an impression was being spread broadcast by newspapers that we were mere pupils and dependents of yours. You indignantly denied that you were responsible for it. When I went to France I found everywhere an impression that we had taken up aeronautical studies at your special instigation . . . in short, that you furnished the science and money while we contributed a little mechanical skill, and that when success had been achieved you magnanimously stepped aside and permitted us to enjoy the rewards. I cannot remember that I ever spoke for publication regarding the matter. . . . However, I several times said privately that we had taken up the study of aeronautics long before we had any acquaintance with you; that our ideas of control were radically different from yours both before and throughout our acquaintance; that the systems of control which we carried to success were absolutely our own, and had been embodied in a machine and tested before you knew anything about them and before our first meeting with you; that in 1900 and 1901 we used the tables and formulas found in books, but finding the results did not agree with the calculations, we had extensive laboratory experiments and prepared tables of our own which we used exclusively in all our subsequent work; that the solution to the screw-propeller problem was ours; that we designed all our machines from first to last, originated and worked out the principles of control, constructed the machines, and made all the tests at our own costs; that you built several machines embodying your ideas in 1901 and 1902 which were tested at our camp by Mr. Herring, but that we had never made a flight on any of your machines, nor your men on any of ours, and that in the sense in which the expression was used in France we had never been pupils of yours, though we had been very close friends, had carried on very voluminous correspondence, and discussed our work very freely with you.

Wilbur Wright

May 14, 1910

I am in bad health and threatened with nervous exhaustion. . . . Your letter of April 28th was gratifying, for I own that I felt very much hurt by your letter of January 29th, which I thought both unduly angry and unfair as well as unjust.

I have never given out the impression, either in writing or speech, that you had taken up aeronautics at my instance or were, as you put it, pupils of mine. I have always written and spoke of you as original investigators and worthy of the highest praise. . . .

The difference in opinion between us, i.e., whether the warping of the wings was in the nature of a discovery by yourselves, or had already been proposed and experimented by others, will have to be passed upon by others, but I have always said that you are entitled to immense credit for devising apparatus by which it has been reduced to successful practice.

I hope, upon my return from Europe, that we will be able to resume our former relations.

*Octave Chanute**

* Chanute died that November, at age 79.

47

———⊳•⊲———

"The cheering subsided to a silent prayer . . ."

From the *New York American*, January 1, 1911

While Curtiss and the Wrights battled over the patent issue in courts, both parties formed exhibition teams that toured the nation in 1910 and 1911. The shows were popular—for many people it was the first time they had seen an airplane fly—but due to the primitive state of flying machines, pilot casualties were high. In fact, many attended hoping to see spectacular crashes and blood spilled. The following is an excerpt of the *New York American*'s account of popular Wright pilot Arch Hoxey's fatal accident at the 1910 Los Angeles air meet.

———⊳•⊲———

He started down in a spiral descent. As the little speck gradually grew larger, it could be seen that the daredevil birdman was rushing earthward with one perpendicular swirl after another. At times it seemed as if the craft almost stood on beam end. Even those who had watched him day after day grew afraid. The cheering subsided to a silent prayer for the man in the frail thing of cloth and sticks.

Suddenly, after he had made a waltzing turn around the purlieus of the field, 500 feet up in the air, he attempted another hair-raising bank. But as the craft almost stood on its end, an unexpected puff of gusty wind blew full blast in its rear. Instantly the craft turned over . . . . The cracking of the spars and ripping of the cloth could be heard as the machine, a shapeless mass, came hurtling to the ground in a series of somersaults.

When the attendants rushed to the tangled mass of wreckage they found the body crushed out of all semblance to a human being. The crowd waited until the announcer megaphoned the fatal news and then turned homeward. All flying was over for the day.

48

Down the Hudson River

By Glenn Curtiss (with Augustus M. Post), in *The Curtiss
Aviation Book* (1912)

Blériot's Channel feat left America feeling that it had gotten behind in aeronautics. To fill the gap newspaper magnate William Randolph Hearst and
the *New York World* offered $10,000 to the first aviator to fly between Al-
bany and New York City. Glenn Curtiss, the hero of Reims, stepped up to
the challenge.

To fly from Albany to New York City was quite an undertaking in the
summer of 1910. I realised that success would depend upon a dependable
motor and a reliable aeroplane. In preparation for the task, therefore, I set
the factory at Hammondsport to work to build a new machine. While
awaiting the completion of the machine, I took a trip up the Hudson from
New York to Albany to look over the course and to select a place about
half way between the two cities where a landing for gasoline and oil might
be made, should it become necessary.

There are very few places for an aeroplane to land with safety around
New York City. The official final landing place, stipulated in the conditions drawn up by the *New York World*, was to be Governor's Island, but I
wanted to know of another place on the upper edge of the city where I
might come down if it should prove necessary. I looked all over the upper
end of Manhattan Island, and at last found a little meadow on a side hill
just at the junction of the Hudson and Harlem rivers, at a place called Inwood. It was small and sloping, but had the advantage of being within the
limits of New York City. It proved fortunate for me that I had selected this
place, for it later served to a mighty good advantage.

There was quite a party of us aboard the Hudson river boat leaving New
York City one day in May for the trip to Albany. As an illustration of the
skepticism among the steamboat men, I remember that I approached an
officer and asked several questions about the weather conditions on the
river, and particularly as to the prevailing winds at that period of the year.
Incidentally, I remarked that I was contemplating a trip up the river from

New York to Albany in an aeroplane and wanted to collect all the reliable data possible on atmospheric conditions. This officer, whom I afterward learned was the first mate, answered all my questions courteously, but it was evident to all of us that he believed I was crazy. He took me to the captain of the big river boat and introduced me, saying: "Captain, this is Mr. Curtiss, the flying machine man; that's all I know," in a tone that clearly indicated that he disclaimed all responsibility as to anything I might do or say.

The captain was very kind and courteous, asking us to remain in the pilot house, where we might get a better view of the country along the way, and displaying the keenest interest in the project. He answered all our questions about the winds along the Hudson and seemed to enter heartily in the spirit of the thing until we approached the great bridge at Pough-keepsie and I began to deliberate whether it would be better to pass over or beneath it in the aeroplane. Then it seemed really to dawn upon the captain for the first time that I was actually going to fly down the river in an aeroplane. He apparently failed to grasp the situation, and thereafter his answers were vague and given without interest. It was "Oh, yes, I guess so," and similar doubtful expressions, but when we finally left the boat at Albany he very kindly wished me a safe trip and promised to blow the whistle if I should pass his boat.

Albany afforded a better starting place than New York, because there were convenient spots where one might land before getting well under way, should it become necessary. This was not true of the situation at New York City. As to the advantage of prevailing winds, it seemed to be in favour of Albany as the starting place, and I finally decided to have everything sent up to the capital city. On my way up I had stopped at Poughkeepsie, in order to select a landing place, as at least one stop was deemed necessary to take on gasoline and to look over the motor. We visited the State Hospital for the Insane, which stands on the hill just above Poughkeepsie, and which seemed to be a good place to land. Dr. Taylor, the superintendent, showed us about the grounds, and when told that I intended stopping there on my way down the river in a flying machine, said with much cordiality: "Why, certainly, Mr. Curtiss, come right in here; here's where all the flying machine inventors land."

Notwithstanding the Doctor's cordial invitation to "drop in on him," we went to the other side of Poughkeepsie, and there found a fine open field at a place called Camelot. I looked over the ground carefully, locating the ditches and furrows, and selected the very best place to make a safe landing. Arrangements were made for a supply of gasoline, water, and oil to be brought to the field and held in readiness. It was fortunate that I looked over the Camelot field, for a few days later I landed within a few feet of the place I had selected as the most favoured spot near Poughkeepsie. This

is but one thing that illustrates how the whole trip was outlined before
the start was made, and how this plan was followed out according to
arrangement.

I shall always remember Albany as the starting place of my first long
cross-country flight. My machine was brought over from Hammondsport
and set up; the Aero Club sent up its official representatives, Mr. Augustus Post and Mr. Jacob L. Ten Eyck, and the newspapers of New York City
sent a horde of reporters. A special train was engaged to start from Albany
as soon as I got under way, carrying the newspapermen and the Aero Club
representatives, as well as several invited guests. It was the purpose to have
this train keep even with me along the entire trip of one hundred and fifty-
two miles, but as it turned out, it had some trouble in living up to the
schedule.

The aeroplane, christened the *Hudson Flier,* was set up on Rensselaer
Island. It was now up to the weather man to furnish conditions I considered suitable. This proved a hard task, and for three days I got up at day-
break, when there is normally the least wind, ready to make an early start.
On these days the newspapermen and officials, not to mention crowds of
curious spectators, rubbed the sleep out of their eyes before the sun got up
and went out to Rensselaer Island. But the wind was there ahead of us and
it blew all day long. The weather bureau promised repeatedly, "fair weather,
with light winds," but couldn't live up to promises. I put in some of the
time in going over every nut, bolt, and turnbuckle on the machine with
shellac. Nothing was overlooked; everything was made secure. I had confidence in the machine. I knew I could land on the water if it became necessary, as I had affixed two light pontoons to the lower plane, one on either end, and a hydro-surface under the front wheel of the landing-gear.
This would keep me afloat some time should I come down in the river.

We bothered the life out of the weather observer at Albany, but he was
always very kind and took pains to get weather reports from every point
along the river. But the newspapermen lost faith; they were tired of the
delay. I have always observed that newspapermen, who work at a high ten-
sion, cannot endure delay when there is a good piece of news in prospect.
One of those at Albany during the wait, offered to lay odds with the others that I would not make a start. Others among the journalists believed I
was looking for free advertising, and when another of the advertised
starters for the *World* prize reached Albany he was greeted with: "Hello,
old man, are you up here to get some free advertising, too?" One of the
Poughkeepsie papers printed an editorial about this time, in which it said:
"Curtiss gives us a pain in the neck. All those who are waiting to see him
go down the river are wasting their time." This was a fair sample of the
lack of faith in the undertaking.

The machine was the centre of interest at Albany during the wait. It seemed to hold a fascination for the crowds that came over to the island. One young fellow gazed at it so long and so intently that he finally fell over backwards insensible and it was some time before he was restored to consciousness. Then one of the newspapermen dashed a pail of water over him and at once sent his paper a column about it. They had to find something to write about and the countryman, the flying machine, and the fit made a combination good enough for almost any newspaperman to weave an interesting yarn about.

Our period of waiting almost ended on Saturday morning, May 30th. The *Hudson Flier* was brought out of its tent, groomed and fit; the special train provided by the *New York Times* to follow me over the New York Central, stood ready, with steam up and the engineer holding a right-of-way order through to New York. The newspapermen, always on the job, and the guests were watching eagerly for the aeroplane to start and set out on its long and hazardous flight.

Then something happened—the wind came up. At first it did not seem to be more than a breeze, but it grew stronger and reports from down the river told of a strong wind blowing up the river. This would have meant a head gale all the way to New York, should I make a start then. Everything was called off for the day and we all went over and visited the State Capitol. The newspapermen swallowed their disappointment and hoped for better things on the morrow.

Sunday proved to be the day. The delay had got somewhat on my nerves and I had determined to make a start if there was half a chance. The morning was calm and bright—a perfect summer day. News from down the river was all favourable. I determined it was now or never. I sent Mrs. Curtiss to the special train and informed the *World* representative and the Aero Club officials that I was ready to go. Shortly after eight o'clock the motor was turned over and I was off!

It was plain sailing after I got up and away from Rensselaer Island. The air was calm and I felt an immense sense of relief. The motor sounded like music and the machine handled perfectly. I was soon over the river and when I looked down I could see deep down beneath the surface. This is one of the peculiar things about flying over the water. When high up a person is able to see farther beneath the surface.

I kept a close lookout for the special train, which could not get under way as quickly as I had, and pretty soon I caught sight of it whirling along on the tracks next to the river bank. I veered over toward the train and flew along even with the locomotive for miles. I could see the people with their heads out the windows, some of them waving their hats or hands, while the ladies shook their handkerchiefs or veils frantically. It was no effort at all to keep up with the train, which was making fifty miles an hour. It was like a real race and I enjoyed the contest more than anything else during

the flight. At times I would gain as the train swung around a short curve
and thus lost ground, while I continued on in an air line.

All along the river, wherever there was a village or town, and even along
the roads and in boats on the river, I caught glimpses of crowds or groups
of people with their faces turned skyward, their attitudes betokening the
amazement which could not be read in their faces at that distance. Boat-
men on the river swung their caps in mute greeting, while now and then
a river tug with a long line of scows in tow, sent greetings in a blast of white
steam, indicating there was the sound of a whistle behind. But I heard
nothing but the steady, even roar of the motor in perfect rhythm, and the
whirr of the propeller. Not even the noise of the speeding special train only
a few hundred feet below reached me, although I could see every turn of
the great drive-wheels on the engine.

On we sped, the train and the aeroplane, representing a century of the
history of transportation, keeping abreast until the Hudson had been
passed. Here the aeroplane began to gain, and as the train took a wide
sweeping curve away from the bank of the river, I increased the lead per-
ceptibly, and soon lost sight of the special.

It seemed but a few minutes until the great bridge spanning the Hudson at Poughkeepsie, came into view. It was a welcome landmark, for I
knew that I had covered more than half the journey from Albany to New
York, and that I must stop to replenish the gasoline. I might have gone on
and taken a chance on having enough fuel, but this was not the time for
taking chances. There was too much at stake.

I steered straight for the centre of the Poughkeepsie bridge, and passed
a hundred and fifty feet above it. The entire population of Poughkeepsie
had turned out, apparently, and resembled swarms of busy ants, running
here and there, waving their hats and hands. I kept close watch for the
place where I had planned to turn off the river course and make a landing.
A small pier jutting out into the river was the mark I had chosen before-
hand and it soon came into view. I made a wide circle and turned inland,
over a clump of trees, and landed on the spot I had chosen on my way up
to Albany. But the gasoline and oil which I had expected to find waiting
for me, were not there. I saw no one for a time, but soon a number of men
came running across the fields and a number of automobiles turned off the
road and raced toward the aeroplane. I asked for some gasoline and an automobile hurried away to bring it.

I could scarcely hear and there was a continual ringing in my ears. This
was the effect of the roaring motor, and strange to say, this did not cease
until the motor was started again. From that time on there was no disagreeable sensation. The special train reached the Camelot field shortly
after I landed and soon the newspapermen, the Aero Club officials, and
the guests came climbing up the hill from the river, all eager to extend their

congratulations. Henry Kleckler, acting as my mechanic, who had come along on the special train, looked over the machine carefully, testing every wire, testing the motor out, and taking every precaution to make the remainder of the journey as successful as the first half. The gasoline having arrived, and the tank being refilled, the special train got under way; once more I rose into the air, and the final lap of the journey was on.

Out over the trees to the river I set my course, and when I was about midstream, turned south. At the start I climbed high above the river, and then dropped down close to the water. I wanted to feel out the air currents, believing that I would be more likely to find steady air conditions near the water. I was mistaken in this, however, and soon got up several hundred feet and maintained about an even altitude of from five hundred to seven hundred feet. Everything went along smoothly until I came within sight of West Point. Here the wind was nasty and shook me up considerably. Gusts shot out from the rifts between the mountains and made extremely rough riding. The worst spot was encountered between Storm King and Dunderberg, where the river is narrow and the mountains rise abruptly from the water's edge to more than a thousand feet on either side. Here I ran into a downward suction that dropped me in what seemed an interminable fall straight down, but which as a matter of fact was not more than a hundred feet or perhaps less. It was one of Willard's famous "holes in the air." The atmosphere seemed to tumble about like water rushing through a narrow gorge. At another point, a little farther along, and after I had dropped down close to the water, one blast tipped a wing dangerously high, and I almost touched the water. I thought for an instant that my trip was about to end, and made a quick mental calculation as to the length of time it would take a boat to reach me after I should drop into the water.

The danger passed as quickly as it had come, however, and the machine righted itself and kept on. Down by the Palisades we soared, rising above the steep cliffs that wall the stream on the west side. Whenever I could give my attention to things other than the machine, I kept watch for the special train. Now and then I caught glimpses of it whirling along the bank of the river, but for the greater part of the way I outdistanced it.

Soon I caught sight of some of the sky-scrapers that make the sky-line of New York City the most wonderful in the world. First I saw the tall frame of the Metropolitan Tower, and then the lofty Singer building. These landmarks looked mighty good to me, for I knew that, given a few more minutes' time, I would finish the flight. Approaching Spuyten Duyvil, just above the Harlem river, I looked at my oil gauge and discovered that the supply was almost exhausted. I dared not risk going on to Governor's Island, some fifteen miles farther, for once past the Harlem river there would be no place to land short of the island. So I took a wide sweep across to the Jersey side of the river, circled around toward the New

York side, and put in over the Harlem river, looking for the little meadow at Inwood which I had picked out as a possible landing place some two weeks before.

There I landed on the sloping hillside, and went immediately to a telephone to call up the *New York World.* I told them I had landed within the city limits and was coming down the river to Governor's Island soon.

I got more oil, some one among the crowd, that gathered as if by magic, turned my propeller, and I got away safely on the last leg of the flight. While I had complied with the conditions governing the flight by landing in the city limits, I wanted to go on to Governor's Island and give the people the chance to see the machine in flight.

From the extreme northern limits of New York to Governor's Island, at the southern limits, was the most inspiring part of the trip. News of the approach of the aeroplane had spread throughout the city, and I could see crowds everywhere. New York can turn out a million people probably quicker than any other place on earth, and it certainly looked as though half of the population was along Riverside Drive or on top of the thousands of apartment houses that stretch for miles along the river. Every craft on the river turned on its siren and faint sounds of the clamour reached me even above the roar of my motor. It seemed but a moment until the Statue of Liberty came into view. I turned westward, circled the Lady with the Torch and alighted safely on the parade ground on Governor's Island.

General Frederick Grant, commanding the Department of the East, was one of the first officers who came up to extend congratulations and to compliment me on the success of the undertaking. From that moment I had little chance for anything except the luncheons and dinners to which I was invited. First came the luncheon at the Astor House given by the *New York World,* and then the big banquet at the Hotel Astor, presided over by Mayor Gaynor and attended by many prominent men interested in aviation. The speeches were all highly laudatory, of course, and there were many predictions by the orators that the Hudson river would become a highway for aerial craft, as it had for steam craft when Fulton first steered the old *Clermont* from New York to Albany.

On the trip down from Albany I carried a letter from the mayor of that city to Mayor Gaynor, and delivered it in less time than it would have taken the fastest mail train. My actual flying time was two hours, fifty-one minutes, the distance one hundred and fifty-two miles, and the average speed fifty-two miles an hour.

From Albany to Poughkeepsie is eighty-seven miles, and by making this in a continuous flight I had, incidentally, won the *Scientific American* trophy for the third time. It now became my personal property, and its formal presentation was made at the annual dinner of the Aero Club of America for that year.

49

———⇒•◦•⇐———

Finding His Wings

By Adelaide Ovington

In Europe, Blériot's company was flooded with orders for copies of his now-famous *Blériot XI,* and with the orders came pilots to train. So he opened a flying school at Pau, outside of Paris, where many early aviators first took to the sky before heading out on the exhibition circuit. Among them was the dashing Earle Ovington, who met his future wife, Adelaide, on his way to fly in America. She tells of it in her book *An Aviator's Wife* (1920).

———⇒•◦•⇐———

"In bed," the aviator replied.

The table gasped.

"Evidently you didn't catch our question," the Captain stated with dignity. "Miss Alexander asked where you learned to fly."

"Exactly. And I answered 'in bed.' I learned to fly in bed," Mr. Ovington repeated quietly. "Every morning for fifteen minutes I sat up in bed with a pillow between my knees for a controlling lever. My feet rested on an imaginary steering bar connected by wires with the rudder. Sitting thus, I took many flights."

"A good safe way to fly," jeered the Irishman.

"More sensible than it sounds," the aviator retorted. "Believe me, there were some hair-raising side-slips and horrible deaths during those early flights. As time went on, however, I grew expert. The control of my imaginary craft became more and more subconscious. Soon I was making long flights at great altitudes! I flew over hundreds of miles of beautiful imaginary country, through fleecy imaginary clouds, over bleak imaginary mountain ranges, without making a single mistake in the control of my machine."

"I guess it wasn't so easy when you tried the real thing," sneered the Irishman.

"Well, no, it wasn't. But the many flights I made between the sheets enabled me to handle a machine much more quickly when I finally tried it in the air. For instance, one evening I was circling the field and became so spellbound gazing at the splendour of the setting sun that I forgot what I was doing. Before I realized that anything had happened, the earth was coming toward me at a dizzy pace. I had fallen into a bad side-slip. But the thing had happened to me so many times in bed that I knew just what to do to regain control. If I hadn't, sunsets upon this planet would have been a thing of the past for me."

"Where did you learn to fly—er—when you weren't in bed?" asked the Englishman.

They were all very much interested by now. Even the Irishman, I noticed, didn't miss anything that was said.

"I studied flying at Blériot's school at Pau, a beautiful winter resort in the south of France. It surely was an ideal place for aviation. A green field, level as a lawn, extended for miles in every direction, with the quaint little village of Pau on one side, and the snow-capped Pyrenees on the others. The weather was wonderful. Although it was January, we embryo birdmen used to lie around on the grass, without coats, waiting for our turn to fly."

"It strikes me," put in the Irishman, "that you did most of your flying in a recumbent position."

Mr. Ovington laughed good naturedly. "You mustn't get me started on aviation if you don't want me to talk."

"Oh, but we do!" we chorused. The Senator jumped in with the question:

"Why are there so few successful aviators?"

"Because flying is a subjective mental process. Expressed in more popular language, a good aviator flies instinctively. The subjective or subconscious mind—that portion over which we have so little control and which wanders around when we are asleep—works more efficiently in some people than in others. When its action is very rapid, it may be relied on in emergencies to a far greater extent than the sluggish objective part of our mental make-up. On the other hand, the objective mind—that portion of my brain I am using now in talking—acts slowly and is liable to many errors. It can't be relied on in flying a man-made bird. The manipulation of an airplane is like walking a tight rope; the flyer is continually balancing himself upon the invisible currents of the air."

"I suppose that explains why so few aviators become really expert," the Senator observed.

"Why, yes. Leblanc, Blériot's right hand man, told me that ninety per cent of his students should never have attempted to leave the ground; eight per cent would make fairly safe flyers under normal conditions; and the remaining two per cent were born flyers."

"So you think the born aviator is a man who flies subjectively?"

"Unquestionably. When the real emergency arrives he does the right thing at exactly the right time without having to think about it. Looking back upon his narrow escape, he wonders what made him act as he did.

The made flyer, however, who relies on his objective mind, is pretty sure to do the wrong thing in a crisis, and gives the daily press a chance to add another name to its long list of the martyrs of the air."

With this final remark Mr. Ovington rose from the table. He patted the Irishman on the shoulder.

"All done, now," he said soothingly.

"Well, that wasn't so bad," grinned the Irishman.

Later, every one turned up on deck for an afternoon of sports. To our astonishment the aviator laid aside his book and took part in all the events. Even more to our astonishment, he won prize after prize—all, in fact, except the last one. By that time we were almost more surprised to see him lose. He and the Irishman were playing "Are you there, brother?" and he deliberately let his opponent knock him out. I don't know to this day whether he did it because he was ashamed to take any more prizes, or because of the kick which the son of Erin had given the steward.

We found afterward that the birdman had held the all-round championship in college for two years, so it wasn't strange that he was able to beat these business men at his own game.

That evening Mr. Ovington joined me on deck, while Betty was over at the rail studying the stars with the Irishman. Dropping into the chair beside me the aviator pulled out a calabash pipe and asked if he might smoke.

"I reckon you don't know I'm a Virginian. I love the smell of good tobacco."

He filled his pipe. Then he produced a small, leather-covered book from his pocket and began turning its pages meditatively. "I don't know whether you'd care to see it," he said with a diffidence that sat oddly on him. "It's my diary."

"About Pau?" I asked eagerly.

"Yes, mostly. It's nothing much but it may serve to make you laugh."

"Oh, do let me see it!" I cried, reaching out my hand. What a story I would have to tell Betty now!

"Wonder if there's light enough here for you to read."

"Oh, yes," I replied, opening the book at the first page.

"*Jan. 16th.* Usual fifteen minute flight in bed. Only killed once.

"I didn't mind last night when they put me in room thirteen at the Hotel de Londres, at Pau, but imagine my surprise to see 13 on the slip they asked me to sign when I registered at Blériot's school. I'm going to prove that 13 is a lucky number for me.

"No trials today as too windy. "Blériot, Leblanc, Legagneux, and Morin all made flights. Was so impatient to fly I kept my eyes glued to the anemometer. Flying looks like great sport. Introduced American base-ball and it made a big hit. Leblanc, in his monoplane, plays with the Ville de Pau like a cat with a mouse."

"What was the 'Ville de Pau'?" I asked, looking up from the diary.

"A big dirigible balloon—a sort of baby Zeppelin. It used to pass over our heads three times a day with its fourteen passengers."

He began to smoke and I turned the page.

"*Jan. 17th.* Still too windy for students. Can make imaginary flights now with safety. Fellows laughed at me at first but after several of them had met with horrible deaths when they tried to imitate me I had them practising all over the field. More base-ball. I'll be fit to join the Nationals if this windy weather keeps up.

"*Jan. 18th.* First trip in Blériot, twice the length of field 'grass cutting.'* These Anzani engines may not be good motors but they are great atomizers. The castor oil was dripping off my nose when I got back. Brown, one of the students, tried to bore a thirty foot hole in the high fence around the aerodrome—and succeeded. That's his third smash. 'Dutchie' broke his leg and was taken to a hospital. He fell thirty feet and was thrown out when he hit the ground.

"*Jan. 19th.* Again too windy, according to old 'Wooden Shoes'."

"Who was 'Wooden Shoes'?" I looked up to enquire.

"One of our instructors, a short, square little man with a big temper. He usually wound a scarf round his neck as though he had the croup and stuck on his head a queer little cap with a knob on the top of it. He got his name from the fact that he always wore wooden shoes."

I laughed as I took up the book again.

"This afternoon, as we were lying on the grass, 'bump!' came a little Demoiselle monoplane from apparently nowhere and landed in our midst. It turned out to be a student from a nearby aerodrome. His motor had stopped in mid-air and he was forced to volplane† to the ground. After some tinkering he limped away, swinging like a pendulum. These watch-charm airplanes may be all right for consumptives, but they don't look as if they could lift a life-sized man three inches. A hard landing in one of them would mean an engine through the back of the head, an iron spike between the shoulder blades—for the control rod runs up your back—and a none too soft seat on terra firma.

"*Jan. 20th.* My, but flying is the king of sports! We grass-cutters are not supposed to fly until we have practised lawn-mowing for a week or two, but I managed to get in ahead of the game. As I peddled the bicycle I had hired for five francs a week over to the aviation field this morning, I prayed that old Wooden Shoes would be in a good humour, for I hoped that he would let me try my luck in the air. He of the dainty footgear told me to do some grass-cutting, but under no circumstances to leave the ground.

"The grease-covered mechanics wheeled out one of the patched up machines kept especially for 'taxi-drivers,' like myself, and I clambered into

---

* taxiing
† glide

the cockpit. The cane-bottom seat was not more than ten inches wide and its back consisted of a strip of three-ply veneer, three inches wide and a quarter of an inch thick. To make it still lighter it was bored full of holes. The French certainly do peel down their machines to make them light! I had been told to steer for a pylon at the other end of the field, and as my little monoplane bumped unevenly over the ground, I must have concentrated too much on that pylon and not enough on what I was doing. I pressed my feet so heavily on the rudder cross-bar that the back of the seat gave way, and I slipped over on to the bottom of the fuselage, pulling the elevator control toward me as I went. Not realizing in the least what had happened, I scrambled back into position as quickly as I could. Instead of being on the ground as I supposed, I was three hundred feet in the air, and still rising! Didn't I thank my lucky stars, then, for the practice I had had flying in bed! Except for that, I wouldn't be here tonight writing this diary. Between wiggling the rudder with my feet, warping the wings to keep the horizon where it belonged, and pushing and pulling the elevator to stop the earth from jumping up and down, I had a busy sixty seconds.

"I boldly struck out around the field and had no difficulty in making the first turn. It was so much fun I kept on and made another. As I neared the finish line I could see old Wooden Shoes waving me down as if he had gone mad. I was beyond his reach, though, and decided to take another turn for good luck. About half way on this last circuit my motor began to cough molten metal out of the exhaust valves, and the tail of the machine began to droop. I realized that I must come down instantly. It was easy enough to glide downward, but my lack of experience as to the sensitiveness of the controls made me drop at an angle which must have given the onlookers palpitation of the heart. I grazed the roof of a hangar, took several pickets off the fence, and landed on one wheel with a series of bumps, when my oil-cooled Anzani gave out entirely, and died with a consumptive wheeze. Old Wooden Shoes was in a rage. I shall never forget the way his sabots kept time with his machine-gun French as he called me everything impolite he could think of. But I didn't mind. I had really flown!

"Tonight, as I peddled back to the hotel, my thoughts kept pace with my feet. I made plan after plan about what I should do when I returned to America a finished flyer. To think I was a real birdman at last! The dream of Darius Green* had come true for me! I simply could not grasp it. The five miles of road flew under my tires like so many city blocks as I dreamed of triumphs ahead."

"I wish you hadn't stopped your diary there," I said, handing him back the book. "Did you get your license right off?"

"The Aéro-Club of France gave me my 'brevet'—that's what they call a

---

* A popular poem of the previous century, "Darius Green and His Flying Machine," in which the protagonist builds a fanciful aircraft.

pilot's license—after my eighth flight." He slipped the diary back into his pocket and brought out the big book. "We'll be in in a couple of days and I haven't finished this yet."

As he sat there beside me, frowning intently as he read, he might have been miles away. I wondered what his life had been, where he had lived, whether he had brothers and sisters—even a wife, perhaps. No, not a wife, for no man with a wife could ever have been so engrossed in his work. Where was he going? What lay before him? Would he be a conqueror of the air or one of its many victims? Two days more and I might never hear of him again, except, perhaps, to see his name in the paper. Suddenly he closed his book with a bang.

"Let's go look at the stars," he suggested, rising abruptly.

"Like—Betty?"

He looked down with one of his slow smiles.

"Like ourselves."

The night was cold and clear, and the stars flashed down on us in friendly nearness. There they all were—Orion, lifting his starry club to meet the Bull that charged headlong toward oblivion in the western sky; blinding Sirius, the great dog star, and white Capella, "the little she-goat"—even the Twins were there, arm in arm as they'd been for centuries past, their feet in the Milky Way.

We stood for a long time watching the stars. He was strangely silent, even for him. I proposed a walk and he fell into step at my side. When he still said nothing I thought he must be tired and decided it was time to go below.

"You must think me an awful bore," he apologized, staring at me with troubled eyes, "but I'm in the dickens of a mood tonight."

I wanted to tell him that I didn't mind but felt he understood without my saying anything.

With that we said good night and I went down to my cabin. Hours later I awoke to hear solitary footsteps pacing the lonely deck, and I wondered if they could be his.

50

⇒•≺

How a Woman Learns to Fly

By Harriet Quimby, in *Leslie's Illustrated Weekly* (1911)

During its nascent days, aviation's glass ceiling stood around six feet off the ground. When one Blanche Scott approached Orville Wright for lessons, he told her that women were too nervous to fly. Yet in March 1910 Charles Voisin taught his lover Madame la Baronne de Laroche; the world's first female pilot received France's thirty-sixth pilot's certificate. Then in 1911 America's Harriet Quimby, a drama critic for *Leslie's Illustrated Weekly*, signed up for lessons at the Moisant School of Aviation on Long Island.

⇒•≺

Garden City, Long Island, May 15th, 1911. Americans are called an inquisitive race. I am satisfied that this is true. I am also satisfied that curiosity is not confined to the women. Here I am, a novice with a fortnight's experience in the Moisant School of Aviation, at Hempstead Plains, Long Island, and yet I have forty-seven letters, thirty of them from women, eagerly asking how to learn how to fly. Though my actual experience so far amounts to little more than what is known as "trimming the Daisies"—in reality, skimming over the grass on a wheeled machine, with occasional jumps of from ten to twenty-five feet into the air—I do feel qualified to tell a beginner how she must dress and what she must do if she expects to be a flyer.

If a woman wants to fly, first of all she must, of course, abandon skirts and don a knickerbocker uniform. I speak of this particularly, because so many have asked me about my flying costume. It may seem strange, but I could not find an aviation suit of any description in the great city of New York—and I tried hard. In my perplexity it occurred to me that the president of the American Tailors' Association, Alexander M. Grean, might be a good advisor; and he was, for it did not take him long to design a suit which has no doubt established the aviation costume for women in this country, if not for all the world, since the French women still continue to wear the clumsy and uncomfortable harem skirt as a flying costume. My suit is made of thick wool-back satin, without lining. It is all in one piece, including the hood. By an ingenious combination it can be converted in-

stantly into a conventional appearing walking skirt when not in use in
knickerbocker form.

The speed with which the aviator flies and the strong currents created
by the rapidly revolving propeller directly in front of the driver compel the
latter to be warmly clad. There must be no flapping ends to catch in the
multitudinous wires surrounding the driver's seat. The feet and legs must
be free, so that one can readily manipulate the steering apparatus; for the
steering on a monoplane is not done by a wheel guided by the hand as in
an automobile. One who has to run a motorcycle or an automobile successfully is all the better qualified to begin his lessons as an aviator. Without experience of this kind, the noise of an unmuffled motor in an airplane
will be nerve-racking.

The first lesson of the beginner in an airplane is intended to accustom
her to the noisy jarring vibration of the engine. Before the student climbs
into her seat, she will discover why it is well to cover her natty costume
with washable jumpers or overalls. Not only the chassis of the machine,
but all the fixtures are slippery with lubricating oil, and when the engine
is speeded a shower of this oil is also thrown back directly into the driver's
face. It is interesting to know that castor oil is used as a lubricant for high-
tensioned engines, like the Gnome.

The first instruction that my preceptor, Andre Houpert, gave me after
taking my seat in the monoplane was regarding the manipulation of the
switch, so that no injury would result to the mechanic who was cranking
the engine directly in front of me. The school machine I use is a Moisant
monoplane, fitted with a Gnome engine of thirty horse-power. Four sturdy
mechanics held on to the rudder until I had speeded the engine to the necessary velocity to start the aeroplane across the field. Under the impetus of
a rapidly revolving propeller, the machine swept ahead, sometimes on the
ground and, as the engine gained speed, sometimes a little above it. The
aviator's first lesson is to learn to steer his airship in a perfectly straight line
for a distance of a mile or over. This looks very easy, until you discover that
an aeroplane possesses the perversity common to all inanimate objects. It
always wants to go the other way, instead of the straight way that you seek
to direct. Your first dash across the field and back takes two minutes, if no
mishap occurs. After two dashes of this description, a discreet teacher will
dismiss you for the day. You have had all that your nerves ought to be asked
to stand. In the best schools of France—a land famous for its aviators—
no pupil, however apt, is permitted to have a longer daily lesson than five
minutes at the onset of his course; and Monsieur Houpert, who is a graduate of a leading French school of aviation, follows this plan. When we
read about Grahame-White or some other noted aviator learning to fly to
altitudinous heights after only three days' lessons, we must bear in mind
that these three days do not represent all the time required in training, but

simply the aggregate of hours devoted on many consecutive days to short lessons. Though I have been a student at the Moisant school for almost two weeks, my actual time in the monoplane would not exceed half an hour—yet I am already called a flyer!

After learning how to make a straight line on and off the ground, you are next taught how to manipulate the wings, so that when you leap off the ground you may preserve your balance in the air. Having accomplished so much, you are prepared for further instruction given in a course of lectures in connection with field practice, regarding emergencies requiring special knowledge. You are not yet prepared to make an application for a pilot's license, but are well on the way to reach your goal. Like learning to swim, the first requisite of one who would learn to fly is confidence and the knowledge that you can do it. The future mastery of the swimmer's art depends upon himself and how much time he can give to the recreation. The same may be said of the would be flyer.

Everyone asks me "how it feels to fly." It feels like riding in a high powered automobile, minus bumping over the rough roads, continually signaling to clear the way and keeping a watchful eye on the speedometer to see that you do not exceed the limit and provoke the wrath of the bicycle policeman or the covetous constable. Other questions that everybody asks are, "How much does it cost to learn to fly and what is the cost of an aeroplane?" The Moisant course of lessons requires a month and the price is $750. A monoplane of the best kind in this country costs from $6,000 to $7,000.

PART TWO
[AUGUST 17, 1911]

Four o'clock in the morning! The light is just dawning as the telephone at the Garden City Hotel summons me to rise. The birds are chirping. The air is heavy with the odor of the fields, the trees and the flowers. It is the time when nature seems to be at rest, and is, therefore, especially adapted for a lesson in flying. This is the reason why the students at the Moisant Aviation School must submit to the penalty of an early contemplation of nature, whether they appreciate it or not.

The student of aviation must be the earliest riser of all students in search of knowledge, for all the lessons can be given only while the air is still and while the little signal flag on the field clings close to its mast. Dressing in a hurry and waiting for a moment to enjoy the healthful precaution of a cup of hot coffee poured from a faithful vacuum bottle, the student is soon on the way across the field to the hangers, where the aeroplanes, with expanding white wings, are silently awaiting their flights. The activity of instructors and students here is in striking contrast with the quiet of the sleepy hotel just left. Even the little white dog with a black spot on his forehead, the much petted mascot of the school, is alert and seems thoroughly interested in the goings on. An anxious look is directed from time to time to a little red flag on the end of a tall bamboo pole, placed in the middle of the aviation field, and there is considerable misgiving as the light piece of bunting flutters from its mast. Each one hazards a guess as to the possibility of a flying lesson. All hope that the wind is not too strong or too puffy, but all fear that it may be, for this is not an unusual experience. Professor Houpert, the instructor, settles that matter by walking out into the open with an anemometer and measuring the velocity of the breeze, which he may report as blowing four or five miles an hour. If it is over this, the school is called off for the day, for a student of aviation who ventures into anything more than a six-mile wind, especially with a low-powered school machine, is almost certain to come to grief. This little measuring instrument resembles a small windmill, with cups instead of blades, and the strength of the breeze is measured by the rapidity with which the cups revolve.

If Professor Houpert's verdict is favorable, there is a general scurrying toward the dressing rooms, where the students cover their natty aviation costumes with homely, one-piece mechanic suits, calculated to withstand any kind of wear and tear as well as oil. Each student picks up a chair and drags it from the hanger to the field, so as to rest comfortably until his or her turn comes to take a lesson. The beginner takes his first lesson in grass cutting. This means that he mounts the machine, the motor is started and he attempts to guide it as it moves swiftly on its wheels over the long stretch of grass to the far end of the aerodrome. Here a mechanic is posted to await the student's arrival, turn his machine around and start him back again over the course. He is, indeed, a promising student if he has made anything like a straight line in his grass cutting. If he succeeds in doing this five or six times without mishap, he is permitted to take short jumps of two or three feet in height in the air as he rushes across the field. An irreverent newspaper man termed this feat kangarooing, which name seems to fit the performance pretty well. It is at the kangarooing stage that the fascination of flying begins.

There is no exaggeration regarding the much reported sense of fascination which accompanies a flight, however low, through the air. The feel of the first freedom experienced as the wheels leave the ground makes the student eager for a longer flight. It is not surprising that sometimes a fledgling will forget what the instructor says and elevate his planes, which, of course, like a flash, shoots the machine higher into the air. Finding himself much higher than he expected to go, he is more apt to seek a sudden descent, involving both a breakage and humiliation.

As the seniors enjoy the discomfitures of a freshman at college, so do the senior students of aviation enjoy the antics of the grass cutter. The length of time that the would-be aviator remains in the kindergarten class depends largely upon himself. It is no disgrace to spend weeks at the early stage of instruction, for some of the world's best flyers have been the slowest to learn. Nor should it be forgotten that the lessons, depending on weather conditions, must necessarily be irregular. Learning to fly is like learning anything else. It requires patience and stick-to-itiveness to master the art. It requires these qualities, also, to learn to drive an automobile, but it does not follow that one who can run an automobile can drive a flying machine, for there is no similarity in the control of the two. But one who has easily learned how to drive an automobile and to pilot it with a clear head through congested traffic will undoubtedly find his experience an aid in learning to fly. I state this as the result of my own experience.

It is, indeed, a time for rejoicing in the school when Professor Houpert informs the student that he has graduated from the rather clumsy kindergarten machine and is to take his first flight in a lighter and more powerful machine fitted with a sensitive control. This means that he is really going to fly. The humor of the aviation school differs from any other. The students are invariably a light-hearted and a jolly crowd, seeing and enjoying the funny sides of things. A great deal of good natured banter is exchanged between those who return from a flight and the students who have watched them. Although one young fledgling reached a height of only ten feet or so and that only one fraction of a minute, he returned with an exciting tale of having fallen into an air hole and a laughable explanation of how he dexterously straightened his machine and returned to earth with safety. Another created a roar of laughter, when he returned from a kangerooing trip, by his account of being attacked by a vicious sparrow on the way. M. Vedrine, who crossed the Alps and startled the world by reporting that in transit he had been attacked by an enormous eagle, has nothing on the students of the Moisant school.

The fascination of flying is not confined to students. Despite the early hour in which the lessons are given, spectators hover about the field, wandering over from Garden City or Mineola. Not infrequently an automobile party appears on the scene, and I have observed that the most interested are always the ladies accompanying these parties, and they are usually in majority.

It was a happy day for me when Professor Houpert told me that my grasscutting days were over and that I was ready for a flight in the air. It was the day I had longed for with an expectancy that I cannot describe, the fascination of flying had such a hold upon me. Every student tells me that he has the same feeling, except those who have had a mishap which has tested their nerve too much. A flying student cannot expect to go through the course of instruction without some breakage, for the most skillful of flyers have their bad moments. It must be remembered that the flying machine must be in perfect working order and that one false move of the student invites disaster. It may be only a broken fork or wheel or perhaps a chip off the propeller, but it is enough to disable the machine and put it out of commission until repairs have been thoroughly made. It is a remarkable fact that thus far the records show that only one beginner has had a fatal casualty. I refer to the case of Mlle. Moore, a student of a bi-plane school in France, a few weeks ago.

The second machine in which I was to take my first flight in the air differed in essentials from the first one, known as the grass cutter. The latter is equipped with three wheels, so that it can roll over the ground smoothly, while the former has two wheels in front and a skid instead of a wheel behind. The student must, therefore, rise above the ground promptly or run the risk of injuring the dragging skid. The chassis of the flyer is lighter than that of the grass cutter and the power of the former is considerably increased. The student who takes his first real flight is instructed to fly straight across the field and to alight near where a mechanic stands waiting to turn him around for his return trip. His first lesson as a freshman is intended to teach him to manage his machine while running over the ground. His first lesson as a graduate is to learn how to cut his pathway through the air. While grass cutting, the freshman learns how to steer. While air cutting, the graduate must not only steer, but he must learn the more difficult task of warping his wings and of manipulating his elevating and lowering planes. The warping is done by a wheel resembling the steering wheel of an automobile and which rests directly in front of the pilot. This wheel, by a movement back and forth, elevates or lowers the plane. After one successful straight-away flight, I was instructed by my pleased instructor to fly across the field and to turn around and come back without alighting at the other end. The fundamental requirements of a good student are that he shall be able to make a good ascent and a safe landing. These are the most difficult accomplishments of a flyer. When he has mastered them he has learned his lesson pretty well. After learning to make a circuit of the aerodrome, the student is asked to do what is considered difficult—a right-hand turn. After having done this without mishap, he is then capable of attempting to make a flight in the form of a figure eight, which is the essential requirement before he can secure the much coveted pilot's license from the Aero Club of America. I have frequently been asked how I felt when I first really went up into the air to a height of one hundred feet, which at the present writing is my personal record altitude but I must reserve this recital for a subsequent article.

PART THREE
[AUGUST 24, 1911]

The thrill of pleasure with which the eager and anxious university student after years of patient endeavor secures his diploma has been mine. It takes four years of study to win a college diploma. It takes a much shorter time, if you have a competent instructor and if fate deals kindly with you, to secure your license to pilot an aeroplane. The question has been so often asked me since I have been honored by receiving the first pilot's license granted to a woman in the United States—"How long did it take you to fly?"—that I feel that I must answer this and perhaps some other questions to which I have referred in preceding articles. I took my first lesson in flying at the Moisant Aviation School at Hempstead Plains, Long Island, May 10th. I qualified for my pilot's license by passing the required tests of the Aero Club of America, representing the federation of aero clubs of the world, on the morning of Tuesday, August 1st. This does not mean, however, that I spent all this time learning to fly. My lessons altogether aggregated only thirty-three and the actual time spent on each lesson was from two to five minutes. This is the stipulated time allocated to students at each lesson in all the leading schools of aviation in France. That my course of instruction covered as many weeks as it did was really due to adverse weather conditions, for there are many days when the winds prevent even the most experienced aviators from venturing out. The gratifying evidence of my success was contained in the following letter which, it is needless to add, I prize most highly:

AERO CLUB OF AMERICA
297 Madison Avenue
New York

August 2d, 1911
Miss Harriet Quimby
225 Fifth Ave.
New York City
Madam:

We take pleasure in informing you that at a meeting of the Executive Committee held this afternoon, you were granted an Aviation pilot's license of the Aero Club of America. The book is all made up and lacks only the signature of our acting president, which will be obtained to-morrow morning.

We find that the only other Aviation pilot's license granted to a woman under the 1911 rules is that of Mme. Draincourt, of France, who passed the tests on a Caudron biplane.

Should no mail advices to the contrary reach us within the next few days from Europe you can accordingly consider yourself the only woman to have qualified under the 1911 rules on a monoplane.

Regarding the landing made by you at the close of your first distance test on August 1st, we would say that accurate landing is not a record internationally recognized, so that we do not know how this performance compares with the best made in Europe. We can state, however, that, at this date, it is the most accurate landing ever made in America on a monoplane under official supervision.

The American record for accurate landing is 1 foot 5-1/2 inches by Mr. Sopwith on his biplane; we do not officially make any distinction between types of aeroplanes in this record; we can not see, however, how there can be any objection to your landing being referred to as an "American record for monoplanes" at this date, as this is what it is in fact.

> Yours Sincerely,
> G. F. Campbell-Wood
> Secretary

The following day my pilot's license was forwarded to me. It was neatly bound in leather and looked very much like a gentleman's pocketbook. It reads as follows:

> Federation Aeronautique Internationale, Aero Club of America.
>
> The above-named club, recognized by the Federation Aeronautique International as a governing authority of the United States of America, certifies that Harriet Quimby, having fulfilled all the conditions required by the Federation Aeronautique Internationale, is hereby licensed as an aviator.

This paragraph written in French, German, Russian, Italian and Spanish, appears on the opposite side:

> The civil, naval and military authorities, including the police, are respectfully requested to aid and assist the holder of this certificate.

And now as to the tests which were required to obtain the much coveted pilot's license. I found that I was obliged to comply with the new regulations adopted by the International Aeronautical Federation at its meeting, October 28th, 1910. A license can be granted only by an organization governing aviation in its own country and represented in the international federation. In the United States the Aero Club of America is entitled to this distinction. The applicant for a license must be at least eighteen years of age and must pass three tests, namely—two distance tests, consisting of covering without touching the ground a close circuit not less than five kilometers (3.107 miles) in length, the course to be indicated by two posts not more than five hundred meters (about 1,640 feet) from each other, and the aviator to change his direction at each post, so as to make an uninterrupted series of figure eights. Applicants are required to make an altitude flight to a minimum height of fifty meters (about 164 feet) above the starting point. He is also required as a further test in landing to stop his motor not later than the time when the machine touches the ground and to stop his aeroplane at a distance of one hundred and sixty-five feet from the point designated before the flight. The landings are an important consideration, for unless they are properly made the issue of a license is discretionary. Accompanying my pilot's license were three printed reports, carefully filled out and duly signed, testifying to all the recorded details of the trial flights and landings.

Interest centers naturally about the trial flights and how they are made. Quite unexpectedly on the afternoon of July 31st, while attending my class on the aviation grounds, I was told by my instructor that I must be prepared early the next morning to try for my pilot's license. It was the goal coveted by every student in the school and I was therefore not a little elated to hear that at last my turn had come to make the attempt. It was to be at five o'clock in the morning. At eight-thirty in the evening I was off to slumberland. I confess that sleep was disturbed by many visions. Much to my disappointment, by telephone in the morning, which was to have awakened me for the trial flights, came this message from my instructor. "The fog is thick enough to cut with a knife. Don't come over until I send my motor car for you and your party as the field is clear." Meanwhile, Mr. G. F. Campbell-Wood and Baron D'Orcy, representing the Aero Club, who had come to Garden City to supervise the test, appeared in the lobby at the hotel as agreed upon the evening before, and, incidentally, it must be said that it is an evidence of the true sportsman's spirit for gentlemen like these so cheerfully to give their time at any hour to supervise the tests of the Aero Club. It must be remembered that sometimes, on account of unfavorable weather conditions, the officials chosen for these occasions must wait patiently for hours and even for days until they can complete their work. So it is plain that it must be in some degree a labor of love. In spite of M. Houpert's message our eagerness to begin the work at hand ruled the hour. So we climbed into the surry, thoughtfully provided the evening before by the club officials, and driving through the thickest kind of unheavenly mist we groped our way in the dim morning light to the aviation field. The fog seemed to grow thicker every step we took and when we reached the hanger we could scarcely distinguish objects fifty feet across the way. As for the field itself, it was not in sight. It was absolutely blanketed in fog. I turned appealing eyes toward my instructor. He shook his head and in his customary laconic style remarked, "We must wait." And we waited and waited and waited, with how much patience I need not recite. There was gloom without gloom within the hanger. But we were cheered by the hopeful voice of the chief mechanician prophesying that in half an hour the sun would surely assert itself and clear the field. And it did. *Through fleecy clouds and seas of azure blue, Oh, shining sun, thy light shines always true.*

At six-thirty the field was clear and our monoplane was rolled out. The field already had been laid out with two posts set apart at the required distance from each other. The flying machine was rolled to the left of one of the posts so as to give sufficient room to make the ascent and the turning around the first post and to complete it around the second post at the far end of the field and return, making altogether a figure eight. At the first post stood Mr. Wood and at the second Baron D'Orcy. A red flag indicated the positions. The officials were there to see that the circles were made outside and inside the posts as required. In the center of the field a spot indicated by white canvas several feet in diameter was chosen as the landing place. The tests require that the monoplane shall stop within the radius of one hundred and sixty-five feet from the spot. When all was in readiness I was helped into my seat and was eager for the start. I knew that the sooner it was begun, the quicker it would be over. It only remained for the chief mechanic to turn the propeller and thus crank the engine. Now came the last word from my patient and thoughtful instructor, M. Houpert. He explained to me that he would stand not far from the first post and if I lost count while making the five eights in the air, he would signal me on the completion of the final one and I would know it was time to land. The signal was to be the waving of his handkerchief. A moment after the propeller began its revolutions of fourteen hundred and fifty a minute, my machine rolled speedily along the ground for fifty feet or so, then responded promptly to the elevating plane and rose quickly to the air.

In less time than it has taken to write it I was sixty or seventy feet up and circling the second post at the far end of the field. Glancing down I caught a glimpse of the waving hand of Baron D'Orcy, who was watching the flight from his post. Reaching the middle of the field on my return trip I could easily distinguish my instructor, whose signal I was to await. Further on I could see the little group of friends and students of the school, seated about or standing, all with upturned eager faces. Their voices could not reach me, but their waving signal evidenced their interest. Round and round I went, the faithful little engine sending out its steady whirr, which always delights the heart of a pilot. What did I think of? I thought more of my engine than anything else, for if it failed me I would be obligated to pitch my machine and glide down, a feat I had never attempted. If it continued to hit on every cylinder it meant the speedy accomplishment of my purpose. What did I see? I saw Captain Baldwin's hangers at the end of the field, I saw the cluster of our own hangers at the west, the domes of Garden City in the background, a glimpse of the ocean at the south and

Long Island Sound on the north. One who has not made an ascension can scarcely comprehend the clearness with which objects beneath the aviator can be discerned. The ruts in the road, a dog running across the road, the tops of chimneys and almost every blade of grass are plainly pictured below. I am not surprised at the recent statement that the aeroplane can make the submarine easily distinguishable in any harbor and that it will, therefore, seriously interfere with the usefulness of the latter as a weapon of war. How did I feel? I felt like a bird cleaving the air with my outstretched wings. There was no thought of obstruction or obstacle. There was no fear of falling because the mastery of a well-balanced machine seems complete.

It may not seem credible, yet the easiest thing that a flyer can do is to fly in an unbroken circle to the left. It is like the use of the right hand because it seems to be the natural direction to go. To make the turn to the right is much like endeavoring to use the left hand by a right-handed person. Hence the severest part of the Aero Club's test is that which requires an applicant for a license to make not only the turn to the left, but also to completely reverse it and make the turn to the right. Furthermore, this must not be done one or two times, but ten times, five of them consecutively in two successive trials.

It was six-forty-two in the morning, according to the official record, when the first trial flight began, covering a distance estimated at about twelve miles, and the flight ended at six-fifty-one. I kept no track of the number of eights I made, but I depended upon Professors Houpert's signal when the five had been completed. I spoke of the difficulty of making the turn to the right and the left turn being comparatively easy, but I did not add that the guidance of a machine to either left or right is not difficult to one who has learned his lesson. The circle can be made without banking, which means balancing the machine to cut the corners short, just as running around a corner one would shift from the perpendicular, and a great many in making their turns keep the machine at a comparative level by taking the turn wider. But the more confidence the aviator gains in himself and his machine, the more he is going to bank his corners.

Was I happy when I saw the signal of Professor Houpert, indicating that I had safely gone through the first half of the test? Honestly, I was. Not because I was tired, for driving a monoplane takes little physical strength. Not because I was timid, for I had been too intent on my work for that, but because I felt that my task was half accomplished, and in my frame of mind it seemed to me that half done was all done. I have been fortunate in all of my landings at my school lessons and this test, so dreaded by many, gave me little apprehension. Approaching the point designated before my flight as the place where I should descend, I lowered my planes and made a sharp descent from an altitude of seventy-five feet, then straightened my machine and skimmed the surface of the ground, cutting off the engine just before I reached the ground, then rolled across the grass toward the canvas patch. Before I could leave my seat, my instructor, the Aero Club representatives, Captain Baldwin and my classmates and friends were heaping their congratulations upon me. I was not as presentable as I might have wished, for my face was completely covered with castor lubricating oil, which had been used freely on the engine.

Waiting for a few moments for the engine to cool, I started on the second flight at seven-twenty-two and again completed the five eights and landed at seven-thirty-one. My altitude was the third and final test. Again my faithful monoplane was put into service. The flight began at seven-forty-five and ended six minutes later, and then I was once more on earth to receive the welcome greeting of friends whose encouraging words had made my success doubly pleasant. I hope no one will accuse me of being conceited or even proud when I say in conclusion that the honor I sought and prize most highly is that of having secured the first pilot's license ever granted to a woman in America.

13. With the propeller of Harriet Quimby's Blériot XI turning over, the famed aviatrix receives last-minute instruction in compass navigation while mechanics and observers help brace her brakeless flying machine. Note the flotation bag in the open fuselage.

51

Canvas, Steel, and Wire

Quote by Cal Rodgers

After the great publicity generated by the Albany-to-New York flight, William Randolph Hearst put up a $50,000 prize for the first pilot to fly across the United States, provided he did so in under thirty days. Among those willing to try was Cal Rodgers, who flew the *Vin Fiz Flyer,* a special Wright airplane sponsored by a grape drink manufacturer. But with the thirty-day deadline running out and Rodgers only as far as Chicago, a reporter for the *Chicago Record Herald* asked if he would continue.

"I am bound for Los Angeles and the Pacific Ocean. Prize or no prize that's where I am bound and if canvas, steel, and wire together with a little brawn, tendon, and brain stick with me I mean to get there. The $50,000 prize however, seems to be practically out of the question. The conditions state that I must be there by Oct. 10 . . . I'm going to do this whether I get $50,000 or 50 cents or nothing. I am going to cross this continent simply to be the first to cross in an aeroplane."

Though it took him forty-nine days, sixty-nine stops, and five major crashes, on November 5, 1911, Rodgers finally reached California. Only two wing struts and the rudder remained of the original machine that left Brooklyn that September. No first-person account of the trip survives; Rodgers died in a plane crash less than five months later.

14. September 17, 1911: Cal Rodgers departs Sheepshead Bay, Brooklyn,
on the first flight across the contiguous United States.

52

➤➤◦◄━━

The Sensation of Flying

By Claude Grahame-White

The big question from the groundbound was, "What is it like?" Pilot Claude Grahame-White provides some impressions in his 1911 book, The Story of the Aeroplane.

➤➤◦◄━━

A great many people have flown, and yet very few of them have given anything like a good explanation of what the sensations of flying really amount to. The explanation of this is fairly simple. It is extremely difficult for anybody to say exactly what he felt like when in the air.

The sensations are complex. The speed is great. Impressions come into one's mind at a very great rate. The result is that, when a man is back on the ground again, he is generally only able to gasp, and to wonder himself really what it all was like.

Naturally, when he is in a frame of mind like this, a man can scarcely be expected to give a very clear and a very lucid description of what it feels like to fly. More than one person, I am sure, has made a painstaking effort to analyze his sensations.

The result, however, has never been particularly happy. I myself have been interviewed times without number as to my sensations in performing some particular flight. I am afraid, from the interviewer's point of view, my replies have never been particularly satisfactory. There is, as a matter of fact, a great deal of humor in this desire of people who remain on the ground to hear from others exactly what it is like in the air.

I remember, on some of the early occasions when flying, judged purely from the point of view of flying, was a far greater novelty than it is now, having seen incidents that amused me very much.

At one aviation meeting, a rather celebrated person was taken up for a flight. After making two or three circuits of the aerodrome, he was brought safely back to earth again. Immediately, half a dozen reporters, scenting a good "story," thronged round him, and began to question him closely as to his impressions.

He gasped a little, tried to straighten himself out and exclaim, "It was great." This observation, although very expressive, was scarcely ample enough to suit the men who had hoped to write half a column at least as to the views of this particular individual. So they waited a little, patiently, and then tried again. Evidently they hoped that the confusion of his rush through the air would pass away, and that the famous personage would, after all, say a few things that would be really noteworthy.

But his second declaration was scarcely more informing than his first. It was: "It's absolutely ripping." And although the newspaper men, true to their reputation for painstaking, did not desert him for some time, they practically failed altogether to get anything of a descriptive nature from the famous personage as to the sensations of flight.

The whole business amused me more than a little. The person in question was very well known, and particularly well known for his fluency of speech. It was, therefore, a striking illustration to me of a fact that I had realized before.

The first time a man flies the sensation is almost more than he can realize or express. The sensation, so to speak, sweeps his mind clear. He comes back to earth with nothing more than a sense of largeness and a good deal of awe. I mean, in the explanation given below, to convey in quite a matter-of-fact way really what happens when you start out on a flight in an aeroplane.

The first thing that one does is to take one's seat in the driver's position. In a biplane, the type of machine which I shall describe, one's accommodation is a small wooden seat. Some pilots, with a view to comfort, place a cushion on it. Others whom I have known, when undertaking a long cross-country flight, have removed the small wooden seat fitted by the makers, and have substituted a comfortable wicker-work arm-chair. But such luxuries are only thought of, as a rule, by the very old hands.

In a biplane the pilot's seat is located in the center of the front of the lower main plane. To your right hand, as you sit, there is a lever. It is in the form of an upright metal rod, which moves on a universal joint. Wires lead away from it, by which you control the various planes of the machine. For instance, fixed out in front of you, on long wooden rods, is the elevating plane.

This is so made that it will tilt up and down, acting in unison with a small plane, having a similar motion, which is attached to the tail of the machine. This tail, in the form of two small planes, fixed one above another, is thrown out on wooden outriggers at the back of the main planes.

The rod, by a simple movement forward and backwards, actuates these elevating planes, as they are called. The rod has another function also. It moves from side to side, and in so doing operates what are known as the "ailerons." These are small planes hinged to the rear edges of the main planes.

Their work is very interesting. As the aeroplane passes along through the air it is being struck all the time by wind gusts. Some of them hit the planes more on one side than another. The result is that the machine heels over a little sideways.

This is where the ailerons come into action. What the pilot does when he sees his machine beginning to drop on one side is to move his controlling lever slightly in the opposite direction to that upon which the aeroplane is falling. This action draws a wire, and lowers the ailerons—there are two of them—on the edges of the plane which is depressed. These ailerons, when tilted down, have the effect of raising the side of the machine which is heeling over.

With this simple control, the lateral stability of the machine is effected. There is one other controlling function which the pilot has to remember. As he sits in his driving seat he places his feet on a cross-bar, which is so made that it will move to and fro on a central pivot. From this cross-bar, on either side, run wires. These are carried right back to the tail of the machine, where they actuate a rudder which is exactly like that of a ship.

When the pilot wants to turn to the left, he pushes his foot forward on that side. The rudder comes round, and the aeroplane, obedient to its helm, moves round in the desired direction. Behind the pilot, as he sits perched in his seat, with the controlling lever in his right hand, and his feet on the rudder bar, are the engine and the propeller. Below him as he looks down are the skids and running wheels which carry the aeroplane along the ground when it is starting on or returning from a flight.

The preliminary to a flight is the starting up of the engine. This is effected by one of the mechanics swinging the propeller until the engine gets to work.

To men who fly for the first time the noise of an engine is bewildering. No silencer is fitted. The result is that the engine, when accelerated ready for flight, makes a quite stupendous roar. The method, just before starting, is for the pilot to accelerate his engine and for a number of men to hold back the aeroplane.

This holding-back movement is necessary because when the engine is going "All out" the machine has a very strong tendency to move swiftly forward across the ground.

After he has accelerated, the pilot sits in his seat for a moment or so listening to his engine. If it is running without a miss, and everything seems all right, he lifts up his hand as a signal to the men to release their hold of the machine.

As they do so, it moves forward across the ground. At first its progress is slow, but it soon gathers speed, and when a pace of about thirty miles an hour is gained, the pilot knows that the moment has come to tilt up his elevator and take the air.

Nothing is more graceful than the way in which an aeroplane leaves the ground. It does so without any suggestion of effort. All one sees, in watching it, is that the wheels, which a moment before were on the ground, are now passing along a foot in the air.

On this point, it is curious to remember the experience of passengers, when starting upon a flight. So imperceptible is the change from moving along the ground to rising in the air that very few of them ever know when they have actually begun a flight. What happens is that they suddenly look down and discover that the ground has begun to fall away below them.

When you want to rise, you know perfectly well what to do. You tilt your elevator to a little more acute angle and the machine responds at once. Afterwards, well, as one flyer puts it, "You just fly." As you pass along through the air you very soon begin to lose the feeling that your engine is making a very great noise.

You find yourself glancing below. When you are flying fairly close to the ground the fields and country appear to be slipping away very fast. But as you ascend higher you lose this sense of speed. As a matter of fact, at a good height, you seem to be moving quite slowly.

As to the fascination of flight, what is it? I have studied it carefully, and have compared my own sensations with those of others. One of the best definitions you can find of the general feeling a man has when he is flying is that it is a great, curious sense of power.

This may not seem a very satisfactory explanation to the reader, but it is one of the best I can give. I think that, in the back of one's mind when one is flying, is the realization that one is doing something that man has striven in vain to do for many centuries.

It is partly a feeling of conquest. And now you can imagine yourself climbing steadily upwards, with the ground fading away below. There is no finer sensation than this, I imagine. One of the most striking things in connection with flying is the responsiveness of one's machine to every controlling movement. While one is flying it is necessary to be making minor adjustments all the time. With one's rudder bar, for instance, one is always more or less occupied. The movements are, to some extent, instinctive. They are the sort of movements that a bicyclist makes to preserve the balance of his machine. All the time, while you are flying, your machine is being struck by little inequalities of air, and is showing a tendency either to move up or down or from side to side.

Therefore, the movements one makes are very small ones to correct this tendency. One's feet move just a little to and fro upon the rudder-bar. This little "joggling" of the rudder is sufficient to keep the machine on a straight course. As regards the elevator, one is moving the rod in one's hand a matter of an inch or so only, and the same applies to the movements one makes in manipulating the ailerons.

A good deal of misconception exists as to the fatigue involved in making an aeroplane flight. Personally, I have found that fatigue is a negligible quantity, save when one is flying in gusty winds. Then, of course, the constant corrective movements that one is bound to make, and the strain of keeping so incessant a control of one's machine, is apt to have a very fatiguing effect.

But when one is flying under favorable conditions, I do not see that there is any strain at all. Of course, in the earlier days of flying, when engines were not so reliable, there was a certain strain upon a pilot, when flying across country, because he had a feeling in his mind that his engine might stop at any moment.

And the first pilots suffered from strain, no doubt, to a certain extent, because of their unfamiliarity with the air. Now, however, the strain in this respect is becoming less and less. Engines, too, are becoming more reliable. Men understand far better what to do when they are in the air. As a matter of fact, I think there is less actual strain in piloting an aeroplane across country than there is in driving a high-powered car from point to point along the road. Of course, as I have said before, the weather conditions are all important. Sometimes, when flying, pilots suffer from cold. This is notably the case in winter flying.

In high flying, also, more than one airman has returned to earth with his hands completely numbed by the cold.

On a fine summer's day, however, flying is a magnificent experience. Personally I have not experienced any more really exhilarating sensation than one can find in flying under ideal conditions.

There is exhilaration, of course, in driving a well-found car on a good road, but this is a poor thing when piloting an aeroplane is compared with it.

To be in the air! To feel your motor speeding you on! To hold the lever and feel the machine while in flight answer to your slightest move! To look below and see the country unfolding itself to your gaze, and to know that you and you alone are the master of the situation—the man who is doing this wonderful thing! Realization of all these points gives you something of a feeling of awe.

Turning to another phase of flying, I am convinced that a judicious participation in aeroplaning provides a man with a very fine mental tonic. To begin with, he must always be ready for any emergency. I hear people very often talking about "Brain Fag." Business men, too, complain very often that they want a change and need "bucking up." I already foresee that, in the future, flying will come to be regarded as one of the greatest health-givers. It will not be long, in my opinion, before doctors tell ailing men to go in for a course of aviation.

Naturally, before this result is attained, the machine will have to become much more perfect. That there are a number of very health-giving properties in flying, I do not think can be denied.

More than one man in indifferent health who has taken it up has, to my knowledge, improved quite remarkably in his physique. Of course, in its present stage, flying requires much more concentration and ability than will be the case in a few years' time. Its development as an amusement is only dependent on the perfection of mechanical details.

53

———✧———

Why I Looped the Loop

By A. Pégoud

Blériot test pilot Adolphe Pégoud saw a pilot parachute from a stricken machine, then observed the plane undergo some beautiful evolutions on its own before it crashed. He decided that if an aircraft could perform such maneuvers empty, it would do them under a pilot's control as well. Thus, he invented aerobatics. The following is his rationale for his approach to aviation, published in the October 1913 issue of the old *Flying* magazine.

———✧———

When, some years ago, during my rambles in Morocco I read of the then wonderful flights of my elders, the first pupils of the pioneers, there came to me a desire to fly, which, in time, developed into a vocation. To qualify for this vocation it required courage, cold blood, skill, mastery of oneself, a certain amount of disregard for one's life . . . yes, all that . . . . Was I adapted for it? Often times I asked myself that, and I confessed to myself that I believed I had all these qualities.

My experience at the Camp of Satory, where I had the honor of learning the ABC of aviation from the lips of Captain Carlin, decided my future. I felt an imperative desire to do big things, great things, to accomplish feats of utility, to do something to advance aviation or develop greater progress.

Dream of youth, may be . . . . As soon as I was in possession of a Blériot monoplane I defined what I could do to accomplish something worth while. Before long I became what they call an acrobat of the air. I had had experiences for five years as cavalier on land, that made the task of becoming a cavalier of the air really easy.

At this time my dream began to become a reality. To prove that a naval aeroplane does not need floats to be a part of a battleship Mr. Blériot proposed that I would demonstrate how the aeroplane could be hooked to a cable by means of his landing and receiving apparatus. I made this demonstration before the Minister of the Navy.

Then it seemed to me that with my aeroplane I could do almost anything, and, having the assurance of self-mastery and physical strength, I asked Mr. Blériot to allow me to loop the loop in the air, to demonstrate how the aeroplane that I was flying could fly upside down and regain its normal position by a simple exercise of control. In accordance to what I consider my vocation, I wanted to demonstrate to pilots that it is possible to fly with the aeroplane turned upside down; that no matter what happens, the aeroplane does not necessarily have to drop; no matter what position the aeroplane assumes it does not constitute danger; that, given mastery of oneself, a simple maneuver will make the aeroplane reassume its normal position.

Mr. Blériot had confidence in me. After hesitation, which I understood quite well, he made me an aeroplane of the ordinary army type with reinforced trussing.

Meantime, I had the pleasure of demonstrating the Bonnet parachute, letting the aeroplane drop to earth while I was borne down by the parachute, showing the apparatus is as practical as I had thought. Following this demonstration I had the pleasure to fly upside down, and everything came out as I had expected it would and I had told Mr. Blériot.

These experiments are not ended. I want to be able to say to aviators, "You can upset, you can drop perpendicular, you can turn sidewise, you can slide on your wings or on your tail . . . all that is of little importance; your apparatus does not need to lose control—you can make it reassume its normal position by a simple maneuver."

I further want to be able to say: "Even if your life is entirely in danger, here you can have a life saving device, the parachute, with which you can save yourself, letting your aeroplane drop down. You can come to earth without hurt, the parachute breaking your fall."

I shall, maybe, have the satisfaction of having many tell me, as several officer aviators have said to me: "My dear Pégoud, now I don't fear anything."

If my demonstrations show—and I am certain they will—that the security in aeroplanes is a fact, I shall be satisfied. It will seem to me that I will have worked for the good of aviation and for national defense.

54

———⇒•◇•⇐———

Johannisthal Days

By Anthony Fokker (with Bruce Gould), in *Flying Dutchman* (1931)

Holland's first indigenous pilot was Anthony Fokker, the son of a wealthy plantation owner who had built his own monoplane from steel tubing and canvas. The company he envisioned then with schoolmate Fritz Cremer would design and produce some of the most devastating aircraft for Germany in World War I, but at the stunting pilots' hangar in Johannisthal Fokker was just another daring young aviator out to make a name for himself.

———⇒•◇•⇐———

When I came to Johannisthal I changed overnight from being a big frog in a small pool to a very little one in a big pool. Up to that time I hadn't realized what a country boy I was. Not that Berlin overwhelmed me. My innate conceit was too strong for that. But I saw that I still had a long way to go to make my mark in the world. At the first glimpse of my unusual looking airplane a general horse laugh was raised. Older and more experienced pilots, whose reputations were international, regarded my low-wing, aileronless monoplane as a joke. No one around spoke a good word for it. Angered by their jeering, I still didn't want to betray my feelings by blurting out my opinions of them and their planes.

Johannisthal was a thriving little cosmopolis. Aviation was a sport which had attracted daring spirits, ne'er-do-wells, and adventurers from all over the world. There were sober, industrious pilots and designers present, too, but they were in the minority. Many of the amateur pilots were rich men's sons, who found this spot a fertile ground for the sowing of wild oats. Dazzled by the dare-deviltry of these men, beautiful women from the theatre and night clubs hung around the flying field, more than a little complaisant, alluring—unstinting of favors to their current heroes.

Excitement out of the air centered in the gay, sportive little café, run by Papa Senftleben, attached to the field, where wine, women and song were permanently on the menu. My drink, "Kaffee Fokker," became famous, because it was so different, a tall beaker of warm milk with an inch of coffee. Pilots and their favorite girls spent most of the midday there, for actual flying lasted only an hour or two after sunrise and before sunset after the wind had died down. It was a hard, dangerous life, but a dashing and reckless one, attractive to youngsters barely out of their teens. There was something of a storybook quality about that heady mixture of brave men and fair women. At night, hastily organized parties raced into Berlin for a tour of all the gay spots. They drank to "a quick life but a snappy one; a short life but a happy one." Frequently, these all-night affairs wound up at dawn with the bleary bravado of a half-drunken flight. The primrose path in the air sometimes ended in a screaming wreck. Everyone then had another drink, quick. But it was soon forgotten.

Of the crack pilots on the field when I reached Johannisthal, a husky German Jew, Willy Rosenstein, was the ace. His name was on everyone's lips; his picture everywhere. Flying a Rumpler Taube, one of the most successful of the early German airplanes, with his breath-taking banks, twenty to thirty degrees steep, he never failed to thrill the crowd. A favorite in the air and in Senftleben's café, he was cocky and king. Whatever he said about another pilot or his plane was reverently noted. That was everyone's opinion thereafter.

Striding into our hangar two or three days after we had arrived, he took one withering look at my funny plane where I had set it up, and laughed. It was as good a way to kill yourself as any, he commented, and walked away. The hangers-on trooped out after him, laughing, leaving me wanting to throw a wrench at his thick head. I was automatically expected to crash on my first flight.

There was no friend to tell me how gawky and countrified I looked at the time. Just turned twenty-two, I probably appeared as hopeless as my plane to all those smartly dressed people. I had never given a thought to clothes. All my spare time during the day, while the other pilots were sleeping or in the casino carousing, I spent working on my present airplane, or drawing up plans for a new type. If possible, I caught a nap after lunch; if not, I went without. Those who remember me in Johannisthal admit that I was anything but prepossessing; that I was usually grimy and tousle-haired, with my nose invariably in a cylinder head and my face and hands smeared with oil. When I flew I wore ordinary workclothes or overalls. The other pilots dressed in dashing flying suits, and carried helmets and goggles with conspicuous carelessness. I wouldn't have known how to speak to any of the beautiful girls hanging around even if one of them had spoken to me, but none did. I didn't even realize that I was supposed to be missing anything.

No matter how much I disliked Rosenstein for belittling my plane, I didn't want to underestimate his skill. I was out at dawn to watch him the first flying day. He could fly. Handling his Rumpler with practiced ease, he not only had a knack for airmanship, but he was a showman as well.

What I saw, however, made me feel better. I could make steeper banks and sharper curves than his. Pretty soon I would show him.

I had accepted the hospitality of a hangar from the Dixie Motor Company. This bit of frugality proved a very foolish thing, but I was yet to be initiated into the tricks played on the unsophisticated. On Saturday and Sunday afternoons big crowds trooped out from Berlin to watch the flying at Johannisthal. Having set up the plane and tuned up the engine, I was all ready for my first Saturday.

As every pilot got a proportionate share of the entrance fee, dependent upon the actual time he spent in the air, there was great rivalry to be aloft the longest. Rosenstein usually got the biggest purse for the day. No sympathy was wasted on those pilots whose planes were out of commission. The fewer in the air the more money each one received.

I scented no danger in this. In fact, I confided to the Dixie pilot I was going to try to stay up longer than anyone. He knew I would remain in the air as long as my gasoline held out because he had seen me flying in Mainz. And he had been so generous in lending me part of his hangar that I did not suspect his friendliness. He just grinned and told me not to take any wooden pfennigs. I thought he was feebly trying to be funny, and went out for lunch.

At four o'clock, when the wind had died down, I wheeled my plane out in front of the hangar. Methodically, I primed the motor with the aid of a mechanic. Now was the time to show these fellows who was from the country. Smiling in anticipation of their amazement, I spun the propeller. The engine took hold immediately with a quick explosion, and I ducked under the wing to get into my pilot's seat. While I was still scrambling under the wing, the engine coughed and died. I backed out angrily, primed the motor with gas once more, and tried again. The same result. I thought the gas was clogged and tinkered with the carburetor. For nearly a quarter of an hour I kept this up—priming, swinging the propeller, ducking under the wing thinking everything was fine—only to have the engine gurgle and die. A crowd seemed to collect as if by magic. One might have thought they had been told to expect a funny show. They offered jeering comments, suggesting that perhaps I did not really want to fly, that I was afraid. Unable to understand why my motor should start to readily but die almost as speedily, I was boiling with rage.

The rest of the flyers were all in the air making money, while I was wearing out my arm swinging the fool propeller. There was only a brief time to find out what was the matter because it became dark shortly after five o'clock. The mechanic and I looked over the motor carefully, trying to ignore the jibes we heard plainly enough. Everything seemed in tiptop order. The damn' engine should start, did start when primed, and ought to keep on running.

I had strained the gasoline into the tank with my own hand. Surely, it was all right. Still, it was obvious that something mysterious had happened. Might as well look at everything.

Opening up the carburetor, we found inside it a whitish deposit that looked like wax. I didn't know what it was, but I knew that it couldn't have strained through the chamois skin I had used. I looked into the gasoline tank, but could see nothing. Nevertheless, we drained it thoroughly, and put in fresh gas.

The motor started with a bang and purred smoothly.

But by that time it was too late to join my competitors in the air. I could only curse the sabotage which had kept me on the ground.

The next day I learned that it was sugar which had been dropped into my gas tank. It is a sure trick to keep the motor from running. If there were to be too many aloft, sugar was put into the tanks of the unsuspecting, so that the others could make more money.

There wasn't a chance of finding out who had pulled off the stunt. No more shared hangars to save money, however! I moved out that same evening and hired my own hangar. That night I slept under the plane, and henceforth always kept a guard on it. My mechanic brought me sandwiches.

Sunday was as good a flying day for crowds as Saturday. During the afternoon, however, it was windy. Only two pilots got ready to go up, Rosenstein and Wsewolod Abramowitch. The latter, a Russian and a fine pilot, flew a Wright biplane. No one seemed to expect me to fly. They were still laughing over the sugar trick.

There was more wind than I had ever flown in before, probably four or five miles an hour. If the top of the grass barely moved in the wind, it was regarded as "stormy weather." It wasn't an ideal day for a début at all. On the other hand I would make a lot of money. The pilots' share would only be divided three ways. Probably I would make as much as 700 marks. Moreover, it was a chance to gain a reputation at one stroke. If I could go aloft when only Rosenstein and Abramowitch dared hazard the wind, there would be no doubt about the quality of my airplane.

A regular pilot made a terrific fuss about flying. There couldn't have been more folderol if he had been departing for a trip around the world. His admirers and assistants acted as if he might never return. A mechanic fidgeted with his flying suit, and put his crash helmet on his head elaborately. Then his current girl rushed up excitedly, threw her arms around him and kissed him dramatically. He patted her on the back in his best pooh-pooh manner, whereupon she kissed him again. While all this was going on before a gaping crowd, more mechanics wheeled the airplane out from the hangar with the ceremony usually reserved for a racehorse in the paddock. Shouting to the crowd standing around to get out of the way, they walked the plane out to the flying line. Only then would the pilot get into his seat, and look about in a grim, grand way. The mechanic started the engine, ran around the wing to shout something unintelligible to the pilot, who waved his arms as if he understood. The carefully staged hocus-pocus worked up a great deal of excitement. The crowd, in a fever of anticipation, was on tiptoe for the take-off.

Never accustomed to much personnel, I scorned such romantic foolishness. Starting my engine myself and clambering into the seat, I taxied my plane out from the hangar to the field and was up in the air while the crowd was still walking along towards the sound of a motor from my hangar.

The amazement on the faces of the people as I soared over them nearly a hundred feet high after the first round of the kilometer square field was worth seeing. Everyone had been so perfectly sure that I would crash! No one conceded that an airplane could fly without ailerons. When they saw that mine did, they immediately concluded that I was a great pilot, capable of handling a ship in which anyone else would break his neck. The next day newspapers wrote up my flight as if it were an astounding feat.

When I came into Senftleben's café for supper, I got more attention than I wanted. Persons entirely unknown to me begged for my autograph. Women, who had remained completely unaware of my existence, smiled fondly. Young, inexperienced, I hardly knew why they were smiling. The sudden change in attitude was something of a nuisance, except that Rosenstein came over to introduce himself, shake my hand, and to congratulate me on my flying and on my plane. Aviation was the whole of my life. To interest me a woman would have had to be a flyer herself. I was working day and night and had no time for play.

The way I lived was to get up at five o'clock or earlier every morning, roll out my ship and, if conditions were right, fly. After a hop I would go to Senftleben's for breakfast, and perhaps to my combined office and sleeping quarters on the second floor. Most of the other pilots, who had likewise been up early, then went to bed until noon. I went back to the hangar to work. As long as my father was financing me I felt I owed it to him to spend all my time getting ahead. I kept right on sending enthusiastic letters to him, asking for 4,000 or 5,000 marks more. Soon I would begin paying him back. He maintained faith in me, though protesting more and more about how much money he was pouring into aviation.

My reputation not only as a flyer but as a designer increased at Johannisthal faster than my income. We were still building the plane in which I planned to teach Fritz. Constantly we expected to make ends meet by exhibition flying, yet the end of the month always showed us in the red. Any day we hoped to sell a plane, but so far, purchasers were skittish.

When the first army officials visited my combined hangar and shop, Fokker-Aeroplanbau, I would have offered to build them a plane for the bare expense of manufacture if they would have taken it. They left only "interested."

It was six months later that they came back suggesting a cross-country flight from Johannisthal to the military field at Doberitz, about thirty kilometers [19 miles] away, as a test of my plane for army use. I readily assented.

Although I had kept close to the airdrome during exhibition flights, the hop to Doberitz was far from difficult for me. Carefully grooming the plane against accident, I made the trip without incident, landing on schedule before a small group of officers assembled for the occasion. They were impressed, but it was not until I returned from Russia that they were "sold." Then, two planes were ordered, for 10,000 marks, as a result of my increased reputation, and we started their manufacture at once.

A short time later I embarked on a much more ambitious cross-country hop from Berlin to Hamburg, two and a half hours in the air. It necessitated the installation of auxiliary fuel tanks. Because I was not a good navigator—and never will be—an army officer came along as passenger. As soon as we left Johannisthal and swung towards Hamburg, I turned over the rudder to him. The plane, being automatically stable, required no other attention. He kept the course, and we made the flight with no trouble, though I spent most of my time wondering what was going to happen.

After that important flight, showing what my plane could do, it occurred to me that the Dutch Government, which was known to be in the market, might buy from me. I planned to fly from Berlin to The Hague, but dislocated my arm in a flying accident three days before the scheduled departure. A Dutch friend of mine, Bernard De Waal, who had learned flying in another school, persuaded me that the long distance flight would be a great advertisement. He made the 400-mile trip with only one stop at Hanover—on May 13, 1913. I took the train. At The Hague, to explain my arm in a sling, I told them I had slipped on a greasy floor.

We received a fine reception and big writeups in the press. Movies were made and we could go nowhere without being cheered. I believed that my own Government would surely give me an order after all the public fuss made over us. It was a duplication of the enthusiastic Haarlem turnout. But I had the usual difficulty seeing a big general in a small army. When I finally gained entrance to General C. T. Snyders, he promised only that his staff officers would look into the matter. One did come to Johannisthal later, flew and liked our plane, but we got no orders. Instead, the Dutch Government, to my intense disappointment, ordered Farman planes from France.

In later years, General Snyders turned out to be a good friend, but that was after the War, when my plane had proved itself on the German Front, and I came back a famous man. The War had turned him into an aviation enthusiast and he was one of the pioneers in organizing the Holland-India flight. No doubt he put too much dependence on his subordinates at that time. Our one-stop flight from Berlin clearly showed that the plane had superior qualities.

Out of the whole trip I gained nothing but expenses. De Waal talked me into letting him fly back to Berlin. I must have had a hunch. I instructed him, in a pinch, to land on trees to break his fall. They were soft. But when a rocker arm of the 100 h.p. Argus engine broke, he found an even softer spot in a farmyard, plopping down in the squashiest manure pile for miles around. It seemed all too fitting an end. The plane was badly damaged and had to be shipped by train to Johannisthal.

It was in 1912 that the aviation world was electrified by the news that the Frenchman, Pégoud, had looped the loop. He was the first flyer in the world to perform that hairraising stunt. People paid thousands of dollars to watch him. Lincoln Beachey came out of his retirement, to learn the thing he had never dared to do. Finding out how it was done, he returned to flying—and his death in 1915.

One of Pégoud's first demonstrations outside France was at the Johannisthal flying field in 1913, not long after my return from Holland. His Blériot monoplane, with an enlarged elevator, had a reinforced upper structure to stand the strain when it turned over. Pégoud was strapped to his seat to prevent his dropping out when he hung head down at the top of the loop. The day I saw him, along with thousands of others, he made three loops, but most of his flying was only spectacular curves.

My biggest ambition was to match his stunt.

And I was actually the first in Germany to loop.

Pégoud's looping crystallized my idea of abandoning the automatically stable feature of my airplane. Pilots were beginning to feel safe in the air. Confident of controlling their planes, they were demanding greater maneuverability so they could perform stunts. My ship was too stable; it resisted efforts to fly in any but a normal manner. Stability was no longer a dreaded problem; more power had given us the control which we lacked at first. Therefore I abandoned the whole automatic type and went to conventional design, warping the wings, however, instead of using ailerons, at first.

In general appearance, the first plane I constructed after that decision greatly resembled the French monoplane types, but from a detailed engineering standpoint it was radically different. For the first time I used a rectangular fuselage of welded steel tubes. The wings were wood, covered with fabric, and braced with cables. As soon as I finished and test-flew the new plane I decided to try my first loop.

Nobody had ever told me how; I only knew that I had seen it done. The loop seemed to require the use of great speed. On the other hand, pulling an airplane sharply up at terrific speed puts a tremendous strain on the wings. Something is likely to buckle. After I had flown around, testing out my plane gingerly like a man putting his toe in a cold water bath, I glided down and yelled to my mechanics to watch me—I was going to try a loop.

When I had gotten some altitude, I began to wish I hadn't promised anything. I found that I was thoroughly scared, too frightened to make a start. While trying to get up my nerve, I pretended to be getting more altitude, all the time wishing my motor would stop or something would happen which would permit me to withdraw with honor. Several times I dropped the nose to pick up speed, but each time I nosed up for the loop I leveled out again like a balky horse refusing a fence. I kept wondering whether I had made the plane strong enough to stand the strain, and went over every detail of construction in my mind to assure myself of the stoutness of each part. I felt in a worse position than a pilot who trusts blindly to others. Finally, I saw that the motor wasn't going to quit. The mechanics were stretching their necks to watch; I was simply in for it. So I set my teeth and thought, "Some day you must die, it might as well be now." With that, I pushed the nose far down, picked up speed until the wind whistled through the guy wires, and pulled up sharply on the elevator.

The airplane staggered fearfully, turned over like a flash on its back, and for a moment my feet slipped off the rudder as we hung there, upside down. I prayed for my straps to hold. Then over we came in a steep dive towards the ground out of which I pulled as rapidly as possible. In a minute the airplane was back again in normal flying position.

I had flown my first loop and was still alive!

That was the way I felt, exclamation mark and all.

I had looped at 1,500 feet altitude and come out of it losing only about 200 feet.

The story of my first loop was printed in newspapers all over Germany. Offers for exhibition flights came pouring in. A promoter took hold of the whole matter for me and lined up a German flyer, who had bought an old Blériot, like Pégoud's, and said he would loop, too, although he had never done it before. The promoter closed one contract after another in a whole string of cities. Everybody was anxious to see an airplane loop. People hardly believed it could be done, even though they had read about it.

Coblenz was the first city on our schedule. Thousands crowded out to the flying field to see the famous loop-the-loop airman. The first time aloft I confined myself to steep banks and spectacular curves. I found I didn't want to loop. The thought of doing it still scared me to death. If I could possibly get out of it, I didn't intend to loop. I stunted brilliantly instead. When I landed I found the public wildly enthusiastic. They had never seen such an intricate combination of banks and curves. In fact, some banks were so steep that many people thought I had actually looped.

Unfortunately an army flyer on the committee knew better. He complained that I had failed to live up to my contract. We were to receive 10,000 marks for three days, with 500 marks for expenses. A proportionate part of the purse was paid after each flight. There had not been as big a gate as had been expected. People could see the flying outside the field as well as inside. My failure to loop gave the committee a chance to refuse to pay the second installment.

The promoter, thoroughly frightened at the committee's threat, told me that if I did not loop we would lose most of the money. He persuaded me to go up again, and I flew around wondering whether I had the nerve to loop for that crowd.

I remembered that strain the plane underwent and how it shuddered when I pulled up sharply after the preliminary dive. Probably the wings would simply fold up under the excessive strain. Still I had done it once. Thinking it over carefully, I decided that this time I would not pull up so sharply. Maybe it would loop a little easier.

Before I could change my mind I dived the plane and pulled it up gently. In two seconds I was on my back without much strain and with less loss of speed than the first time. Then I nosed over easily and pulled up again to normal flying position.

That felt a lot better. I tried it again a little slower this time, making for a perfect loop. The plane swung into it with practically no undue strain.

I suddenly discovered I knew how, and from that time on enjoyed the trick, a favorite stunt with airmen once they get the knack. Nowadays, pilots do it for setting-up exercise in the morning.

On landing, everybody except the committee seemed satisfied. They had to dig into their pockets to pay for the thrill of those outside the field.

The tour continued, but the other pilot didn't seem to want to loop. He banked and curved steeply, just as I had done the first day, but couldn't get up his nerve to go the whole way. In fact he never did loop throughout the whole series of exhibitions, but demanded fifty per cent of the takings just the same. Understanding how he felt, I didn't have the heart to complain.

At Frankfurt we flew on the Zeppelin airport and I got some experience in showmanship which was of advantage to me demonstrating planes in later days. I found it was possible to thrill the public without really endangering myself. Audiences wanted to believe one was going to break one's neck, and then see one save it spectacularly. The Zeppelin hangar was at the side of the field opposite the public. Taking off in the direction of the hangar I flew low, directly at it. At the crowd's distance it was impossible to judge accurately the narrowing space between me and the building. The spectators held their breath momentarily expecting me to crash. While they were gasping, I zoomed high over the hangar and disappeared by dropping down behind, playing leapfrog. Everyone waited tense, for news of the expected crash. Flying below the roof and in line with the building I circled wide, over a forest. Hidden by the trees, I was out of sight for several minutes. Most of the crowd had given me up for lost. While they stood strained, waiting for the electric news of a crash, I suddenly shot up behind them and flew over their heads waving. Landing quickly, I jumped out and the crowd spontaneously ran towards me yelling their heads off, carrying me off on their shoulders and begging me to sign photographs. Hundreds of people offered real money for a passenger flight; invitations to parties poured in. I refused both. I was unwilling to risk other people's lives, and too tired to attend parties. It required all my time to keep the plane in working condition. Looping the loop was now the easiest part of the performance, but it looked the hardest and always was the biggest attraction of the exhibition.

Our first tour ended with a big demonstration in Johannisthal, where I was hailed as the most daring pilot in Germany. Many army officers, who in late 1913 were beginning to take up flying, were present to watch me loop and stunt.

I remembered how, only a year before, I had come to Johannisthal, to be jeered at. It pleased me to know that Rosenstein was among those who were now watching me enviously.

Cities all over Germany, which we had missed on the first swing around the country, were clamoring for our appearance. I continued these exhibition flights right up to the War. The newspapers wrote fabulous stories about my spectacular flying, exaggerating its danger. They alarmed my father, who sent me a postcard, urging me to quit.

"Now you are famous," he wrote. "Now is the time to stop. The only thing you can do next is to break your neck."

I am still flying.

55

———➤•◄———

"A short life, full of consequences"

From the diary of Bishop Milton Wright

While aviation continued its breakneck development in Europe, in America it was stymied by the withering grasp of the Wrights' patent suit. Wilbur fought the infringers until, in a weakened state, he died in 1912.

———➤•◄———

Thursday, May 30, 1912

This morning at 3:15 Wilbur passed away, aged 45 years, 1 month and 14 days. A short life, full of consequences. An unfailing intellect, imperturbable temper, great self-reliance and as great modesty, seeing the right clearly, pursuing it steadily, he lived and died. Many called—many telegrams (probably over a thousand).

Bishop Milton Wright's diary

56

⇒·•·⇐

The Credulous Farmer

By Grover Loening, in *Our Wings Grow Faster* (1935)

While war loomed on Europe's horizon, and with the airplane's role yet un-certain (though the best minds now predicted that it would add geometri-cally to the devastation), common folks still held the flying machine in a somewhat laconic awe.

⇒·•·⇐

On another day out at the Simms Station Field,* we were all watching some engineers who were taking borings of the soil and rock formation with the usual little one-inch boring drill. This was part of an extension survey being made for flood-prevention work in the Miami valley, which had just recovered from its disastrous 1913 flood.

Thinking to have some fun, Orville turned to an old farmer who was standing near and asked him what they were doing out there.

"Wal," said the farmer, "I guess they're fig'ring as to get rid of the water by drilling them there holes."

"Oh, but they won't get rid of much water that way," said Orville.

"I dunno," said the farmer, spitting out a chew of tobacco with deliber-ation; and then, turning to the airplane standing there, he nodded his head towards it and said, "I never tho't this derned thing'd fly."

* A cow pasture outside Dayton, now part of Wright-Patterson Air Force Base.

INDEX